Sophie Grigson's Meat Course

The Channel 4 television series **Sophie's Meat Course**
was produced by Wall to Wall Television

SOPHIE GRIGSON'S
MEAT COURSE

Photographs by Jess Koppel

Network Books

For Florence and William

Network Books is an imprint of BBC Books,
a division of BBC Worldwide Publishing,
BBC Worldwide Limited, Woodlands,
80 Wood Lane, London W12 0TT

First Published 1995
Reprinted 1995 (twice)
© Sophie Grigson
ISBN 0 563 37173 0

Photographs © Jess Koppel
Stylist Roisin Nield
Home economist Lyn Rutherford
Illustrations by Kate Simunek
Animal motifs by Bobby Jones

Printed and bound by Butler and Tanner Ltd., Frome
Colour separations by Radstock Reproductions Ltd., Midsomer Norton
Jacket printed by Lawrence Allen Ltd., Weston-super-Mare

CONTENTS

ACKNOWLEDGEMENTS

This is the third book I have written for Network Books and I remain most grateful to be working with such a friendly and patient team. I would particularly like to thank Heather Holden-Brown and Deborah Taylor, who don't bat an eyelid at the piecemeal way I deliver my manuscript, and deal with any discrepancies so discreetly. Frank Phillips I have to thank for the design, while I return again to thank my friend, photographer Jess Koppel, who along with food stylist Lyn Rutherford and stylist Roisin Nield, always come up with such refreshing, sympathetic and thoroughly edible photographs.

Much of what I know about meat has been gleaned from the Godfreys in Highbury, who run one of the best butcher's shops I've come across. Their meat is superb, their advice sound. More recently, Graham Portwine of Covent Garden has been my mentor and co-presenter on the television series that inspired and accompanies this book. Big thanks are due to Sue Shephard, of Channel 4, for commissioning the TV series in the first place and firing us all with enthusiasm.

At Wall to Wall Television, the company who made the series, I owe much to Charlotte Black, our long-suffering producer, and Kathy Myers, director. Caroline McCool, our production co-ordinator, did an amazing job scheduling and rescheduling and keeping everyone in the right place at the right time – worth her weight in gold. Excellent and thorough researchers Sadie Hennessy, Sue Davison and Tracy Cavalier combed the country to unearth tremendous butchers and producers. Filming meat is not an easy task, but cameraman Chris King managed to make almost every shot look like some earthy, rosy-hued still-life painting and deserves a huge round of applause. Thanks too, to those other people, too many to name, who worked so very hard to finish the series in time and, of course, to the meat producers who opened their doors to our crew. Last but not least, a quick thank you to Divertimenti, who helped so generously with equipment.

Invaluable though the help of all these people has been, I owe the greatest debt of all to my husband, William, who has put up with my absences, and my crises, and endless lumps of meat strewn around the kitchen, so very patiently. I couldn't have done it without him. On the home front, I would also like to thank Annabel Hartog who has tested most of the recipes in this book, stumbling only at the thought of skinning testicles, as well as Michelle King for keeping me organized, Susie Elliott for keeping the house organized, and Mandy Atkins and Zoe Devonshire for keeping my daughter organized and happy.

INTRODUCTION

Surprisingly enough, under the circumstances, I don't eat a great deal of meat. Don't get me wrong, I love meat, but I just happen to like fish and vegetables and pulses every bit as much. Meat plays an important part in many of the meals we eat in our household, but no more so than other types of food. When I do choose to cook meat, I want it to be the best, I want it to taste superlative and if it does then I'm quite happy to settle for less in terms of quantity. If it doesn't, then to be frank, I'd rather do without.

This book is all about meat, but its aim is not to encourage readers to eat vast hunks of flesh day in day out. The idea is more to help you relish the prospect of a meat dish, rather than to take it for granted. It may be something as simple as a grilled chop or as grand as a rib roast of beef, it may be a classic like steak and kidney pudding or an exotic curry. Whatever, the skills of buying and handling the meat at the heart of the dish are all important, though by no means taxing. This book will, I hope, instil you with the confidence to insist on the highest quality and give you the knowledge to recognize it.

Of course, it is all very well knowing what you are after, but finding it is not necessarily as easy as it should be. The choice of meat available from supermarkets has improved considerably in recent years, but a supermarket can never offer the kind of service provided by a good butcher. With few exceptions, you get what there is, wrapped in clear film and no questions asked, or at least none answered by the staff who are unlikely to know a great deal about what they sell. Who is going to tell you how long it was hung for? Or what breed it came from? Or what kind of lives the animals led?

I used to rely upon a marvellous family of butchers for all my meat when I lived in London. Whenever I needed advice on a cut for this dish or that, I would just ring and ask their opinion, knowing full well that it would be sound and that they would then supply me with exactly what I needed. Since moving away from the big smoke some months ago, I have still to find any supplier to match their standards. I'm sure there must be one somewhere near, but he has yet to reveal himself. A shame, as in this country we are capable of producing some of the best meat in the world. It just so happens that we consumers are also palmed off with a great deal that is hardly worth bothering with.

My checklist for a good butcher runs something like this: a) the shop is pleasant to walk into, clean, tidy, sweet-smelling; b) the meat is displayed well and hygienically; c) the staff are helpful, knowledgeable and enthusiastic; d) they stock free-range meat (though not necessarily exclusively); e) they know where it came from and the breeds; f) the meat is properly hung; g) they are pleased to prepare special cuts on order, skilled enough to cut them well and interested enough to ask what I'm going to do with them.

It's a long list but it is by no means an unreasonable list. A butcher who is justifiably proud of his trade, his skills and his knowledge of meat would take all these points for granted. Besides, meat, any meat, is expensive, so it is perfectly reasonable for the customer to demand a high level of service.

The better the quality of the meat, the easier it is to cook well. An old-fashioned, lovingly cured rasher of bacon will make a memorable bacon butty, worthy of high praise. Fast-cured, modern, mass-produced bacon makes a sandwich that is no more than fodder. Same process, radically different result, and that goes for any recipe you care to mention, from the simple to most complicated.

The recipes I've chosen for the book cover an enormous breadth of styles, and still I've had to leave out many that I would like to have included. There just isn't room in this one volume to squeeze in every good meat dish I've ever come across, not to mention all those I've yet to discover. Similarly, I've had to be selective about the meats chosen, in order to do them some sort of justice. I've left out things like kid and ptarmigan, which are not so widely available, and, rather regretfully, passed up on the opportunity to experiment with some of the incoming oddities, such as ostrich and llama, which may well prove to be the big hits of the future. Only time will tell.

Meanwhile, there should be enough in the pages that follow to keep any carnivorous cook in business for the time being. Ostrich and llama can wait.

RECIPE NOTES

As usual, the first advice must be to stay firmly with either imperial weights (the sign of us oldies) or metric (for the new generation of cooks), not switching from one to the other willy nilly. Note that all spoon measurements are rounded, though this can be taken loosely where flavourings are concerned. In the few instances where it matters seriously (e.g. with baking powder), the recipes were tested with a 15 ml tablespoon and a 5 ml teaspoon, my one concession to modernity. All eggs are size 2.

Where olive oil is listed in the ingredients, I would always use extra virgin olive oil, though if you prefer a lighter taste, refined olive oil can be used instead. By and large, herbs should be fresh, but where I think dried herbs work well as an alternative, I've listed them too. With bay leaves, it doesn't matter much either way, as long as dried ones haven't been hanging around for ever and a day. Pepper (black, not white) should always be freshly ground, as should nutmeg.

Timings are always approximate, to be read as guidelines rather than precise entities. So many things can affect cooking times – pan size, hob heat, oven temperature, thickness of a chunk of meat – that any cook must take some responsibility for the success of their own cooking. Judge by eye, by taste, by common sense. Always adjust seasonings to suit yourself and no-one else.

Beef

Beef

Standing slap bang next to a bull, even a young one, is not my idea of fun, but I did it (under protest) and felt enormously brave. I even patted and stroked the creature and was finally forced to admit that he did seem extremely docile and friendly. Mind you, this was no ordinary bull, but a prize-winning half-grown pure-bred Aberdeen Angus. His softly curled coat was as dark as midnight, shampooed and burnished to a high gloss, all ready for show. 'At least', I thought to myself, 'if he does turn nasty, I will have been gored by a class act.'

Beef has the honour of being considered the king of meats, and that makes Aberdeen Angus king of kings. There are other less common breeds which produce meat that is as succulent and full of flavour, but you are not very likely to come across them in the butcher's shop. Generally speaking, if you want the best roast in the world, then you had better ask for Aberdeen Angus. Most of what is sold comes, in fact, from Aberdeen Angus crossed with other types of cattle, but the essential flavour and beautifully marbled flesh remain the salient characteristics of the superior beast.

Though we eat less beef these days than we used to, we still think of it as the most British of meats, and we're not the only ones. The French nickname for the Brits has long been 'les rosbifs' (say it aloud), while other countries envy us the quality of our beef. Sadly they might well change their minds if they sampled some of the second-rate stuff that is often palmed off on the unsuspecting buyer. It's not difficult to pick out a prime joint of beef, but you do have to know what you are looking for. Prime roasting beef is about the most expensive meat to be had, but it really is worth the extra cost. Think of it as an occasional treat, a rare splurge. Far better to thrill to the taste of the best only a few times a year, than to be bored by the mediocre on a regular basis.

HOW TO SPOT GOOD BEEF

First of all, do not be seduced by brightly coloured, rosy-red beef, with a minimal covering of snowy white fat. It may look pretty, but this is no beauty contest. The best beef will have been thoroughly hung – for weeks rather than days. The muscle will have matured from that glaring red to a deep, rich browny-burgundy and the fat should have developed to a creamy tone that may verge on being yellow, depending on both the animal's diet and age. Cattle that have been mainly grass-fed will have yellower fat.

If you are shopping for a prime roasting joint, ignore lean-looking meat. A good marbling of fat throughout the meat is an essential characteristic, for two reasons. Firstly it brings with it true flavour; lean beef will be dull in comparison. Secondly it provides an inner and outer basting, helping to keep the meat moist and juicy as it cooks. In fact, whatever the cut, fat should never be considered an encumbrance.

CUTS AND COOKING

As a rough rule of thumb, when it comes to beef, those parts of the animal at the top, along the centre back to the rump end, are the tenderest and that makes them well-suited to fast cooking methods such as roasting, grilling and frying (of course, they can also be cooked in many of the slower ways, too). The shoulders and lower legs, the bits that are worked hardest when the animal is alive, yield up tougher cuts which are usually cheaper and blessed with sackloads of flavour, but they require long and gentle cooking.

ROASTING

The larger the joint the better. Forerib is the best of all, but sirloin comes a close second. Fillet makes a quick, meltingly tender roast, but will need to be thoroughly larded. The flavour of fillet is milder than say, rib. Topside and silverside are less highly rated and although they can be oven roasted, it's probably more sensible to pot-roast them. Like fillet they are both very lean (though not quite so tender), so in the dry heat of an oven they need to be helped along either with a coating of thin fat tied around them, or generous larding. Both need frequent basting as they cook.

GRILLING, BARBECUING AND FRYING

These are all fast methods of cooking which are ideal for steaks – rump, sirloin and fillet, not to mention the big boys T-bone and Porterhouse for serious meat eaters.

STIR-FRYING

Rump and fillet are well-suited to this fastest of cooking methods and should be cut into evenly-sized, narrow strips.

POT-ROASTING

Brisket, thick flank, topside, silverside.

STEWING AND BRAISING

Shin and leg, brisket, thin flank, chuck and blade, neck and clod, skirt. Anonymous cubes of 'stewing steak' will generally require a longer cooking time than similar-looking cubes of 'braising steak'.

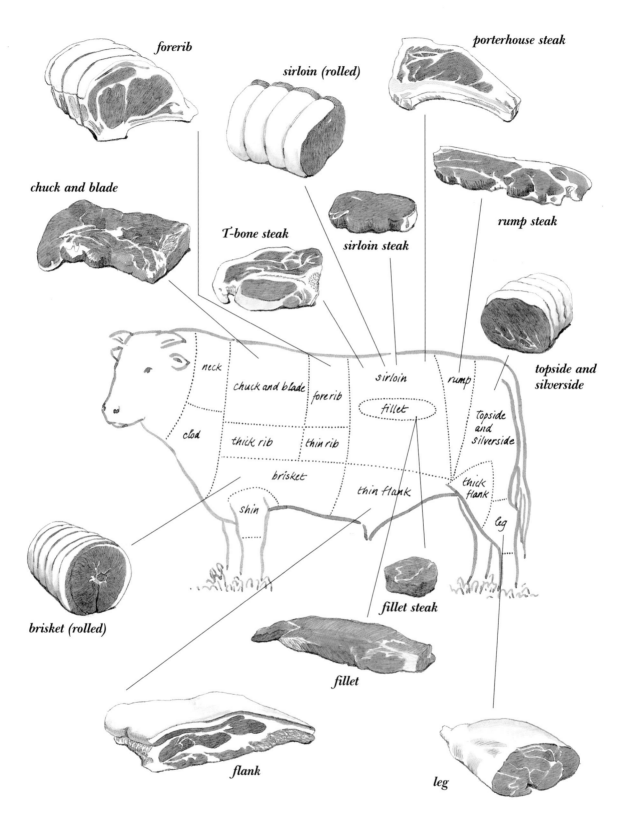

forerib

sirloin (rolled)

porterhouse steak

chuck and blade

T-bone steak

sirloin steak

rump steak

topside and silverside

neck

chuck and blade

forerib

sirloin

rump

fillet

Topside and silverside

clod

thick rib

thin rib

brisket

thin flank

thick flank

shin

leg

brisket (rolled)

fillet steak

fillet

flank

leg

See Alternative Names for Meat Cuts, page 311.

ROASTING A JOINT OF BEEF

Beef

I prefer to roast good-quality beef at a high temperature initially, then at a reduced temperature for the main body of the cooking time. I do sometimes cook the meat right through at a high temperature if it is absolutely tip-top and on the bone (see Rib Roast of Beef with English Mustard on page 20). Frequent basting (every 20–30 minutes) is essential and it may be necessary to protect the meat with foil if the exterior threatens to burn. The foil should be removed for the last 5–10 minutes of the cooking time.

The bigger the joint, the better it will roast; small joints have a tendency to dry out and be less succulent. Left-over beef is marvellous cold, and will feed the family happily for several days if need be. Meat, when roasted on the bone, tends to have a better flavour and looks more dramatic. The bone conducts heat through the meat, so that it cooks more evenly. A boned and rolled cut, on the other hand, is much easier to carve.

Either way, the meat must be left to rest for 20–30 minutes once it is done if it is to be enjoyed at its best. Turn the oven off, leave the door ajar and let the meat sit in the gentle warmth while you make the gravy, have a drink or eat the first course. This process allows the meat to re-absorb some of its juices, making it moister and heightening flavour. Don't worry about it losing too much heat. A large joint holds its heat very well.

Feeding a table full of people, some of whom like their meat rare, some of whom like it well done, presents no problem. The outer ends of a decent-sized joint will always end up fairly well cooked, while the interior remains pink. My advice, in general, is always to cook beef rare.

CALCULATING ROASTING TIMES

When it comes to roasting, you have to be prepared to undertake a simple bit of mathematics. Use a calculator if necessary! Timings worked out this way are not 100 per cent accurate, but they give an idea of when to start checking your joint to see if it is done.

Weigh your joint of meat after it has been prepared, i.e. fully trimmed or with the stuffing in it, if there is one. Multiply the given time per pound or per half kilo (see below) by the number of pounds or twice the number of kilos of weight. This is the length of time needed to cook the meat after the oven temperature has been reduced. For instance, if you have a fine piece of sirloin on the bone, weighing in at 4½ lb, that you want to cook rare, it will need four and a half times 14 minutes (after the initial 20 minutes at a high temperature), i.e. about 63 minutes. Metrically, 4½ lb is 2 kg, so four times 15 minutes, which gives about 60 minutes – 3 minutes difference in the calculation of the cooking time won't matter as this is merely a rough indication of timing anyway.

Beef

ROASTING TIMES AND TEMPERATURES FOR BEEF

Start the joint off at 240°C/475°F/Gas Mark 9 for 20 minutes, then reduce the temperature to 190°C/375°F/Gas Mark 5 for the final cooking time.

Rare:	13–15 minutes per 500g
	12–14 minutes per lb
Medium:	20–22 minutes per 500g
	18–20 minutes per lb
Well Done:	25–28 minutes per 500g
	22–25 minutes per lb

TESTING FOR DONENESS

The most accurate method is to use a meat thermometer. Push it into the centre of the thickest part of the meat, without coming too close to the bone, before the joint goes into the oven. If you have to protect the meat with foil as it cooks, make sure that the dial of the meat thermometer stays outside the foil so that it can be easily read.

The thermometer will record the temperature at the centre of the meat, but remember that as the meat rests after the oven is turned off it will continue to cook in its own residual heat. So turn the oven off when the meat is still a few degrees short of being done to your liking. For rare beef, the meat thermometer should read 55°C/130°F (reaching a temperature of 60°C/140°F as it rests), for medium beef 65°C/150°F (reaching a temperature of 70°C/160°F as it rests), and for well-done beef, 75°C/170°F (reaching a temperature of 80°C/180°F as it rests).

If you don't have a meat thermometer, a metal skewer is your next best bet. Plunge the skewer into the heart of the meat and leave for 30 seconds. Pull it out and place the tip on the inside of your wrist. If it is cold, then the meat is not yet done. When it is warm, the meat is rare, when fairly hot it's medium, and when it's very hot it's well-done.

MAKING A STEW

Most stews are made by the same standard method. What makes the difference is the ingredients. Some use water as the basis of the sauce, others take wine, beer or stock. The classic bouquet garni may include a strip of orange zest or a sprig of rosemary, while elsewhere spices, chillies or soy sauce add their zest to the whole.

While there may be some peculiarities in the method of this or that stew and while there may be some stews where the meat is not browned first, on the whole this is the way to go about the process, and it applies not only to beef stews but to most other types of meat stew as well.

1
PREPARING THE MEAT

Trim off chunks of gristle and huge globs of fat, but don't be too zealous about cleaning out every last particle of fat. Some fat will add to the flavour of the stew. If using a cut like shin of beef, don't mistake the slightly translucent walls of connective tissue for gristle. These are what make this cut so brilliant for stewing, and they will melt down as the meat cooks to produce a rib-sticking sauce.

The size of the pieces of meat will vary from one stew to another, usually dictated by tradition rather than expediency. It's probably better to err on the side of larger rather than smaller pieces of meat as they will shrink as they cook. Besides, stated sizes are just guidelines; no-one seriously expects you to get out the ruler before you wield your knife.

As always, a sharp knife makes trimming and cutting meat a doddle. A blunt knife turns it into a chore.

2
BROWNING

Let's get one thing straight, browning, or searing as it is sometimes called, does not seal in the juices. That's an old wives' tale, and it would be the ruination of a good stew if it were true. You would end up with nice-tasting bits of meat in totally tasteless liquid, instead of a well-balanced mixture of meat in a coating of beautifully fragrant sauce.

Browning serves a quite different function, to caramelize the natural sugars in the exterior of the meat. This intensifies the deep savouriness and gives the characteristic, enticing dark colour to the finished stew. Knowing how to brown meat properly is the key to making a good stew. Some recipes tell you to coat the meat in flour before browning. If you do, leave it until the very last minute, coating the meat a few pieces at a time and putting them straight into the frying pan. If the meat is not floured, dry it on a tea-towel or kitchen paper just before browning.

Heat the fat in a wide heavy-based frying pan (a high-sided pan will slow down the browning process) over a high heat. To brown thoroughly, the fat must be scarily hot. Fry the meat in two or three batches, according to the capacity of your pan. Never, ever overcrowd the pan. There should be plenty of room to turn the meat easily.

If you put too much meat in the pan at one fell-swoop, the temperature of the fat will fall dramatically, the meat juices will start to ooze out, swamping the base of the pan, and the meat will steam instead of browning. It won't work.

If you get it right, the surface of the meat will immediately begin to colour and any liquid will be instantly evaporated. Turn the pieces only when the underneath has browned. This process serves to colour the whole stew, so don't hoick the meat out when it is merely a shade darker than it was to start off with. This process is not called browning for nothing. Take the meat as dark as you dare, without actually burning it!

3
THICKENING

You can thicken a stew when the meat goes into the oven by sprinkling a tablespoon or two of flour over before adding the stock. Some stews need no thickening at all, but if the sauce still looks watery by the time the meat is done, you can take remedial steps.

If the juices taste rather insipid, strain them off into a wide frying pan, then boil them down until reduced to a syrupy consistency. Taste and adjust the seasoning and pour back over the meat and vegetables, which you have been keeping warm in the oven. If the juices taste fine, you can thicken them by stirring in beurre manié. To make this, mash equal quantities of butter and flour together. Set the casserole dish over a low to medium heat, and stir in small knobs of beurre manié until the sauce begins to thicken. Cook for a few minutes without boiling. Taste and adjust the seasoning just before serving.

4
DEGLAZING THE PAN

After browning the meat, the frying pan will be speckled with delicious browny residues which carry a good deal of flavour and should not be wasted. Pour out any excess fat left in the pan, then pour in the deglazing liquid – wine, beer or spirit, stock or even water – and bring up to the boil, stirring and scraping in all those residues. Pour over the meat.

5
LIQUIDS

Usually the liquid that forms the basis of the stew is heated up before being added to the meat. For instance, if it has been used to deglaze the frying pan. If not, you will either need to bring the casserole up to a simmer on the hob, or put it first into a hot oven (around 200°C/400°F/Gas Mark 6) for about 20–30 minutes until it begins to simmer.

6
COOKING

Stews are best cooked at a very lazy simmer, more of a relaxed burble really, for a good long time. This can be done on top of the stove, but is probably easier in the oven where it is less likely to burn on the base. The temperature should be around 170°C/325°F/Gas Mark 3, but check once in a while and adjust the temperature as necessary. Never try to rush the cooking by increasing the temperature. It won't do any good, and may even toughen the meat, or worse still burn the base of the casserole. The meat is ready when it is, as the Americans say, 'fork tender', i.e. a fork slips easily into it with practically no resistance. If it is cooked on the bone, then it will part easily from the bone with no effort.

7
SKIMMING

More often than not, a thin layer of oily fat will have risen to the surface of the stew by the time it is cooked. If you wish to serve the stew straight away, then you can skim this off first by tilting the pan so that the fat runs together and can be more easily spooned out without bringing too much of the precious stew itself. Once you've disposed of as much as possible this way, let the stew settle again, then blot off the surface fat with pieces of kitchen paper – just lay them flat on the surface for a few seconds then lift off. Don't expect to remove every last speck unless you have the patience of an angel.

It's far easier to degrease a stew when it has been cooked a day in advance. Let the stew cool, then cover and refrigerate overnight. By the next day the fat will have congealed to a thin and rather unsightly layer. Most can be lifted off with a slotted spoon and Bob's your uncle.

8
GETTING AHEAD

There are three very good reasons for cooking a stew a day (or even two) in advance of when you want to eat it. The first is that it saves you all that bother and worry about timing on the day of the meal. The second is that you can degrease it much more easily (see above) and the third is that 99 times out of a 100, it will actually taste all the better for reheating. Don't ask me why, but I bet you it will.

However, when you do come to re-heat the stew, make sure you do it thoroughly. Bring it to the boil and let it simmer for 5 minutes. You may find that you have to add a little extra water to thin down the juices.

Beef

GRILLING A STEAK

Ask for your steaks to be cut 2.5–3.5 cm (1–1½ in) thick. If they're cut too thin, they'll end up being leathery. Make sure the steaks are at room temperature before grilling; take them out of the fridge and let them sit for a good half an hour in the kitchen, loosely covered so that the meat can 'breathe'. Pre-heat the grill (or barbecue) thoroughly, turning it on to full-power for at least 5 minutes before you start to grill. Brush both the grill rack and the steaks with a little oil or melted butter. Season with pepper only.

Grill close to the heat until browned, then turn and brown the other side. This will probably be enough for a 'blue' or rare steak. If the steaks are to be cooked further, reduce the heat, or move the grill rack a little further away from the heat. Exact timing will depend on the thickness and cut of the meat and the power of your grill. You can tell how it is doing by pressing the meat with the tip of your finger, but it takes experience to get it right. A blue steak will be very soft, offering no resistance at all. Rare steak will be soft and spongy. Medium rare will feel a little firmer. Medium steak will offer some resistance and will feel just firm to the touch. If you must cook it well-done, which seems a shame as it won't be half as succulent and juicy, the steak will feel solid. You can also use the less elegant method of testing, which is to cut into the steak with a knife. Not professional, but more accurate for the inexperienced.

Here, as a rough guide, are some approximate grilling times for steaks, assuming they have been cut about 2.5 cm (1 in) thick.

Blue: 1–2 minutes per side
Rare: 2–3 minutes per side
Medium Rare: 2–4 minutes per side
Medium: 3–5 minutes per side

MAKING BEEF STOCK

Beef stock is always a brown stock, made first by caramelizing the bones and vegetables for both flavour and colour, then finished with lengthy simmering. You can now buy pretty good-quality fresh beef stock in tubs in supermarkets, which is infinitely preferable to a stock cube but still can't match a humdinger of a home-made stock.

Buy your bones from the butcher, who should be only too glad to get rid of them. Onion and carrots are essential, but you can omit the celery and/or leek. Never add salt to a stockpot. You may want to reduce the stock down for a sauce so it is far better to season with salt when the stock is being used, rather than when it is being made. If you have a large enough stockpot, it is a good idea to make double the quantity (it freezes very well).

This same method can be used for lamb and veal stock. With lamb stock, I often add a good slug of Marsala or Madeira to the pan.

1.5 kg (3 lb) beef bones	1 leek, trimmed and quartered
1 large onion	4 sprigs of parsley
2 carrots, quartered	2 bay leaves
1 tablespoon oil	1 large sprig of thyme
1 celery stalk, quartered	

Put the bones in a roasting tin and roast at 220°C/425°F/Gas Mark 7 until they are richly browned, turning them every now and then. This is a surprisingly slow process and could take an hour or more. Keep checking them. Quarter the onion, but don't peel it. Turn the onion and carrots in the oil and add to the roasting tin after half an hour.

Once both bones and vegetables are well browned (but not burnt – take out any pieces that are looking perilously dark), tip them into a large stockpot and add the remaining ingredients. Cover very generously with cold water and bring slowly to the boil, skimming off any scum that rises to the surface. Leave to simmer gently for at least 4 hours, 6 is better. Top up with water as necessary.

Leave to cool, then strain. Chill in the fridge until any fat has congealed on top and scrape it off. If you aren't going to use the stock immediately, either freeze as it is, or, to save space in the freezer, reduce down further.

TO FREEZE STOCK

Measure the amount of stock you have and make a note of it. Pour it into a wide frying pan and boil hard until reduced right down to a few spoonfuls. Cool then pour into ice-cube trays and freeze. Divide the amount of stock you started off with by the number of ice-cubes (i.e. if you started off with 1.5 litres (3 pints) and you have 6 cubes' worth, then each cube is the equivalent of 250 ml (½ pint) of stock). Then you'll know how much diluted stock each ice-cube represents. Once frozen, drop the ice-cubes into a freezer bag and label.

When needed, take the required number of ice-cubes, place in a measuring jug and top up with enough hot water to make up to the original quantity.

RIB ROAST OF BEEF WITH ENGLISH MUSTARD

Forerib is the best of all roasting joints. It is the grand roast beef of Old England, the joint that made, and still makes, foreigners and natives alike drool. Almost as essential as the grand joint itself are the sandwiches made from the left-overs, so it's important to invest in a generously proportioned piece of beef that will look impressive on the table and keep everyone well-fed for a couple of days.

Ask the butcher to prepare the joint for you, trimming it nicely, but without removing too much of the fat as this is what gives such a good flavour and protects the meat from drying out. To make carving easier, ask the butcher to chine the joint, i.e. loosen the chine or backbone so that it comes away easily once the joint is cooked.

The hot mustard forms a thin crust on the beef, but mellows in the heat of the oven, so serve a little more alongside.

SERVES 8

3.5 kg (8 lb) forerib of beef
1 generous tablespoon traditional hot English mustard
Salt and freshly ground black pepper

Pre-heat the oven to 220°C/425°F/Gas Mark 7. Weigh the joint and calculate the cooking time, allowing 14 minutes per 500 g (13 minutes per lb) plus 15 minutes for rare meat, 18 minutes per 500 g (16 minutes per lb) plus 20 minutes for medium, 22–27 minutes per 500 g (20–24 minutes per lb) plus 25 minutes for well-done.

Place the joint in a roasting tin, fat-side up. Smear the mustard over the fat and season with salt and pepper. Roast for 30 minutes or so, then cover with foil to prevent burning. When done (see page 14), remove the foil, turn off the heat, open the door a crack, and leave the roast to relax in the oven for 30 minutes (or transfer to a warm place to relax if you are making Yorkshire pudding). Serve with Yorkshire pudding and Horseradish and Walnut Sauce (see page 23).

Carving a rib roast

1. *Holding the meat in place with a fork, loosen the meat from the rib bones with a carving knife.*

2. *Carve the meat down towards the rib bones in thick or thin slices, according to preference.*

YORKSHIRE PUDDING

When I shared a flat in student days with a Yorkshireman, he insisted that the Yorkshire pudding (which he made to accompany not just beef, but any type of roast meat) must be served before the meat in the traditional style. This was a most delicious economy measure. The pudding, soggy with juices from the joint under which it had been roasted, served to fill up hungry stomachs before the meat arrived. That way a smaller joint could be stretched around many people and with any luck there would still be enough left for the following day.

These days, I like my Yorkshire pudding rather crisper on the surface (though I dislike those little individual puddings which always seem to be all crust and no moist interior at all) so I put it into the oven as the roast comes out. By the time the meat is fully rested and ready to serve, the Yorkshire pud is puffed and browned and ready to dish up.

Crisp, tender Yorkshire pudding also makes a marvellously homely but indulgent dessert when served with lashings of condensed milk or golden syrup and some cream!

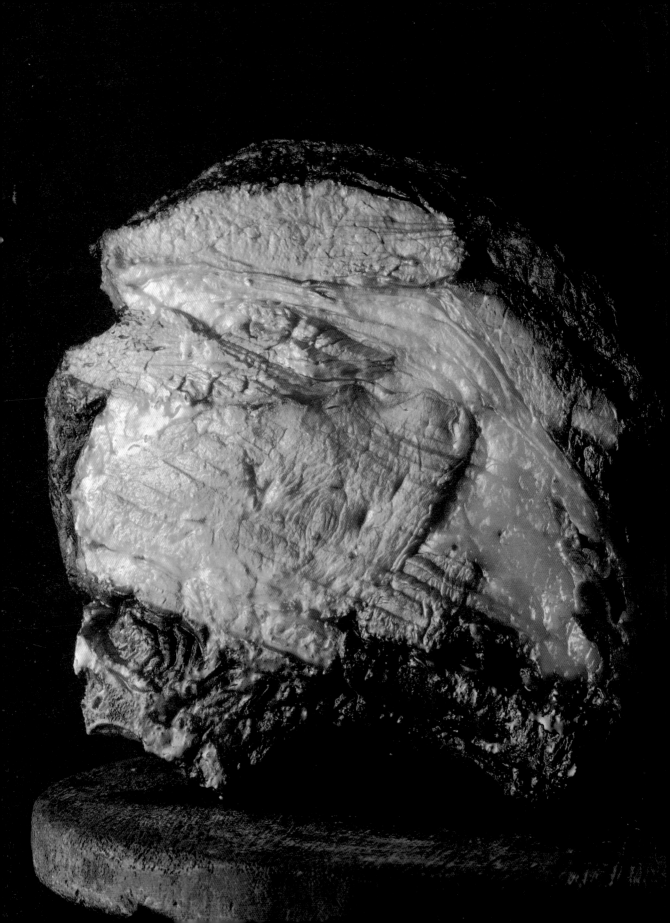

250 g (9 oz) plain flour	300 ml (10 fl oz) milk
A pinch of salt	300 ml (10 fl oz) water
3 eggs	2–3 tablespoons dripping or oil

Either pre-heat the oven to 220°C/425°F/Gas Mark 7, or turn it up that high when your joint of beef is nearly cooked, if it is being done at a lower temperature. Sift the flour with the salt into a bowl and make a well in the centre. Add the eggs and a generous splosh of milk. Begin to stir in the flour, gradually adding the rest of the milk, then the water until you get a smooth, creamy batter.

Put a baking sheet into the oven. Pour the dripping or oil into a roasting tin or shallow oven-proof dish and place it on the baking sheet in the hot oven. Leave for 10–15 minutes to heat through thoroughly (at this point take the meat out of the oven to rest, assuming it is cooked). Quickly remove the dish from the oven, give the batter a stir and pour it in. Return the dish of batter to the oven, setting it on the baking sheet and bake for 25–30 minutes until well-risen and browned. Serve as soon as possible.

HORSERADISH AND WALNUT SAUCE

Neat creamed horseradish is one of the classic accompaniments to roast beef, but if you've got a really good joint in the oven, take a little time to make this most luxurious horseradish sauce.

75 g (3 oz) shelled walnuts	1½–2½ teaspoons lemon juice
350 ml (12 fl oz) whipping cream	½ teaspoon sugar
1½ tablespoons creamed horseradish	Salt and freshly ground black pepper

Pre-heat the oven to 200°C/400°F/Gas Mark 6. Spread the walnuts out on a baking sheet and roast in the oven for 4–7 minutes, shaking once or twice, until they turn a shade or two darker. Tip into a metal sieve and shake to remove the loose papery skin. Cool and chop.

Whip the cream and mix with the remaining ingredients, then fold in the walnuts. Taste and adjust the flavourings. It should be punchy, but not hot enough to take the roof off your mouth.

BARBECUED FILLET OF BEEF
WITH MUSTARD BUTTER

A whole fillet of beef is just the right shape and size for barbecuing and it makes a glamorous centrepiece for a summer party. It's not cheap, but there's no waste and it will taste marvellous.

Since fillet is so lean, it has to be marinated for as long as possible to keep it moist in the dry heat of the barbie. It will take up far less space than, say, 10 pork chops, so you can fill in the gaps around the meat with vegetables that grill well — aubergine, courgettes and peppers, perhaps. If you start the vegetables off 5–10 minutes before the beef, you or a helper can peel and chop them as appropriate while the meat finishes cooking.

SERVES 8–10

1 fillet of beef, weighing about 1.5–1.75 kg (3–4 lb)	4–5 garlic cloves, cut into thin slivers
	Salt

———— *For the marinade* ————

3 tablespoons sherry vinegar	2 sprigs of thyme, bruised
150 ml (5 fl oz) olive oil	1 sprig of rosemary, bruised
2 shallots, sliced	1 tablespoon coarsely crushed black pepper

———— *For the butter* ————

175 g (6 oz) butter, softened	3 tablespoons chopped parsley
4 tablespoons coarse-grained mustard	Freshly ground black pepper

Ask the butcher to prepare and tie the fillet with string at regular intervals so that it keeps its shape. Make slits in the meat and push in slivers of garlic. Settle the meat in a close-fitting plastic bag. Mix together all the marinade ingredients and pour over the meat. Knot the bag tightly, sit it in a shallow dish (it's bound to leak slightly) and pop into the fridge. Leave it to marinate for at least 8 hours, preferably 24 or better still 48 hours, turning occasionally.

To make the butter, mix together all the ingredients thoroughly. Pat into a neat roll on a sheet of silver foil. Wrap up and chill until needed.

Remove the meat from the fridge at least half an hour before cooking. Drain, reserving the marinade. Barbecue the fillet over a high heat, turning to brown on all sides, then move to a slightly cooler spot on the barbecue (or raise the grill rack), and cook for a further 18–25 minutes, basting frequently with the marinade and turning every 5 minutes or so. Season with salt and rest on a plate at the side of the barbecue for 10 minutes.

Slice the beef and serve each portion with a pat of mustard butter perched on top.

OLD-FASHIONED BEEF AND CARROT STEW WITH PARSLEY DUMPLINGS

SERVES 4 – 6

2 onions, sliced

50g (2 oz) dripping or lard

900 g (2 lb) chuck or shin of beef,
cut into 5 cm (2 in) cubes

Seasoned flour, for dusting the meat

900 g (2 lb) carrots, cut into
2.5 cm (1 in) lengths

1 bouquet garni (see page 33)

750ml (1¼ pints) beef stock,
or 300 ml (½ pint) water and
450 ml (15 fl oz) stout or Guinness

Salt and freshly ground black pepper

—— *Dumplings* ——

100 g (4 oz) self-raising flour

½ teaspoon baking powder

¼ teaspoon salt

50 g (2 oz) shredded suet

2 tablespoons chopped parsley

Pre-heat the oven to 170°C/325°F/Gas Mark 3. Fry the onions in half the dripping in a wide frying pan over a medium heat until lightly browned. Transfer to a casserole dish. Dust the meat with the seasoned flour and fry in batches over a high heat in the same fat as the onion, until browned all over. Add more fat as needed. As the meat is done, add it to the casserole. Tuck in the carrots and bouquet garni, season and sprinkle over a tablespoon of flour.

Pour the stock or water and stout into the frying pan and bring up to the boil, stirring and scraping in the residues on the bottom of the pan. Pour over the meat and season. The liquid should cover the meat; if necessary, add a little more stock or water. Cover the casserole, transfer to the oven and cook for 2 hours until the meat is tender. There should be enough sauce to poach the dumplings but if it looks a bit dry, stir in some boiling water.

Meanwhile, get down to making the dumplings. Sift the flour with the baking powder and salt. Stir in the suet and parsley and add just enough water to make a slightly sticky dough. With floured hands, roll into small balls about the size of a quail's egg.

When the meat is about ready, dot the dumplings over the surface of the stew and return it to the oven, covered, for 30–40 minutes, or until the dumplings are puffed and tender and cooked through. Baste them once or twice with the stew's juices as they cook. Serve the stew and dumplings hot and steaming.

THAI BEEF SALAD

(Yam Nua Yang)

I ate very little beef when I was in Thailand. The sight of butcher's stalls in markets, open to the sun and awash with flies, was enough to put anyone off eating most meat in fact. However, I pushed that to the back of my mind when it came to this salad. Back here, where you can be sure of getting high-quality, tender steak, I think it tastes even better than it did on its home patch.

Raw vegetables are added to contrast with the meat and the spice of the dressing. I've chosen tomato and cool cucumber, although others, such as sweet peppers or carrots, could be used instead. The beef and the dressing can be prepared in advance, but don't put the salad together until the very last minute. It makes a good and fairly substantial first course for 6 people, but can also be served as a main course for 4.

SERVES 4 – 6

450–675 g (1–1½ lb) high-quality lean steak, such as fillet, rump or sirloin	2 small, thin red chillies, seeded and thinly sliced
Oil, for grilling or frying	6–8 lettuce leaves
3 tablespoons freshly squeezed lime juice	Chopped coriander
3 tablespoons fish sauce *(nam pla)*	Chopped chives
1 tablespoon sugar	½ cucumber, peeled and
4 shallots, thinly sliced	sliced 5 mm (¼ in) thick
2 garlic cloves, crushed	2 tomatoes, cut into eighths

The meat can either be grilled or roasted.

To grill: heat the grill until hot then brush the steak with oil and grill close to the heat until browned on the outside, but still rare inside.

To roast: pre-heat the oven to 240°C/450°F/Gas Mark 8. Heat a little oil in a flame-proof dish until it is very hot. Add the meat and brown it quickly over a fierce heat. Transfer to the oven and roast for 10–15 minutes.

Whichever method you use, err, if anything, on the side of undercooking rather than overcooking the beef as it will continue to cook a little in its own heat as it rests. Leave to cool for at least 5 minutes, then slice thinly.

Mix together the lime juice, fish sauce and sugar, stirring to dissolve the sugar. Add the shallots, garlic and chillies. Make a bed of lettuce on a serving dish and pile the beef in the centre. Spoon over the dressing and scatter with coriander and chives. Arrange the cucumber and tomato around the edge.

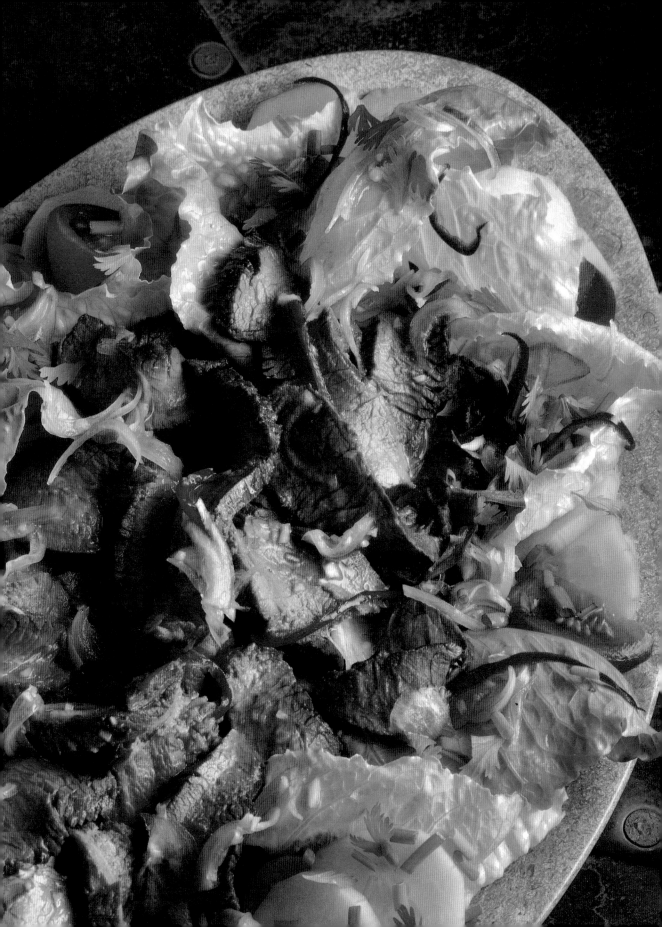

Beef

MARINATED STEAK SANDWICH

❦

For years I was put off the concept of the steak sandwich by the awful things that were served up in that name in so many pubs and restaurants. Pappy bread encasing a strip of leather is not my idea of good food. It took an evening at the Eagle, in Farringdon Road, London, to put me straight about the joys of a real steak sandwich. This version is based on what I ate that night.

SERVES 2, VERY NICELY THANK YOU

2 x 175–200 g (2 x 6–7 oz) slices rump steak, cut 1–2 cm (½–¾ in) thick

1 loaf of ciabatta

A generous handful of frisée lettuce

Salt and freshly ground black pepper

——For the marinade——

70 ml (2½ fl oz) red wine

3 tablespoons olive oil

1 garlic clove, crushed

½ small onion, chopped

½ tablespoon chopped parsley

¼ teaspoon dried thyme

½ tablespoon balsamic vinegar

2 peppercorns, crushed

—— For the dressing ——

2 tablespoons olive oil

½ tablespoon balsamic vinegar

Place the steaks in a shallow dish then mix together all the marinade ingredients and pour over. Turn the steaks so that they are nicely coated, cover and leave to marinate for at least 2 hours, preferably overnight, turning occasionally.

To make the dressing, whisk the oil into the vinegar, half a tablespoon at a time, then season to taste. Cut the ciabatta into 2 pieces, then split each in half lengthwise. Put back together and wrap in foil.

Heat the grill or barbecue until very hot. Remove the steaks from the marinade and brush off any debris. Grill for 2–3 minutes on each side, a little longer if you like your steak well done, then season with salt and pepper. While it grills, warm the foil-wrapped ciabatta on the grill, or in the oven, whichever is more appropriate. Toss the frisée in just enough dressing to coat it.

Unwrap the ciabatta, sprinkle the cut sides with the remaining dressing then lay the frisée on the bases, cover with the steak and clamp on the tops. Eat.

FLAVOURED BUTTERS TO SERVE WITH GRILLED STEAK

A prime steak, perfectly grilled, needs very little in the way of embellishment. A pat of flavoured butter perched on top, melting gently in the heat of the meat, is just right. These butters can be made well in advance and stored in the fridge, or even the freezer, ready to be used at the drop of a hat. Beurre Maître d'Hôtel is the classic accompaniment for grilled steak, but the three others all make excellent finishing touches.

Don't save them for steaks alone. Try dolloping them on hot vegetables or in baked potatoes.

Beurre Maître d'Hôtel – Lemon and Parsley Butter

MAKES ENOUGH FOR 6 STEAKS

100 g (4 oz) lightly salted butter, softened

1 teaspoon finely grated lemon zest

1½ tablespoons lemon juice

3 tablespoons finely chopped parsley

Freshly ground white or black pepper

If you have a food processor, put the butter in the bowl and set the blades whizzing. Add the lemon zest, juice, parsley and pepper. As soon as it is all smoothly amalgamated, scoop out onto a sheet of greaseproof paper, shape into a cylinder and roll up. Chill in the fridge until needed (it will keep for up to 4 days), and then slice and lay a couple of slices on top of each grilled steak just before serving.

If you don't have a processor, make sure that the lemon zest and parsley are very finely chopped, then beat into the butter by hand. Gradually beat in the lemon juice a little at a time and season with pepper.

Beurre aux Fines Herbes

MAKES ENOUGH FOR 6 STEAKS

100 g (4 oz) lightly salted butter, softened

1½ tablespoons lemon juice

1½ tablespoons finely chopped parsley

1 tablespoon chopped chives

1 generous teaspoon chopped tarragon

Freshly ground white or black pepper

Make as for Beurre Maître d'Hôtel.

Double Mustard Butter

Beef

100g (4 oz) lightly salted butter, softened

1 tablespoon coarse-grained mustard

½ tablespoon Dijon mustard

1½ tablespoons finely chopped parsley

A little freshly ground black pepper

Mash all the ingredients together thoroughly (don't blend in a food processor or you'll smooth out the nice knobbly grains in the coarse-grained mustard). As soon as it is all amalgamated, scoop out onto a sheet of greaseproof paper, shape into a cylinder and roll up. Chill in the fridge until needed (it will keep for up to 4 days), and then slice and lay a couple of slices on top of each grilled steak just before serving.

Blue Cheese Butter

100 g (4 oz) lightly salted butter, softened

100 g (4 oz) blue cheese (e.g. Stilton, Roquefort, Gorgonzola)

2 tablespoons finely chopped parsley

1 tablespoon finely chopped chives

Put all the ingredients in a food processor and whizz until smooth, then roll and chill as above.

If you don't have a blender, make sure the parsley and chives are very finely chopped. Mash the cheese to a paste then beat in the herbs. Stir into the butter until smooth and evenly mixed. Roll and chill as above.

Beef

CAPTAIN'S COMFORT

❦

This Danish stew is definitely not sophisticated food; it's basic, filling, peasanty stuff and none the worse for that. In fact, it is just the kind of thing that I love after I've had a surfeit of trendy, char-grilled Italian this or that with something salsa and whatever the latest vinegar seasoning happens to be.

There is no way you could possibly call Skipperlabskovs (its Danish name) trendy or fashionable. It is made of little more than meat and potatoes all cooked up together in a large pot until the potatoes go mushy and absorb the nice meaty gravy. It will never look pretty, but it tastes great. Real comfort food, and you don't even have to brown the meat.

SERVES 4

450 g (1 lb) chuck steak	3 bay leaves
675 g (1½ lb) floury potatoes	6 peppercorns
50 g (2 oz) butter, plus extra to serve	3 tablespoons chopped spring onions
1 large onion, chopped	Salt and freshly ground black pepper
600 ml (1 pint) stock or water	

Cut the steak into 2.5 cm (1 in) cubes. Peel the potatoes and cut into 2.5 cm (1 in) cubes. Melt the butter in a large flameproof casserole or pan and add the chopped onion and meat. Cook gently, stirring, until the onion is tender but not browned.

Add the stock or water, salt, bay leaves and peppercorns. Bring up to the boil, cover and simmer for 1½ hours. Add the potatoes and continue simmering, half-covered, for a further 45 minutes or so, stirring every now and then until the potatoes disintegrate to thicken the 'stew'. By the end of the cooking time you should have a thick mixture — soupier than mashed potatoes, but just about thick enough to eat with a fork. If necessary, add a little more water as it cooks, or boil off some of the liquid at the end if it isn't thick enough.

Adjust the seasoning and sprinkle with the spring onions. Serve in big dollops with a knob of butter on top of each and accompany with rye bread.

CARBONNADES À LA FLAMANDE

Beef

Made with beer and plenty of onions, this stew may be rather less chic than a daube de boeuf (see page 36), but it is just as welcome on a chilly evening. What I really like about it is the contrast between the crisp mustardy layer of bread on the top, and the tender meat and juices underneath.

If you make the stew in advance don't put the bread on top until after you've begun to re-heat it on the day of serving.

SERVES 4 – 6

900 g (2 lb) shin of beef

About 2 tablespoons vegetable oil

2 onions, sliced

2 garlic cloves, chopped

3–4 tablespoons seasoned flour

300 ml (10 fl oz) brown ale or stout

1 tablespoon light muscovado sugar

1 bouquet garni (see below)

Salt and freshly ground black pepper

——— *For the crust* ———

40 g (1½ oz) butter, softened

1½ tablespoons Dijon mustard

6 slices French bread

Pre-heat the oven to 170°C/325°F/Gas Mark 3. Cut the beef into strips about 1 cm (½ in) thick, 8 cm (3 in) long and 2.5 cm (1 in) wide. Heat 2 tablespoons of oil in a large frying pan, add the onions and fry over a moderate heat until tender. Add the garlic and continue cooking for 2 minutes, then scoop the onion and garlic out of the pan and put them in the bottom of an oven-proof casserole.

Raise the heat under the frying pan and add a little more oil, if necessary. Toss the meat in the flour and brown in two batches. Transfer to the casserole.

Reduce the heat under the frying pan and pour in the beer. Bring up to the boil, stirring and scraping in all the residues. Stir in the sugar, then pour over the meat and onions. Add the bouquet garni and season with salt and pepper. Add enough water to just cover the beef. Cover and cook in the oven for 2½–3 hours, stirring occasionally and adding a little more water if it begins to get dry.

Meanwhile, mash the butter with the mustard and spread it thickly on the bread slices. Place the bread buttered side up on top of the stew. Return to the oven and cook, uncovered, for a further 30 minutes, or until the bread is crisp and lightly browned on top. Serve immediately.

Note: To make a bouquet garni, take 1 bay leaf, 2 sprigs of parsley and 2 sprigs of thyme and tie them together with string.

BEEF, GUINNESS
AND MUSHROOM STEW

Guinness gives a dark, rich savoury satisfaction to a beef stew while mushrooms underline the deep flavour — I usually add a few right at the beginning of the cooking time then supplement the stew with freshly cooked mushrooms at the last moment. If you can't get shiitake mushrooms, replace them with large, meaty flat-caps.

SERVES 6

900 g (2 lb) shin of beef	2 tablespoons tomato purée
Seasoned flour, for dusting	½ tablespoon sugar
50 g (2 oz) butter	1 bay leaf
2 tablespoons sunflower oil	2 sprigs of thyme
2 onions, roughly chopped	2 sprigs of parsley
100 g (4 oz) button mushrooms	1 sprig of rosemary
750 ml (1¼ pints) Guinness,	225 g (8 oz) shiitake mushrooms
Murphy's or any other stout	Salt and freshly ground black pepper

P re-heat the oven to 170°C/325°F/Gas Mark 3. Trim the beef and cut into 2.5 cm (1 in) cubes. Toss lightly in seasoned flour. Heat a third of the butter and 1 table-spoon of the oil in a frying pan and brown the meat briskly in batches, without overcrowding the pan. Transfer to the casserole. Add a little more butter and oil to the pan and fry the onions until lightly browned. Scoop into the casserole. Finally fry the button mushrooms and add those to the casserole too.

Pour the Guinness into the pan and bring up to the boil, scraping in the brown residues from frying. Stir in the tomato purée and sugar, then pour into the casserole. Tie the herbs together in a bundle with string to make a bouquet garni and add to the casserole with the salt and pepper. Cover and transfer to the oven. Cook for 2–3 hours or until the meat is very tender. Check occasionally, and if necessary add a little hot water.

Remove the stalks from the shiitake mushrooms and discard. Slice the caps thickly. Heat the remaining butter in a frying pan and sauté the mushrooms, then stir into the casserole and return to the oven for 5 minutes. Discard the bouquet garni, adjust the seasoning and serve.

DAUBE DE BOEUF

This is France's most famous beef stew and it comes, perhaps not surprisingly, with many variations. When it is good (and this version is) it is wonderfully fragrant and aromatic. The name comes from the earthenware dish it is cooked in, a daubière, with a fat pot-belly that narrows to a relatively small rim. Essential to its flavour are red wine, brandy and dried orange zest. Serve the stew with buttered and parsleyed noodles.

SERVES 6 - 8

3 sprigs of thyme	3 large carrots, scraped and sliced
1 bay leaf, snapped in two	675 g (1½ lb) tomatoes, skinned,
2 sprigs of parsley	seeded and roughly chopped
1 strip of dried orange zest	1 tablespoon tomato purée, optional
225 g (8 oz) unsmoked streaky bacon, in a	3 garlic cloves, crushed
single piece, or thick-cut, cubed	50–100 g (2–4 oz) pork rinds, diced
3 tablespoons olive oil	600 ml (1 pint) fruity red wine
2 large onions, sliced	50 ml (2 fl oz) brandy
1.5 kg (3 lb) chuck or rump of beef, cut into	Salt and freshly ground black pepper
5 cm (2 in) squares, about 2.5 cm (1 in) thick	

Pre-heat the oven to 150°C/300°F/Gas Mark 2. Tie together the herbs and orange zest with string to make a bouquet garni. Fry the bacon in the olive oil until lightly browned. Scoop out and spread over the base of an oven-proof casserole. Now fry the onions over a moderate heat in the same fat, until golden, and add to the casserole.

Dry the meat carefully, then brown in the fat over a high heat in three batches. Arrange on top of the onions. Add the bouquet garni, the carrots, tomatoes, tomato purée, if using, garlic, salt and pepper. Cover with the pork rinds.

Pour the excess fat out of the frying pan and pour in the wine. Bring up to the boil, scraping in the brown residues from frying. Pour over the contents of the casserole.

Add the brandy to the pan, warm quickly and set alight at arm's length either with a match, if you cook over an electric hob, or by using the gas flame, tilting the pan so that the warm brandy ignites. When the flames die down, pour the brandy into the casserole too. Add enough water to almost cover the contents.

Cover tightly and place in the oven. Cook gently for 3–4 hours, stirring once or twice, until the meat is marvellously tender. After 3 hours, check the state of the liquid. If it is a little watery, uncover the pan and let it reduce down. When meat and sauce are ready, skim off what fat you can and serve.

Optional Extras

Olives

225 g (8 oz) black olives, stoned

Stir into the stew half an hour before it is done.

Persillade

2 tablespoons chopped parsley

1 garlic clove, very finely chopped

Mix together and sprinkle over the stew just before serving. You can use the olives and persillade together if you wish.

Anchovies and capers

4 tinned anchovy fillets, chopped   2 tablespoons chopped parsley

1 tablespoon capers, chopped   1–2 garlic cloves, chopped

Mix together all the ingredients and either stir into the stew half an hour before it is cooked, so that the flavours mellow out into the sauce, or sprinkle over the stew just before serving for a sprightlier, brassier taste.

Beef

BŒUF À LA MODE EN GELÉE

Bœuf à la mode is the perfect dish for a summer-time party – it can be served either hot or cold, depending on the weather. The instructions below are for the cold version, neatly set and moulded to be cut in wedges. However, if the weather is abysmal, you can skip the last part and serve the beef hot, sliced, with the carrots alongside, and the reduced stock as a sauce.

Either way, cook the beef at least one day in advance. It's not a quick dish to make, but it needs little attention and can be left to cook or cool while you get on with something else.

SERVES 6-8

1.5–1.75 kg (3–4 lb) piece of topside	4 allspice berries
75 g (3 oz) streaky bacon, cut into strips	2 bay leaves
3 tablespoons oil	2 large sprigs of thyme
3 tablespoons brandy	1 sprig of rosemary
1 large onion, chopped	3 sprigs of parsley
2 celery sticks, sliced	600 ml (1 pint) red wine
2 garlic cloves, peeled and halved	900 ml–1.2 litres (1½–2 pints) beef stock
675 g (1½ lb) carrots, sliced	Salt and freshly ground black pepper
2 calf's or pig's trotters	

Lard the beef with the bacon by making holes in the beef and pushing the strips of fat deep down into the meat with the aid of a thin-handled teaspoon, a skewer, or a proper larding needle. Dry the meat thoroughly and then brown in the oil. Transfer to a deep casserole dish.

Warm the brandy and set it alight (either with a match or by tilting it into a gas flame) and pour over the beef. Once the flames have subsided, add the onion, celery, garlic, 100 g (4 oz) of the carrots, the trotters, spices and herbs (but no salt). Pour over the wine and enough beef stock to come three-quarters of the way up the beef. Bring gently to the boil, cover and simmer very gently for about 4 hours, turning the beef occasionally.

When it is done, ladle out enough stock to cook the rest of the carrots in, then leave the beef to cool for 2–3 hours in the remaining stock. Cook the carrots in the stock, seasoning lightly with salt and pepper, then leave to cool before straining and reserving both the stock and carrots.

Remove the beef from its stock and tear into shreds. Strain the stock, mix with the carrot stock, then boil until reduced to 600 ml (1 pint). Taste and adjust the seasoning.

Line a bowl with about half the carrots, pack in the meat and then the remaining carrots. Pour over the stock and leave overnight in the fridge to set. Just before serving, sit the bowl in hot water for a few seconds, then turn out onto a serving plate.

Beef

STEAK TERIYAKI

Japanese teriyaki sauce is dark, sweet and sticky and sets off a juicy steak beautifully. If you can get real sake and mirin (from oriental food stores) then the sauce will be especially good, though dry and sweet sherry stand in quite well.

SERVES 2

2 sirloin steaks, about 2.5 cm (1 in) thick
Sunflower or vegetable oil
2 tablespoons sake or dry sherry
2 tablespoons dark soy sauce

2 tablespoons mirin or sweet sherry, or sake plus 1 tablespoon sugar
1 teaspoon sugar

Cover the base of a heavy frying pan with a very thin film of oil. Place over a high heat. When it is searingly hot, place the steaks in the pan and cook for 6 minutes, turning once.

After the first 4 minutes, having turned the steaks, spoon over the sake. Be warned, it will sizzle and smoke. Cover the pan tightly and cook for the final 2 minutes. Transfer the steaks to a warm plate and keep warm.

Add the remaining ingredients to the pan and stir and scrape all the residues into the liquid. Let it boil hard until reduced by half. Return the steaks to the pan, with any juices that have seeped out, and cook for 1 final minute, turning once.

Good Old Hamburgers

When they are made properly, with good minced beef — try asking your butcher to mince some chuck steak or even sirloin steak for you — home-made hamburgers are a great pleasure. I usually grill them, but you could tart them up no end by frying them, then deglazing the pan with a slug of wine, reducing and finishing with some cream and a little mustard to make a luxurious sauce.

Whether you grill or fry, test them for doneness in exactly the same way as you would a steak (see page 18).

SERVES 4

675 g (1½ lb) lean minced beef	1 egg, lightly beaten, optional
½ onion, grated or very finely chopped	Oil, or a combination of oil
½ tablespoon Worcestershire sauce	and butter, for grilling or frying
1 tablespoon very finely chopped parsley	Salt and freshly ground black pepper
Leaves from 2 sprigs of	
thyme, finely chopped	

——— To serve ———

4 buns, split open and lightly toasted	Dill-pickled cucumbers, sliced
on the inside	Tomato ketchup, mayonnaise,
Shredded lettuce leaves	Tabasco, or your favourite relish
Sliced tomato	

Mix the beef with the onion, Worcestershire sauce, parsley, thyme, and salt and pepper. Use your fingers to squelch it all together thoroughly. If the mixture seems rather crumbly, add a little beaten egg to hold it together. Divide into 4 and shape into nice round patties about 2 cm (¾ in) thick, then grill or fry.

To grill, brush each burger with a little oil and grill close to a thoroughly pre-heated grill until browned and crusty on the outside, but still moist and tender on the inside.

To fry, heat a little oil or oil and butter in a frying pan and fry the burgers over a high heat until nicely browned outside and done to your taste on the inside.

Sandwich in the buns together with lettuce, tomato and pickled cucumber, salt and pepper, and whatever sauces or relishes you happen to like best.

CHA BO

(Vietnamese Hamburgers)

This recipe for spiced hamburgers with a hot, sour, sweet and salty dipping sauce is based on one I came across in an American book called The Foods of Vietnam *by Nicole Routhier. It turns plain hamburgers into something marvellously exotic. Tins of coconut milk, rice vinegar and fish sauce are all available in oriental supermarkets and even in some ordinary supermarkets as well. They all keep for ages, so buy them when you see them.*

SERVES 4

4 tablespoons shelled unsalted peanuts

450 g (1 lb) lean minced beef

3 shallots, very finely chopped

4 teaspoons fish sauce *(nam pla)*

3 tablespoons coconut milk

1 teaspoon ground cumin

1½ tablespoons finely chopped coriander

1 teaspoon sugar

A little oil, for brushing

Salt and freshly ground black pepper

—— *For the Nuoc Cham (dipping sauce)* ——

1 small red chilli, seeded and finely chopped

2 garlic cloves, chopped

2 tablespoons sugar

Juice of 1 lime

4 tablespoons rice vinegar or cider vinegar

4 tablespoons fish sauce *(nam pla)*

To make the dipping sauce, pound the chilli with the garlic and sugar to a paste in a mortar. Work in the lime juice, then the vinegar, fish sauce and finally 3 tablespoons of water. Serve in small bowls.

Pre-heat the grill thoroughly. Grind the peanuts to a coarse powder and mix with all the remaining burger ingredients except the oil, kneading well with your fingers to form a cohesive mass. Divide into 4 portions, roll each one into a ball, then flatten to make a patty about 2 cm (¾ in) thick. Brush with a little oil and cook under the grill for about 3–4 minutes on each side. Serve with the dipping sauce.

BEEF LINDSTROM

Beef Lindstrom is the Swedish answer to the hamburger, and a very good answer it is too. The bulk of the patty is made up of minced beef and mashed potato, with capers and finely diced beetroot dotted through them. They are often served with a fried egg on top, a delicious addition but not absolutely necessary.

On the whole I'm not too taken with pickled beetroot, or even ordinary bought cooked beetroot that has been saturated in vinegar. For this recipe however, I make an exception. Since it is finely diced, the sharpness works quite well. Even so, given the choice I'd rather use beetroot that I've cooked myself, minus vinegar.

SERVES 4

450 g (1 lb) lean minced beef	½ onion, grated
8 oz (225 g) cooked peeled potato, mashed	2 tablespoons capers
1 egg yolk	15 g (½ oz) butter and 1 tablespoon oil,
85–150 ml (3–5 fl oz) milk	or 2 tablespoons oil
1 medium-sized cooked or pickled	4 fried eggs, optional
beetroot, finely diced	Salt and freshly ground black pepper

Using your hands, mix the beef thoroughly with the potato, egg yolk, salt and pepper and just enough milk to hold the mixture together without making it too sticky to shape. If you have a food processor, work the mixture in it to make it smoother. Mix in the beetroot, onion and capers. Divide into 4 portions and form each one into a hamburger shape, about 2 cm (¾ in) thick. Fry in the butter and oil mixture or just oil until nicely browned on both sides. Serve as they are or, even better, with a fried egg on top.

Beef

STEAK TARTARE

PER PERSON:

175 g (6 oz) best rump or fillet steak

1 egg yolk, sitting neatly in its half shell

¼ red onion, very finely chopped

1 tablespoon small capers, rinsed

2 cornichons, or small pickled gherkins,
finely chopped

1 heaped tablespoon chopped parsley

2 tinned anchovy fillets, finely chopped

Dijon mustard

Worcestershire sauce

Tabasco

Salt and freshly ground black pepper

As near as possible to the time you wish to serve the steak tartare, trim the meat and either mince or chop it very finely with a sharp knife. If you must use the processor, whizz it in short pulses, scraping down the sides frequently and making sure that you don't turn the meat into a mush.

Make a neat, plump round cushion of the meat in the centre of a plate. Nestle the egg yolk in its shell in the centre. Place little mounds of onion, capers, cornichons, parsley and anchovies around it. Serve it up straight away.

The diner can mix in just what he or she wants of the piquant bits and bobs around the plate, enrich the meat with the egg yolk and spice it up with mustard, Worcestershire sauce, Tabasco, salt and pepper at will.

YUK HWE

(Korean Steak Tartare)

This is the most delicious, Far Eastern version of steak tartare, flavoured with sesame oil, soy sauce, pine nuts and the sweetness of pear. Though I love steak tartare, I like this Korean dish even better. Try to get a Japanese Nashi pear for a measure of authenticity — you sometimes see them for sale in supermarkets and smart greengrocers' — though the extra sweetness of a ripe western-style pear is very appetizing in its place.

SERVES 2 AS A MAIN COURSE OR 4 AS A STARTER

225 g (8 oz) fillet of beef	4 teaspoons sesame oil
½ tablespoon sugar	½ ripe but firm pear
1 tablespoon light soy sauce	Lemon juice, optional
1 teaspoon sesame seeds	1 egg yolk
Freshly ground black pepper	1 tablespoon pine nuts

To make it easier to cut, chill the beef in the freezer for 10–20 minutes until it's firm but not actually frozen. Cut into slices, across the grain, of about 3 mm (⅛ in) thick, then cut into narrow strips of about 3 mm (⅛ in) across and 2.5 cm (1 in) long.

As close as possible to the time you are to serve the beef, mix it with the sugar, soy sauce, sesame seeds, pepper and finally the sesame oil. Core the pear and cut into matchsticks. If not serving immediately, toss in a little lemon juice to prevent browning. Arrange the meat in a neat round mound in the centre of a plate. Arrange the pear pieces around it, then make a dip in the centre and carefully place the egg yolk in it. Scatter with pine nuts. Mix the meat with the egg yolk and pear at the table.

Pan-Fried Strips of Beef in Wild Mushroom and Mustard Sauce

This is a rich and luxurious beef dish, just the thing for a mid-week dinner party or a special treat. Serve it with parsley-speckled noodles to balance the creaminess of the sauce.

SERVES 4

15 g (½ oz) dried porcini

3 shallots, finely chopped

50 ml (2 fl oz) Noilly Prat or other dry vermouth

300 ml (10 fl oz) whipping cream

25 g (1 oz) butter

1 tablespoon sunflower oil

450 g (1 lb) rump or fillet steak, cut into strips 1 cm (½ in) thick, 5 cm (2 in) long, and 2.5 cm (1 in) wide

175 g (6 oz) button mushrooms, halved or quartered

2 tablespoons Moutarde de Meaux or other coarse-grained mustard

Salt and freshly ground black pepper

Soak the porcini in a little warm water for 20–30 minutes until softened, then chop roughly. Let the soaking water settle for 5 minutes, then carefully pour it off into a separate bowl, leaving the earthy grit behind. Reserve the liquid.

Put the shallots into a pan with the vermouth and boil until reduced to a damp mass. Stir in the cream, bring up to the boil and simmer until reduced by a third. Season with salt and pepper.

Melt the butter with the oil in a wide frying pan over a high heat and heat until foaming. Sauté the strips of beef for a few minutes, turning and tossing until lightly browned but no more. Scoop out and reserve.

Add the button mushrooms to the same pan and fry until tender, then scoop out and add to the meat. Pour off any excess fat and add the liquid from soaking the porcini mushrooms. Bring up to the boil, stirring in all the residues in the pan. Add the porcini and simmer for a couple of minutes until the liquid has mostly boiled off.

Return the beef and fresh mushrooms to the pan and pour over the cream sauce. Stir in the mustard. Bring up to the boil and simmer for a minute or so to heat through. Taste, adjust the seasoning and serve.

My Mince

This is how I cook mince and I can think of no special name for it. It is good enough to eat in all sorts of ways, just as it is, spooned over baked potatoes, on pasta with lashings of Parmesan, or as the basis for my own slightly unorthodox cottage pie (see next recipe).

Beef

SERVES 4-6

1 large onion, chopped

1 carrot, finely diced

2 tablespoons olive oil or sunflower oil

1–2 garlic cloves, crushed

675 g (1½ lb) best-quality, lean minced beef

1 x 400 g (14 oz) tin chopped tomatoes

½ red pepper, grilled, skinned and chopped, optional

3 tablespoons tomato ketchup

2 teaspoons Worcestershire sauce, optional

½ teaspoon dried thyme

½ teaspoon ground cumin

Salt and freshly ground black pepper

Cook the onion and the carrot in the oil in a large, wide, heavy frying pan over a medium heat until tender and lightly coloured. Add the garlic and stir for a few seconds, then increase the heat to high and add half the mince. Fry briskly, breaking up the lumps and turning the meat over, until it is lightly browned. Scoop out onto a plate.

Add the remaining mince to the pan and fry in the same way. When it is done, return the first batch to the pan along with the chopped tomatoes, pepper (if using) and all the remaining ingredients. Add 300 ml (10 fl oz) of water. Bring up to the boil and half cover. Simmer gently, stirring from time to time, for about an hour, adding more hot water as needed. By this time the meat should be tender and most of the liquid evaporated away to leave a delicious moist mush. Taste and adjust the seasoning. (I often add a splash more ketchup or Worcestershire sauce at this stage!)

Beef

MY COTTAGE PIE

I use my standard method of cooking mince as the basis for my cottage pie. The result is absolutely delicious and we all tend to end up eating far too much of it.

SERVES 4 – 6

1 quantity My Mince (see previous recipe)

675 g (1½ lb) floury potatoes

65 g (2½ oz) butter

150–300 ml (5–10 fl oz) full cream milk

Salt and freshly ground black pepper

Pre-heat the oven to 200°C/400°F/Gas Mark 6. While the mince is cooking, make the mashed potatoes. Cook the potatoes by boiling them in their skins, baking them in the oven or microwaving them. Peel while still hot and mash thoroughly in a saucepan with 50 g (2 oz) of the butter. Season with salt and beat energetically over a low heat, gradually adding the milk, until the mash is light, fluffy and smooth. Taste and adjust the seasoning.

To assemble the pie, spoon the mince into a pie dish. Dot the mashed potato over the top and smooth down, then make patterns in the surface with a fork. Dot with the remaining butter and bake in the oven until the potato is patched with brown. Dish up immediately.

MEATLOAF

This is another family favourite. Meatloaf is really pâté by another name, though not quite so fancy. But who cares when it tastes this good? It is lovely straight from the oven (make a tomato sauce to serve with it), though it tends to crumble when sliced. Cold left-overs are just as good and will slice more neatly. Excellent with chutney and a salad, or in sandwiches.

SERVES 6 – 8

1 large onion, chopped	350 g (12 oz) best-quality sausagemeat
2 garlic cloves, chopped	2 eggs, lightly beaten
15 g (½ oz) butter	2 tablespoons chopped parsley
1 tablespoon oil	1 teaspoon dried thyme
25 g (1 oz) soft white breadcrumbs	Salt and freshly ground black pepper
675 g (1½ lb) minced beef	

Pre-heat the oven to 180°C/350°F/Gas Mark 4. Fry the onion and garlic gently in the butter and oil until tender. Scrape into a mixing bowl. Add all the remaining ingredients and mix thoroughly. Quickly fry a small knob of the mixture to test the seasoning, then adjust, adding more salt, pepper, parsley or thyme as required. Pack the mixture into a buttered loaf tin or terrine, smoothing down the surface, then bang hard on the work-top to expel any trapped air bubbles.

Bake in the oven for 1–1½ hours until done. To test, pierce the centre with a skewer – the juices should run clear, rather than raw and bloody. Serve hot or cold.

MEATBALLS IN TOMATO SAUCE

This is a pleasingly adaptable recipe that can be served straight, with vegetables and potatoes, or spooned over spaghetti in a more American-Italian style. Either way, I love meatballs in tomato sauce and am always inclined to make more than necessary — they're good to pick at when cold, too!

To serve over spaghetti, you should make half-size meatballs Spoon them over spaghetti that has been tossed in a little lubricating olive oil, mounded up on individual plates, and pass round a bowl of freshly grated Parmesan.

SERVES 4 (OR 6 WITH SPAGHETTI)

1 thick slice white bread	1 x 400 g (14 oz) tin chopped tomatoes
4 tablespoons milk	1 tablespoon tomato purée
350 g (12 oz) lean minced beef or pork	½ teaspoon sugar
3 tablespoons chopped parsley	4 tablespoons red wine or water
3 garlic cloves, crushed	1 teaspoon dried oregano
1 egg, beaten	Salt and freshly ground black pepper
2 tablespoons olive oil	

Remove the crusts from the bread. Tear the bread into small pieces, put it into a bowl with the milk and leave to soften for 10 minutes. Add the minced beef or pork, half the parsley, half the garlic and salt and pepper. Mix well, kneading with your hands to break up the bread. Add just enough of the egg to bind the mixture without making it too sloppy to shape. Scoop up 1 tablespoonful of the mixture at a time and roll into balls.

Heat the oil over a medium heat in a frying pan large enough to take all the meatballs in a single layer. Add the meatballs and fry briskly until browned all over. Now add all the remaining ingredients to the pan, including the rest of the parsley and garlic. Stir gently to mix without breaking up the meatballs. Bring to a simmer, then reduce the heat to low and cover. Simmer for 30 minutes. Taste, adjust the seasoning and serve.

Beef

BOBOTIE

❦

Bobotie is a recipe of South African origin, credited to the kitchens of the slaves and labourers brought in by the Dutch from the Far East, though it is now a national dish. The Malays, as they were known (though they might well have come from other Far Eastern countries) brought their own culinary traditions with them, gradually adapting them to fit the local supplies of food. Bobotie is just one of a legacy of spiced dishes that they gave their new country.

It's a wonderful way to dress up minced beef (or lamb) and, unlike so many minced meat dishes, you don't even have to fiddle around browning and cooking the meat before you put it together with all the other ingredients.

SERVES 4

1 medium onion, chopped	1 tablespoon mild curry powder
1 garlic clove, chopped	½ tablespoon sugar
15 g (½ oz) butter or 1 tablespoon oil, plus a little extra for greasing	2 tablespoons lemon juice
	25 g (1 oz) flaked almonds
1 thick slice bread	75 g (3 oz) raisins
150 ml (5 fl oz) milk	2 eggs
450 g (1 lb) minced beef or lamb	Salt and freshly ground black pepper

Pre-heat the oven to 180°C/350°F/Gas Mark 4. Fry the onion and garlic in the butter or oil until lightly browned. While they are cooking, remove the crusts from the bread and soak the bread in the milk for 2–3 minutes. Squeeze the milk out of the bread and keep both separately.

Mix the fried onion and garlic with the minced beef or lamb, curry powder, sugar, lemon juice, almonds, raisins, salt and pepper and soaked bread, beating to mix evenly. Finally beat in one of the eggs. Spoon into a greased pie dish and smooth down.

Beat the second egg with the reserved milk, salt and pepper and pour over the minced meat mixture. Bake for 55–60 minutes until the top is set and browned. Serve with rice and a fruit chutney.

Lamb

Lamb

One of the signs of spring in our house is the early morning call from the sheep and lambs. As the weather begins to soften, a neighbour's flock is moved into the field below our bedroom window. Their pre-dawn chorus of baaing and bleating is enough to wake the dead. We curse their proximity as we bury our heads under the duvet in search of peace, forgetting that for the rest of the day we will be glad to look out across this field full of woolly backs, thinking it a most peaceful, rural scene.

Sheep are such an integral part of the British countryside that it is hard to imagine it without them. Long may it stay that way, for it is what makes lamb (and mutton if you can get it) such an appetizingly flavoured meat. Nearly all our lambs are raised free-range (though this doesn't necessarily imply organic), out in green pastures where they can frolic and then stroll as they get older and more sedate, grazing to their hearts' content. I'm sad to say that a handful of farmers have turned to indoor, semi-intensive rearing, but they are few and far between. For the most part, those cute little lambs lead a happy, if short, life.

The type of pasture is a key factor to the flavour of lamb. The French rate salt-marsh (*pré-salé*) lamb very highly and that goes for both their own and ours (much of it from Romney or Wales). The taste of the salt-water-washed herbiage is reckoned to add a distinct quality. I once ate salt-marsh lamb at Mont St Michel, raised in the often flooded fields that surround it. It was superbly sweet and tender. The miniature primitive sheep (a leg is just enough to feed two) that dine on seaweed on the island of Ronaldsay are just as succulent and beautifully flavoured. Mind you, damp is by no means essential. In Spain, I ate some of the best lamb chops I've ever come across. They came from Merinos, raised in the arid Extremaduran *dehesa,* slopes dotted with holm oaks. Here they graze on a profusion of intensely aromatic herbs, which filter their way through to the lucky diner.

Our earliest spring lamb is ready just in time for Easter, but it is not necessarily the best. It will have been slaughtered very young (a mere four months old) and though it will be as meltingly tender as butter – assuming it has been hung properly – it won't have had time to develop much depth of flavour. Butchers and producers I've talked to reckon that the best lamb is worth waiting for. Eight months is about right for the perfect balance of tenderness and flavour and that takes you to around mid-summer.

In fact, lamb remains lamb for up to a year, at which point the meat is rechristened mutton. Young mutton, like young lamb, is considered inferior to the more mature stuff. The ideal age for mutton is around 3–4 years. Mutton is a meat that has dropped out of fashion, though heaven knows why. It is not, as some people imagine, tough or overwhelmingly powerful. Properly hung and cooked appropriately, it is every bit as delicious as its younger, more popular sibling, with an intriguing, complex flavour. Mutton really doesn't need to be dressed as lamb.

HOW TO CHOOSE GOOD LAMB

Lamb

Choosing lamb comes down to common sense in many ways. You should be looking for nice, plump-looking joints, which show no signs of drying out from over-exposure, nor of excessive dampness or moisture. The colour of the flesh will vary according to age and pasture, but generally speaking it should be a clear, brownish-pink, with no sign of blood-iness. The fat should be parchment white, dry, brittle and waxy. Don't worry about those coloured stamps that you often find on lamb. They are imprinted with vegetable dye and are perfectly safe to consume. Just ignore them.

Since lamb is an outdoor animal, often born in the chilly late winter or early spring, it will have a generous covering of fat for warmth, which is all to the good. Trim it by all means, but don't be over-zealous about it. On a small joint, say a rack of lamb that will be roasted at a high heat, the fat plays an essential role in keeping the meat moist. Some fat will drip off during the cooking process, and more can be trimmed off after cooking.

Mutton is a rare find, but well worth trying when you do come across it. Good mutton will have a rich browny, almost purple colour to it, but the fat will still be white and dry. Avoid anything that is greyish with yellowing fat.

CHOPS

Chops are all cut from the back of the animal. The classic chops are the loin chops from the centre. At the rear end, they broaden out to give chump chops, larger and meatier, whilst towards the neck end they slim down into more delicate cutlets (you'll need 2–3 of these per person).

Chops are such convenient bits of meat. Just about the right size for one, easy and quick to cook, good to eat. You can throw them under the grill with nothing more than a light brushing of olive oil to prevent them drying out (if you do, make sure the grill is thoroughly pre-heated so that the exterior sears to a nice crusty brown, while the inside stays juicy and moist) or you can dress them up to whatever degree you care to take them.

One of the simplest improvements that I return to time and again is adapted from the cooking of larger legs of lamb, as in the Lamb Chops with Rosemary, Aubergine and Black Olives recipe on page 80 where I stud the chops with slivers of garlic and needles of rosemary. If the schedule permits, a few hours or even a day later, the flavours will have had time to scent the meat subtly. If you're feeling daring, try replacing the rosemary with thin strips of anchovy – not too many – which will melt subtly into the meat as it cooks.

Lamb

Marinating will usually work a little magic — try pouring over a mixture of olive oil, red wine, a shot of wine vinegar, garlic, onion and aromatic herbs such as thyme, rosemary, oregano or marjoram and let the chops sit in their encouraging bath. Other additions might include crushed coriander seeds or cumin, lemon instead of wine and vinegar, fresh mint or tarragon.

CUTS AND COOKING

ROASTING

Being a youthful meat, most pieces of lamb are tender enough to roast, with the exception of scrag or neck, and somehow it always seems to be a less daunting meat to roast than something like beef. Of course, certain cuts are vastly superior to others. Everyone's favourite is a prime leg of lamb, perfect for Sunday lunch, but even more impressive and beautifully tender is a whole saddle or double loin of lamb. The saddle is made up of two loins (which can be roasted separately for smaller gatherings) nestling up against the central backbone, as well as the kidneys.

A rack of lamb makes the perfect two-person joint, taking very little time to cook. A pair of racks can be joined to make either a guard of honour or a crown roast.

Shoulder, blessed with a heavy marbling of fat, is a cheaper alternative to a whole leg and can be roasted both on the bone and off, as well as being suitable for stuffing and rolling. Similarly, breast can be boned, rolled and stuffed for roasting.

POT-ROASTING AND BRAISING

Lamb shanks, or knuckles, are often ignored in favour of the prime cuts, which actually makes them a marvellous bargain. They are best braised or pot-roasted gently until the meat virtually falls away from the bone. In fact, you can pot roast or braise any bit of lamb, though it is hardly necessary, but for me the shanks reign supreme for this cooking method. Pot roasting and braising are perfect for mutton too.

CASSEROLING AND STEWING

Again, any bit will do handsomely, but bony pieces like scrag or middle neck are cheap and have loads of flavour. For Lancashire hotpot and Irish stew and the like, loin chops (of lamb or, more traditionally, mutton) are what's called for. Chump chops are excellent

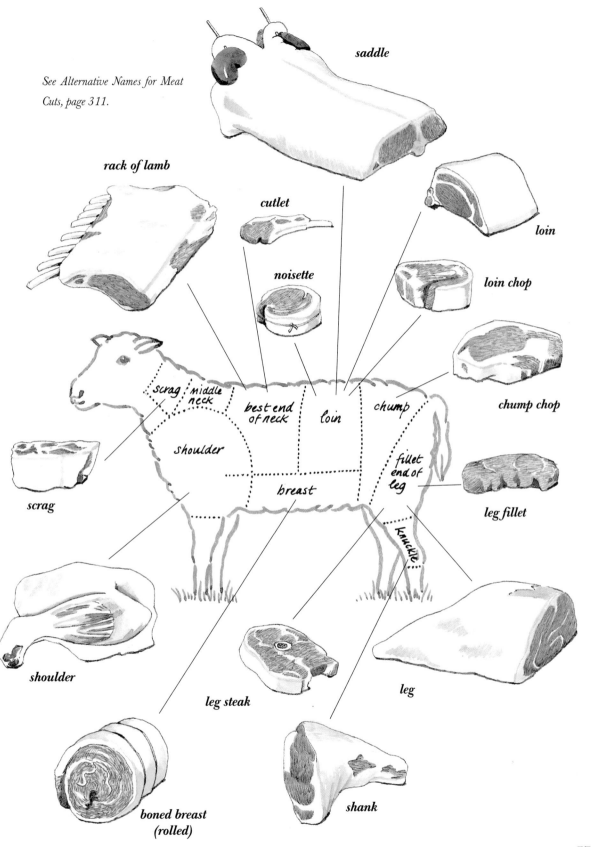

saddle

See Alternative Names for Meat Cuts, page 311.

rack of lamb

cutlet

noisette

loin

loin chop

chump chop

scrag | middle neck

best end of neck

loin

chump

shoulder

fillet end of leg

breast

knuckle

leg fillet

scrag

shoulder

leg steak

leg

shank

boned breast (rolled)

Lamb

too. Although leg is lovely and meaty it is pricey, possibly too pricey for a stew. Shoulder is every bit as good and more economical.

Mutton can be substituted for lamb in many casseroles and stews though it may well need longer cooking. Add a little extra water if necessary.

GRILLING AND FRYING

Chops of all kinds, including the choice little best end cutlets. Leg steaks and shoulder steaks. For kebabs, use leg or neck fillet. An entire butterflied leg of lamb is a stunning centrepiece for a summer barbecue.

ROASTING LAMB JOINTS

Lamb can be roasted pink, which is generally how I prefer it, or well-done, which is more in line with British tradition. Rare lamb, though quite safe to eat, is less of a treat than rare beef. If a decent layer of fat is left on the meat, then it will only need occasional (though regular) basting. The more fat is trimmed off, the more conscientiously you must baste.

A small joint, like a single rack, needs only the briefest blast in a fiercely hot oven. I usually allow a total of 20–25 minutes (depending on size) at 230°C/450°F/Gas Mark 8. If you must have well-done meat, then give it another 5 minutes or so.

A larger joint, like a whole leg, requires a different approach. To calculate the roasting time, allow 13 minutes per 500 g (12 minutes per lb) for rare meat, if that's how you really want it, 18 minutes per 500 g (16 minutes per lb) for medium and 20–22 minutes per 500 g (18–20 minutes per lb) for well-done. Start the meat at 230°C/450°F/Gas Mark 8 and reduce the heat to 200°C/400°F/Gas Mark 6 after 15 minutes. If you use a meat thermometer, take the joint out of the oven when it registers 50°C/125°F (rare, rising to 60°C/140°F as the meat rests), 60°C/140°F (medium, rising to 70°C/160°F as the meat rests) or 70°C/160°F (well-done, rising to 80°C/175°F as the meat rests). If you don't own a meat thermometer, use the skewer test given in the beef chapter (see page 14). Always let the lamb rest for a good 15 minutes or more in a warm place (e.g. the oven, with the heat switched off and the door ajar), during which time the internal heat continues to work its way towards the centre of the meat, raising the temperature at its heart.

TECHNIQUES

CROWN ROAST

Lamb

Though any butcher will prepare a crown roast for you, it's not at all difficult to construct for yourself, as long as you are armed with a sturdy needle, some thread and a thimble.

You'll need two racks of lamb. Ask the butcher to remove the chine bones for you, unless you have a small saw to cut the chine bone (backbone) away just where the rib bones begin. Save them for stock.

Skin the racks of lamb, leaving on a layer of fat. Scrape off the shreds of meat and fat from the tips of the bones, down to about 4 cm (1½ in). Curve each rack into a semi-circle, with the bones curving outwards. If this is tough going you can cut the connecting tissue at the base of the racks between the cutlets, but try not to pierce the meat. Set the racks back to back with the bones curving outwards, and sew them up together at each side using a trussing needle and thick thread or fine string. Stand on a roasting tin and push into a circular crown. Tie a piece of string around the middle to hold the crown in place. Protect the tips of the bones with twists of silver foil to prevent them from burning in the oven. Stuffing the central cavity helps the crown to hold its shape.

1. *Scrape away the meat and fat from the tips of the bones, down to about 4 cm (1½ in). Trim any remaining skin off the racks.*

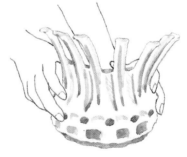

2. *Shape each rack into a semi-circle with the bones curving outwards, slitting the connecting tissue at the base of each rack if necessary.*

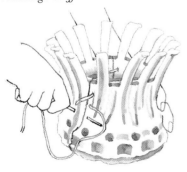

3. *Place the racks together, then sew up each side with a trussing needle. Stand them on a roasting tin and push into shape.*

GUARD OF HONOUR

A guard of honour is almost the inverse of the crown roast, though preparation begins in exactly the same way. Take two racks of lamb, chined (see above). Scrape off the shreds of meat and fat from the tops of the bones, down about 4 cm (1½ in). Now for the difference. Stand the racks face to face, meat inwards, fatty side outward and bones curving towards each other. Adjust them so that the bones interlock, like the swords of a real-life guard of honour. Either sew or tie the base together here and there to keep them in position. Although you can push a stuffing between the two racks, you won't get a great deal in there.

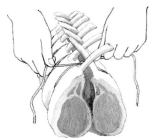

Prepare 2 racks as for step 1 of crown roast (page 59). Stand the racks face to face, bones curving in towards each other, and adjust so that the bones interlock. Sew or tie the base together.

NOISETTES

Noisettes, neat little roundels of tender meat, are usually cut from the loin or the rack of lamb. The first step is to skin the meat. Then, using a short-bladed knife, carefully cut and scrape down between the meat and the bone, stroking the blade against the bone and using it as your guide. Take out the bones. In a rack, you'll have to nick out the plastic-like piece of cartilage lodged between the meat and fat at the thinner end. Next, trim off the gristle nestling under the meat at the other, chunkier end. Carefully pare off any

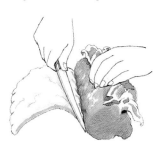

1. After skinning the meat, carefully cut down between the meat and bones to separate them. Remove the bones.

2. Trim the meat of gristle and excess fat. Roll the boned meat up tightly and tie firmly with string at 4 cm (1½ in) intervals.

3. With a very sharp knife, slice down between the strings to make individual noisettes.

excess fat, then roll the boned meat up tightly starting at the thicker, meatier side and progressing towards the thin end. Tie firmly at 4 cm (1½ in) intervals. Using an extra-sharp knife, slice down between the strings to make the individual noisettes.

BUTTERFLYING A LEG OF LAMB

The idea here is to open the leg of lamb out flat, removing the bones so that it can be barbecued or grilled. This is probably the least complicated way to bone a leg (if you want it tunnel boned, leaving a central cavity for the stuffing, then I suggest you ask your butcher to do it, as it requires more precision). First of all, you should know that there are three bones to negotiate and extract and that they run consecutively from the tip to the base, which is the best place to start the boning.

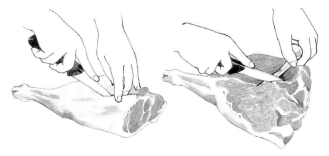

1. *Place the leg on a board with the thinner covering of flesh uppermost. Locate the first bone and slice along the length of it, cutting right down to the bone.*

2. *Cut the meat away from the bone with short strokes, keeping the blade close to the bone and turning the leg as you work. Ease out the bone and then repeat with the 2 remaining bones.*

3. *Open out the meat. Beat with a rolling pin or meat mallet to flatten, then make a couple of slashes through the thickest parts of the muscle.*

Lay the leg on the table in front of you. Prod the meat with your fingers, feeling out the position of that first bone. On one side, there will be a relatively generous covering of flesh, on the other it will be thinner. Turn to the thinner side, then make a cut along the length of the bone, right down to the bone itself. Patiently cut the meat from the bone, excavating round it in short strokes, keeping the blade close to the bone and turning the leg to ease the process. When you get to the knuckle, slice between the bones and ease out the first bone. Here you will find a small knobble of cartilage which can be fairly easily removed.

Repeat the above process with the second bone. The last bone at the narrow end of the leg should be started off in the same way, then when you get near the tip, cut through the fat where the meat has petered away to almost nothing, and remove the bone.

Now you can open your meat out flat. One last process. Take a wooden rolling pin or a meat mallet and bash the thicker parts of the cut side of the flesh to even it out a little. Make a couple of moderately deep slashes through the thickest chunks of muscle, so that the heat can penetrate more evenly and then it's ready to marinate or go straight on the grill rack.

CARVING A LEG OF LAMB

Lay the roast leg on a board, with the meatier side upwards. Hold it firmly in place, either with a carving fork or by grasping the knuckle with one hand. Begin by slicing a narrow wedge of meat, cutting down towards the bone, out of the middle of the joint. Now you can slice the meat on either side. Once that is all off, turn the joint over and slice off the remaining meat on the thinner side, cutting parallel to the bone instead of at right angles.

1. Holding the leg steady with a carving fork or your hand, slice a narrow wedge of meat out of the middle of the joint, cutting down towards the bone.

2. Slice the meat on either side of the initial wedge, before turning the joint over to carve the other side.

LAMB STOCK

Lamb stock is made in much the same way as beef stock (see pages 18–19). I usually add a good slug of Madeira or Marsala or even sweet sherry. A hint of sweetness, though not too much, goes well with lamb.

CROWN ROAST OF LAMB WITH SAGE, LEMON AND CHESTNUT STUFFING

A stuffed crown roast of lamb is one of the most glamorous joints you can place on the table. It is made of two racks of lamb and is usually roasted with a stuffing in the centre. You can, of course, use any stuffing you fancy, though ones with a hint of fruity sweetness, or herb-strewn stuffings, are particularly appropriate.

It's not at all difficult to put together your own crown of lamb if you have a sturdy needle, thread and a thimble, though it is easy enough to buy them fully prepared.

SERVES 6

2 best ends of neck of lamb, or a prepared crown

—— *Stuffing* ——

½ onion, chopped	1 tablespoon lemon juice
1 garlic clove, chopped	40 g (1½ oz) fresh white breadcrumbs
25 g (1 oz) butter	1 tablespoon chopped parsley
Finely grated zest of ½ lemon	1 egg, lightly beaten
2–3 sage leaves, finely chopped	Salt and freshly ground black pepper
175 g (6 oz) cooked, skinned chestnuts, crumbled	

Pre-heat the oven to 180°C/350°F/Gas Mark 4. If your butcher hasn't been kind enough to prepare the crown for you, see the instructions on how to prepare it on page 59.

To make the stuffing, cook the onion and garlic gently in the butter until tender but without browning. Mix with all the remaining ingredients, adding just enough egg to bind. Fill the centre of the crown with the stuffing then cover the stuffing with a piece of foil.

Roast the crown for about 1 hour, removing the foil over the stuffing after 40 minutes. Baste the joint from time to time as it cooks and when it is ready, turn off the heat, leave the door ajar and let the roast rest for 10 minutes. Before serving, remove the foil from the tips of the bones and replace it with cutlet frills, if you have them.

ROAST LEG OF LAMB WITH FLAGEOLETS

Spring green flageolet beans are a classic French accompaniment to a roast leg of lamb, and with some justification. I buy them from Italian delis or good wholefood shops and I believe that some supermarkets now stock them. If you can't find any, then white haricots or cannellini beans are almost as good, especially since it is these that the French in Brittany would use, anyway, which means that you won't be losing out at all on authenticity!

SERVES 6 - 8

1 leg of lamb weighing about 2.75 kg (6 lb)	2–3 tablespoons olive oil
2–3 garlic cloves, cut into long slivers	300 ml (10 fl oz) white wine
Leaves from 2 sprigs of rosemary	Salt and freshly ground black pepper

—— For the flageolets ——

450 g (1 lb) dried flageolet beans	1 bay leaf
1 onion, quartered	2 sprigs of parsley
5 garlic cloves, peeled but whole	1 sprig of thyme
1 large sprig of rosemary	2 tablespoons olive oil

Soak the flageolets overnight in cold water, then drain and rinse. Place in a pan with the onion, garlic, herbs and enough water to cover by about 5 cm (2 in). Bring to the boil and simmer until the beans are tender, about 1–1½ hours. Strain off most of the water that's left and reserve, leaving the beans in the pan. Fish out the herbs and discard.

Liquidize about a quarter of the beans, along with as many of the garlic cloves as you can find, with enough of the cooking water to make a thin purée. Stir the purée back into the pan of beans and re-heat when the lamb is cooked, adding the olive oil, salt and pepper to taste and a little more of the water if needed.

Pre-heat the oven to 230°C/450°F/Gas Mark 8. Prepare the lamb, making slits all over the meat with a small-bladed knife, then pushing in slivers of garlic and rosemary leaves. Rub with olive oil, season well, and place in an oiled roasting tin. Pour the wine around it.

Calculate the roasting time by allowing 13 minutes per 500 g (12 minutes per lb) for rare meat, 18 minutes per 500 g (16 minutes per lb) for medium and 20–22 minutes per 500 g (18–20 minutes per lb) for well-done. Start the meat at 230°C/450°F/Gas Mark 8 and then reduce the heat to 200°C/400°F/Gas Mark 6 after 15 minutes. Baste frequently as it cooks, adding a little water if the juices begin to dry up. When done, turn off the heat, leave the door slightly ajar, and let the meat rest for 20–30 minutes before carving. Skim any fat from the juices and pour into a small jug to serve as a thin gravy, or stir into the flageolets for extra flavour.

Lamb

GIGOT D'AGNEAU BOULANGÈRE – ROAST LEG OF LAMB WITH POTATOES

To be honest, this isn't exactly what the boulangère, *the baker's wife, would be cooking in France. She would use butter, where I've used olive oil. I just happen to love the taste of olive oil with lamb and slowly cooked potatoes and find it a welcome change from the heaviness of butter. She might well be roasting a shoulder rather than a leg, too, if she was sticking firmly with her classic repertoire. If you do substitute a shoulder, then it should be cooked at a slightly lower temperature for rather longer.*

SERVES 6

1 leg of lamb, weighing around 2 kg (4½ lb)

2–3 garlic cloves, cut into thin slivers

Fresh thyme leaves

(or rosemary if you prefer)

Olive oil

Salt and freshly ground black pepper

—— For the potatoes ——

1 large onion, sliced

4 tablespoons olive oil

1.5 kg (3 lb) potatoes, peeled and thinly sliced

3 garlic cloves, crushed

150 ml (5 fl oz) lamb or chicken stock

Pre-heat the oven to 200°C/400°F/Gas Mark 6. Using a small, sharp knife, make slits all over the leg of lamb and push in shards of garlic and thyme leaves. Rub with a little olive oil and season with salt and pepper. Fry the onion in 1 tablespoon of the olive oil until tender. Blanch the sliced potatoes in boiling water for 3–5 minutes until half cooked, then drain thoroughly. Put the lamb in a large, oiled oven-proof dish and arrange half the potatoes and onions around it. Sprinkle over half the chopped garlic and season with salt and pepper. Add the remaining potatoes and sprinkle over the last of the garlic. Season with salt and pepper and pour on the stock. Drizzle over the remaining olive oil.

Roast in the oven for 17–20 minutes per 500 g (15–18 minutes per lb). Rest the joint for 15–20 minutes before serving.

Lamb

ROAST RACK OF LAMB
WITH A HERB CRUST

There is no more perfect joint for two than a tender little rack of lamb. It doesn't come cheap, but for a special occasion it is worth every penny. The meat, cooked on the bone, has an excellent sweet flavour. The cooked rack looks pretty and it hardly takes any time to prepare and roast. This is my favourite way of cooking rack of lamb, with a crisp crust of buttery crumbs flavoured with lots of fresh herbs.

You can doll up the tips of the cutlets with cutlet frills (they're often sold with the rack, in which case, do remember to take them off before the meat goes into the oven, replacing them just before serving). If you buy your rack ready-prepared and they've over-zealously trimmed off every last scrap of fat, then be a little more generous with the butter in the crumbs as this will help to protect the meat from the fierce heat.

SERVES 2

1 rack of lamb	a mixture of parsley, chervil, chives,
25 g (1 oz) stale fine breadcrumbs	marjoram, thyme, savory etc.
20 g (a generous ½ oz) unsalted butter, melted	1 garlic clove, crushed, optional
1½–2 tablespoons chopped herbs such as	Salt and freshly ground black pepper

Pre-heat the oven to 230°C/450°F/Gas Mark 8. If the rack hasn't already been pre-pared, carefully cut off the skin, leaving a thin layer of fat on the chops. Trim the tips of the cutlets, scraping away the scraps of meat and fat, exposing the top 4 cm (1½ in) (see diagram on page 59). Mix the breadcrumbs with the butter, herbs, garlic (if using), salt and pepper in a bowl. Using your hands, keep turning the mixture over until the crumbs have soaked up all the butter evenly. Lay the rack of lamb, fat side upward, in a lightly oiled small oven-proof dish or roasting tin. Pat the crumb mixture firmly and thickly onto the fat side.

Roast the rack for about 20–30 minutes, depending on how well cooked you like your lamb (I usually opt for little more than 20 minutes since it seems a shame to overcook such a choice morsel). If necessary, cover the crumbs loosely with foil towards the end of the cooking time to prevent them from burning. Let the meat rest for 5 minutes, then to serve, simply cut down between the cutlets, dividing the rack in half. It's best to do this at the table, as some of the crumbs are bound to fall off in the process and your fellow diner gets to see how appetizing it looks first.

GRILLED BUTTERFLIED LEG OF LAMB

This is a stunning way of cooking lamb — the inside stays moist and tender whilst the outside becomes a deep crusty brown. Though it works well on an indoor grill, it really comes into its own in the summer months when it can be barbecued outdoors over charcoal; perfect for a party on a balmy July evening.

Put the lamb to marinate the day before cooking if you can, so that it has plenty of time to soak up those Eastern Mediterranean scents of lemon, olive oil and mint. It minimizes effort on the day of your party too, so that apart from cooking the meat, the only thing to do is to throw together the yoghurt and mint sauce that goes so well with the grilled meat.

SERVES 6–8

1 boned leg of lamb (see page 61)

—— *For the marinade* ——

Juice of 2 lemons	2 bay leaves, crumbled
1 onion, chopped	3 tablespoons chopped fresh mint
3 garlic cloves, sliced	or 3 teaspoons dried mint
150 ml (5 fl oz) olive oil	8 peppercorns, lightly crushed

Make a few deep slashes in the lamb at its thickest parts. Lie flat in a shallow dish large enough to take it without folding over. Mix the marinade ingredients. Pour over the lamb. Cover, and leave in the fridge or a cool place for 8–24 hours, turning occasionally.

Pre-heat your grill to its highest temperature and arrange the grill rack so that you can get the meat very close to the heat. Remove the meat from the marinade, brushing off bits of onion and herbs. Strain the marinade, reserving the liquid for basting.

Grill the lamb, cut side up first, very close to the heat, for 5–7 minutes on each side to give a deep brown crust. Re-arrange the grill rack so that the lamb is 10–13 cm (4–5 in) from the heat, and give it a further 12–19 minutes on each side, depending on how well you like it done. Baste the meat with marinade every time you turn it. Keep an eye on it so that you don't allow it to overcook and test it now and again by plunging a knife into the centre — I turn off the heat the moment the scarlet translucence of raw meat disappears, which gives the most perfect succulent pink lamb. Lift the meat onto a serving dish and leave it to relax in a warm oven (or by the side of the barbecue) for 15 minutes before carving. Serve the meat juices with the lamb.

Yoghurt and Mint Sauce

Lamb

SERVES 6 – 8

300 ml (10 fl oz) Greek yoghurt

A handful of mint leaves, chopped

3 garlic cloves, crushed

Salt and freshly ground black pepper

Mix together all the ingredients, adjusting the seasoning to taste. Serve with the lamb.

KORESHT-E REEVAS – PERSIAN LAMB AND RHUBARB STEW

Partnering fruit and meat is common enough in the Middle East, but this recipe may come as a surprise, even so. I usually make it in the spring with forced rhubarb, but you could use ordinary rhubarb, bearing in mind that it will have more of a bite to it. If you use forced rhubarb and like a bracing hit of acidity, use the full 675 g (1½ lb) but if, like me, you like the sharpness more muted, or if you use ordinary rhubarb, then the smaller amount should be sufficient.

SERVES 4 – 6

675 g (1½ lb) boned shoulder or leg of lamb

50 g (2 oz) butter

1 tablespoon sunflower or vegetable oil

2 large onions, sliced

1 level teaspoon ground coriander

1 small bunch of parsley

3 tablespoons chopped mint

450–675 g (1–1½ lb) rhubarb, trimmed and cut into 2.5 cm (1 in) lengths

Salt and freshly ground black pepper

Cut the meat into 5 cm (2 in) cubes. Melt half the butter with the oil in a frying pan and fry the onions until golden. Raise the heat, add half the meat and fry until browned. Scoop out with the onions then brown the remaining meat. Return the first batch to the pan with the coriander, or transfer everything to a heat-proof casserole. Add just enough water to cover and simmer, covered, for 1 hour. Season.

Meanwhile, chop the parsley and mint leaves. Fry in the remaining butter, stirring constantly, for 5–10 minutes. Add them to the stew and continue simmering for a further 30 minutes, with the lid half off, stirring occasionally. Shortly before serving, add the rhubarb. Stir to mix and simmer for 2–4 minutes if it is forced rhubarb, 5–10 minutes if it is ordinary rhubarb. Taste and adjust the seasoning and serve immediately with rice.

LANCASHIRE HOT POT

❧

Forget fancy dishes from the East and the Mediterranean; our own traditional, homely Lancashire hot pot makes a great meal on a cold evening. It is cheap, quick to prepare, and lip-smackingly good. Once you've got it going in the oven, you don't need to bother about it for a couple of hours. No fussing or fiddling. I love it — there's that delicious crisp layer of potatoes on the top, covering tender lamb (or mutton if you can get it) and melting potatoes underneath that just beg to be mashed into the juices.

No doubt Lancastrians would debate the list of ingredients needed to make a genuine hot pot. I've read that mushrooms are added only in Bolton and, in times past, oysters were frequently included as they were cheap and nutritious. I can think of better things to do with oysters these days, but mushrooms do add something special, and I always slip some in. You don't have to brown the meat, but it does improve the colour and flavour.

SERVES 6

6 meaty loin chops, or 12 lamb cutlets

6 lamb's kidneys, halved

50 g (2 oz) dripping or butter, melted

1 kg (2¼ lb) potatoes, peeled and thinly sliced

3 large onions, sliced

225 g (8 oz) flat-cap mushrooms, thickly sliced, optional

300 ml (10 fl oz) lamb or chicken stock, or water

Salt and freshly ground black pepper

Pre-heat the oven to 220°C/425°F/Gas Mark 7. Brown the chops and the kidneys in half the dripping or butter over a high heat, to give them a little colour. Layer the potatoes, chops, kidneys, onions and mushrooms, if using, in a deep casserole, seasoning well between each layer. End with a layer of potatoes, neatly overlapping and covering the contents of the dish. Pour over the stock or water. There should be enough to come about half-way up the ingredients. If you seem to be running short, add a little more water. Brush the remaining dripping or butter over the top layer of potatoes, then season well.

Cover the casserole and place it in the oven. Give it 20–25 minutes to heat through, then reduce the oven temperature to 150°C/300°F/Gas Mark 2 and leave to cook for a further 2 hours. Finally, remove the lid, raise the oven temperature back to 220°C/425F/Gas Mark 7 and cook for a final 20–30 minutes until the top layer of potatoes is browned.

SEAMUS'S IRISH STEW

Like other traditional dishes which were born out of poverty, there are many different versions of Irish stew. Controversy reigns over whether there should be carrots in it or whether one should brown the meat first.

This version was made for me by an old friend, Seamus. When he first made Irish stew as a student, Seamus and his flatmate would get a cheap lamb bone from the butcher, with just a few scraps of meat on it. First thing in the morning, they would throw it into a large casserole with potatoes, carrots and water. By lunch-time it was ready.

These days, he's moved up a little in the world and his Irish stew has become a touch more substantial. The important thing is that whatever cut of lamb you use, and in whatever quantity, it should be stewed on the bone. A 2 kg (4½ lb) shoulder is ideal but 1.5–1.75 kg (3–4 lb) of scrag-end of neck, or neck chops does the job well too. Cut the meat into large cubes or chops, as appropriate.

Seamus usually spices up his stew with a shake of Worcestershire sauce and I have known him to add, most unauthentically, a scant tablespoonful of lightly crushed coriander seeds. In the end, the important thing is that the stew cooks long enough for the potatoes to soften to such a degree that it takes barely any encouragement for them to melt down into the juice to thicken it.

SERVES 6

1. 5–2 kg (3–4½ lb) lamb (see above)

Lard or butter

3 onions, peeled and thickly sliced

675 g (1½ lb) carrots, scraped and cut into thick chunks

900 g (2 lb) potatoes, peeled and halved if large

1 bay leaf

2 teaspoons Worcestershire sauce

Water or stock, to cover

Salt and freshly ground black pepper

Chopped parsley

Trim a fair amount of the fat off the meat and reserve. Cut the meat up into large cubes or chops as appropriate. In a thick-bottomed pan, render down the fat over a low heat. Discard the solid bits and add extra lard and butter if necessary. Brown the meat in the fat then set aside and brown the onion and carrots in the same fat. Drain off any excess fat. Return the meat to the pan with the potatoes, bay leaf, Worcestershire sauce, salt, pepper, and water or stock to cover. Simmer for 2–3 hours until the meat is tender and potatoes are soft and melting. Skim off the fat, remove any very large bones and serve scattered with parsley.

NAVARIN PRINTANIER

This is a perfect spring dish — warming enough to stave off those chilly winds that still blow, but bursting with the freshness and promise of the summer months. To be honest, to make the ultimate Navarin Printanier, you really have to have your own vegetable garden, so that you can harvest the tiny, young vegetables for it on the very day that you cook it. Failing that, choose the smallest carrots, turnips and potatoes you can find, so they can be cooked whole. If your turnips and potatoes are more than about 4 cm (1½ in) across, cut them in half. If you wish, the Navarin can be enriched at the last moment with a slug of double cream or crème fraîche.

SERVES 6

1.5 kg (3 lb) shoulder of lamb, trimmed and cubed	1 bouquet garni (see page 33)
25 g (1 oz) butter	1 garlic clove, crushed
1 tablespoon sunflower oil	225 g (8 oz) small carrots, scrubbed
2 tablespoons flour	450 g (1 lb) small new potatoes, scrubbed
600 ml (1 pint) lamb, chicken or vegetable stock	225 g (8 oz) small white and purple turnips
1 tablespoon tomato purée	350 g (12 oz) shelled peas
	Salt and freshly ground black pepper

Brown the lamb in the butter and oil over a high heat, in several batches. Transfer to a flameproof casserole and pour off all except about 2 tablespoons of the fat from the pan. Add the flour and stir over a moderate heat until you have a light brown roux. Stir in the stock gradually as if making white sauce and then add the tomato purée. Bring to the boil, stirring continuously, then pour over the meat. Add the bouquet garni, garlic, salt and pepper. Cover and simmer gently for about 1 hour.

Now add the carrots, potatoes and turnips and continue cooking for 30 minutes, uncovered, before adding the peas. If necessary, add a little more water or stock if the liquid levels fall low — the aim is to get a creamy, but not over-thick sauce of about the consistency of single cream. Once the peas are in, continue cooking until all the vegetables are tender. Taste, adjust the seasoning and serve.

TAGINE OF MUTTON OR LAMB WITH DRIED FRUIT AND ALMONDS

Lamb

Moroccan tagines take their name from the beautiful wide dishes with conical lids that they are cooked in. They are very aromatic, often combining fruit with meat, and may be sweetened with honey.

This recipe is a delight. It is richly but not overwhelmingly spiced and finished with the crunch of fried almonds and sesame seeds. If you prefer, you can use prunes alone: 450 g (1 lb), or apricots alone: 350 g (12 oz) will do the trick. Only bother with soaking the fruit if it is bone-dry. Most of what we buy these days is only semi-dehydrated, leaving it soft and moist enough to cook with (or eat) straight from the packet.

SERVES 5–6

1–1.25 kg (2¼–2½ lb) boned shoulder of mutton or lamb	2 medium onions, grated or very finely chopped
50 g (2 oz) unsalted butter	225 g (8 oz) prunes
2 tablespoons oil	175 g (6 oz) dried apricots
¼ teaspoon powdered saffron	1 tablespoon sesame seeds
1 teaspoon freshly ground black pepper	1 cinnamon stick
1 teaspoon ground ginger	2 long strips lemon zest
1 teaspoon ground cumin	2–3 tablespoons honey
½ tablespoon ground cinnamon	75 g (3 oz) blanched, halved almonds
	Salt

Cut the mutton or lamb into 4 cm (1½ in) cubes, trimming off any gristle and excess fat. Melt 40 g (1½ oz) butter, mix it with the oil, saffron, pepper, salt, ginger, cumin and ground cinnamon and coat the lamb in the mixture.

Tip into a wide frying pan or shallow casserole and cook over a moderate heat for about 3 minutes to toast the spices. Add the onions, and enough water to cover. Bring to the boil and simmer gently, covered but leaving a small gap for the steam to escape, for 1–2 hours or until the meat is tender.

If necessary, soak the prunes and apricots in water. The prunes can be pitted if you wish, but it's not really necessary. Dry-fry the sesame seeds in a small pan over a high heat until they turn a shade darker.

If it has been soaked, drain the dried fruit. Add to the meat, along with the cinnamon stick, lemon zest and honey. Simmer, uncovered, for a further 30 minutes or so until the

75

sauce has reduced enough to coat the meat and fruit without leaving them swimming (you may even have to add a little water if yours seems to have evaporated too quickly). While it simmers, sauté the almonds in the remaining butter until they are lightly browned, then set aside and keep warm. Taste the tagine and adjust the seasonings. Finally, scatter with the almonds and sesame seeds before serving.

Lamb (or Mutton) and
Vegetable Couscous

Another Moroccan dish, this, and a great way to feed a crowd of hungry people. Couscous is actually the 'grain' (technically a type of pasta, in fact), that is served to soak up the juices of the soupy stew. It is easy to buy these days, not only from specialist shops, but also from most supermarkets. Nearly all of the couscous sold in this country has already been cooked and dried, so just needs rehydrating. It's probably best to follow the instructions on your packet, but I'll tell you my method anyway. I measure out double the volume of hot water to couscous and pour it over the couscous. After 20–30 minutes it will all, or at least nearly all have been absorbed. Any excess should be drained off.

As with the Tagine of Mutton or Lamb with Dried Fruit and Almonds above, in Morocco this dish is more likely to be made with mutton than lamb.

SERVES 8-10

1 kg (2¼ lb) shoulder of lamb or mutton, cut into 5 cm (2 in) cubes

3 onions, cut into eighths

5 large sprigs of coriander, tied in a bunch

½ tablespoon turmeric

2 teaspoons freshly ground black pepper

½ tablespoon ground ginger

½ tablespoon ground cumin

1 teaspoon ground coriander

1 tablespoon olive oil

4 litres (7 pints) water

225 g (8 oz) chickpeas, soaked overnight and drained

450 g (1 lb) tomatoes, skinned, seeded and roughly chopped

450 g (1 lb) carrots, each cut into 3 pieces, then halved lengthways

450 g (1 lb) small to medium turnips, peeled and halved or quartered

450 g (1 lb) courgettes, cut into 4 cm (1½ in) lengths

450 g (1 lb) piece pumpkin or winter squash, de-rinded, seeded and cut into 5 cm (2 in) chunks, optional

450 g (1 lb) potatoes, peeled and cut into 4 cm (1½ in) chunks	Salt
	Harissa or hot chilli sauce, to serve
2 tablespoons chopped coriander	

——— *For the couscous* ———

900 g (2 lb) couscous	Butter

Lamb

Find a generous, accommodating pan to cook the stew in. Dump the lamb or mutton, two-thirds of the onion and the bunch of coriander straight into it, then sprinkle over the spices. Season with salt and then drizzle over the olive oil. Pour in the water. Bring to the boil (allow plenty of time for this), then add the chickpeas. Cover the pan and let the mixture simmer for about 1 hour (1½ hours for mutton).

Now add the remaining onion and all the vegetables and let it all simmer for a further 30 minutes or so, uncovered, until all the vegetables are tender. Taste and adjust the seasoning. Carefully strain off the juices into a serving dish.

Meanwhile, prepare the couscous according to the packet instructions. Dot with butter, pile into a dish, cover with foil and let it steam in a warm oven. Just before serving, pour a couple of ladlefuls of the cooking juices from the big pan over the couscous. Stir briefly and, when absorbed, pile the couscous onto a big plate. Make a well in the centre and put all the bits of meat into it. Arrange the vegetables as prettily as you can over the couscous and meat and take it quickly to the table. Serve the remaining juices alongside so that everyone can make their couscous as moist as they like. Serve with harissa or chilli sauce for those who want to pep the spices up a bit.

Lamb

BRAISED LAMB SHANKS WITH FLAGEOLETS AND ROSEMARY

I could happily eat far more than my fair share of this stew. It is packed to the hilt with marvellous flavours. There's the lamb, of course, the shanks being especially nice mini joints for braising or stewing, but after that come the flageolet beans (if you can't get dried flageolets, you can substitute dried haricot beans), and the tomatoes and chilli. The final perk is a sprinkling of gremolata, finely chopped garlic, lemon zest and parsley, which will lift practically any lamb stew you care to mention. It's something worth considering as a finishing touch with a chicken stew, too, though its classic use is in the Italian Osso Buco (see page 147).

SERVES 4

4 meaty lamb shanks, trimmed	1 bouquet garni (see page 33),
2–3 tablespoons olive oil	including 2 sprigs of rosemary
1 large onion, chopped	675 g (1½ lb) tomatoes, skinned,
1 large carrot, finely diced	seeded and chopped
1 celery stick, finely diced	1 heaped tablespoon tomato purée
3 garlic cloves, chopped	1 dried red chilli
350 g (12 oz) dried flageolet beans,	½ tablespoon light muscovado sugar
soaked overnight and drained	Salt and freshly ground black pepper

——— For the gremolata ———

Finely grated zest of ½ lemon	2 tablespoons chopped parsley
1–2 garlic cloves, finely chopped	

Brown the lamb shanks in the oil in a wide frying pan then transfer the meat to a casserole. Cook the onion, carrot and celery gently in the same pan, until tender and lightly patched with brown. Add the garlic and cook for a minute or so longer, then tip the vegetables into the casserole. Add the flageolets and the bouquet garni.

Tip the excess fat out of the frying pan and pour in 900 ml (1½ pints) of water. Bring to the boil, stirring and scraping in the brown residues from frying. Pour over the casserole and season with pepper but no salt. Either simmer on top of the stove, or transfer to the oven, set to 170°C/325°F/Gas Mark 3, and cook for 1–1½ hours, or until the beans are meltingly tender (but not quite on the point of collapse). Stir in the tomatoes, tomato purée, chilli and sugar, and season with salt (the tomatoes and the salt prevent the beans from softening, which is why you didn't add them earlier – added now, they should prevent them disintegrating). Return to the hob or oven and continue cooking for a further

Lamb

1–2 hours, stirring occasionally, until the meat is so tender it practically falls off the bone.

Remove the chilli. Take a couple of ladlefuls of the beans and juices and blend them in the food processor until smooth. Stir back into the casserole to transform the liquid into a creamy sauce. Taste and adjust the seasoning.

To make the gremolata, mix the lemon zest, garlic and parsley and chop them together very, very finely. Sprinkle over the casserole just before serving.

LAMB CHOPS WITH ROSEMARY, AUBERGINE AND BLACK OLIVES

Lamb and aubergine are often cooked together around the Mediterranean (moussaka is the most obvious example – see page 85). They make a happy pair here entwined with the help of a tomatoey sauce and black olives (kalamata olives are particularly good in this instance). I usually cook this in a heavy cast-iron frying pan, and the colours look so pretty against the black of the metal that I dish it straight up in that. If you don't want to take a frying pan to the table, at least serve it up in some sort of rustic earthenware dish. It's just not the kind of thing for your best porcelain.

SERVES 4

1 aubergine, cut into 2.5 cm (1 in) cubes	3 tablespoons tomato purée
2 garlic cloves	300 ml (10 fl oz) water
4 lamb chops	1 tablespoon caster sugar
Leaves of 1 sprig of rosemary	12 black olives, pitted and sliced
3 tablespoons olive oil	2 tablespoons chopped parsley
1 red onion, sliced	Salt and freshly ground black pepper
½ tablespoon coriander seeds, coarsely crushed	

Put the aubergine cubes in a colander, sprinkle with salt and leave for 30 minutes. Rinse and pat dry. Cut 1 garlic clove into long thin slivers. Finely chop the rest. With a sharp knife, make slits in the chops and push the slivers of garlic and the rosemary leaves down into the cuts. If you have the time, cover and leave the chops to stand for a few hours so that the flavours have a chance to make an impression on the meat.

Take a pan large enough to hold the 4 chops and fry them briskly in 1 tablespoon of the oil until browned on both sides and cooked almost to your liking (I reckon on 4–5 minutes per side). Remove from the pan and set aside.

Now add one more tablespoon of oil to the fat in the pan (aubergines are greedy when it comes to oil) and sauté the aubergine until golden brown and tender (keep the heat fairly high throughout). Scoop out the aubergines and drain on kitchen paper. Reduce the heat under the frying pan, add the last of the oil and and fry the onion until tender. Add the chopped garlic and the coriander seeds and cook for a minute or so longer.

Finally, add the tomato purée, water, sugar, salt and pepper. Stir well, bring to the boil and return the aubergine to the pan. Nestle the chops in amongst the aubergine and simmer for about 2–3 minutes until the sauce is reduced enough to coat the aubergine richly. Stir in the olives and two-thirds of the parsley. Taste and adjust the seasoning, then serve sprinkled with the remaining parsley.

Lamb

GRILLED LAMB CHOPS WITH TOMATO, OLIVE AND ROSEMARY SALSA

Serving a salsa, a fresh-tasting sauce made of finely chopped raw ingredients, with grilled lamb chops is a very modern way of upgrading them into something rather stylish. Though you can warm the salsa through gently, if you prefer, I rather like the combination of sizzling hot meat, with a cool salsa. It also means less last-minute fiddling and one less pan to wash up!

SERVES 4

4 lamb chops	Salt and freshly
A little oil	ground black pepper

—— *For the salsa* ——

225 g (8 oz) well-flavoured tomatoes, skinned, seeded and finely diced	1 teaspoon finely chopped rosemary leaves
5 pieces of sun-dried tomato, chopped	A generous pinch of sugar
8 black olives, pitted and roughly chopped	½ tablespoon balsamic or sherry vinegar
1 shallot, finely chopped	3 tablespoons olive oil
1 garlic clove, crushed	Salt and freshly ground black pepper

Make the salsa at least an hour before eating . Mix together all the ingredients except the salt. Cover loosely and leave at room temperature (or in the fridge if it is for more than 4 hours). Taste and adjust the seasoning, adding a little salt if needed. Either serve at room temperature or warm gently in a small pan.

Brush the chops lightly with oil and grill fairly close to the heat until crusty and brown, turning once. Season with salt and pepper and serve with the salsa.

PAN-FRIED NOISETTES OF LAMB WITH RED WINE AND SHALLOT SAUCE

One of the pluses of noisettes of lamb is that they are quick to cook, and rather elegant into the bargain…certainly more of a dinner party cut than, say, the common or garden chop. Here, they are cooked and then served up with a simple red wine sauce. Very good served with simple accompaniments such as boiled or roasted new potatoes, peas, and glazed carrots or pearl onions.

SERVES 4

25 g (1 oz) butter	1 sprig of thyme
1 tablespoon oil	1 small sprig of rosemary
4 noisettes of lamb	300 ml (10 fl oz) stock
4 shallots, sliced	½ tablespoon redcurrant jelly
1 large glass red wine	Salt and freshly ground black pepper
1 sprig of parsley	

Melt half the butter and the oil in a heavy frying pan and fry the noisettes over a medium heat for about 5–6 minutes each side until just nicely browned and cooked medium rare. Season and keep warm.

Add the shallots to the pan and cook over a gentle heat, stirring occasionally, until meltingly tender. Don't rush this part – give them time to soften and develop a natural sweetness. Now add the wine, then the herbs tied together with a piece of string to make a bouquet garni, and boil down until almost no liquid remains, stirring and scraping in all the residues from frying. Next add the stock and the jelly and bring to the boil. Continue to boil, stirring in the jelly, until reduced by about two-thirds. To finish the sauce, dice the remaining butter and swirl in a few pieces at a time to enrich. Spoon over and around the noisettes. Serve immediately.

ITALIAN CUTLETS

There's something immensely appealing about this very straightforward Italian way of cooking lamb cutlets. Far more interesting than mere breaded fried meat, they are coated in both freshly grated Parmesan and breadcrumbs. All they need then is a squeeze of lemon as they come out of the pan. Keep the accompanying vegetables simple — I'd go for boiled new potatoes and a crisp green salad with plenty of frisée lettuce and rocket leaves in it.

Ideally, you should use a light olive oil to fry the chops, but a mixture of olive oil and sunflower or vegetable oil does the job almost as well. If you strain the oil, it can be used a few more times for frying before it becomes too tainted.

SERVES 2 (OR 3 FOR A LIGHT LUNCHEON)

6 lamb cutlets	Oil for frying
40–50 g (1½–2 oz) freshly grated Parmesan	Salt and freshly ground black pepper
1 egg, lightly beaten	Lemon wedges
Fine white breadcrumbs	

Trim the fat from the tips of the long bone in each cutlet, leaving it bare, so that it makes a nice handle to hold the cutlet with. Season the meat with pepper (the Parmesan will make them salty enough). Spread the Parmesan out on a plate, put the beaten egg in a shallow dish, and spread the breadcrumbs out on another dish.

One at a time, press each cutlet into the Parmesan, turning and patting down gently so that it is evenly coated, then gently shaking off the excess. Next dip the cutlet into the beaten egg, again shaking gently to get rid of large globs. Finally coat evenly in breadcrumbs. If you have the time, let the lamb chops sit around for an hour or more (in which case they should go into the fridge, but must be brought back to room temperature before frying) so that the coating 'sets'.

Heat 2 cm (¾ in) oil in a frying pan over a medium heat. Fry the chops until browned on one side, then carefully turn over and brown the other side. This should take around 4–5 minutes each side depending on how well done you like your lamb. Drain briefly on kitchen paper, then season with salt and pepper. Serve immediately with lemon wedges.

SPICED LAMB CHOPS

This is one of my favourite ways to improve on a chop. The natural acidity of the yoghurt tenderizes the meat (after 48 hours it should just melt in the mouth) and the spices enhance the flavour of the meat without overwhelming it. The spice and yoghurt mixture verges on a tandoori marinade, though without any of the red colouring! Make the cooked chops part of an Indian meal with rice or naan bread and maybe some dhal, or plonk them straight into a more Western setting, by serving them with boiled new potatoes and spinach or broccoli.

SERVES 4

4 lamb loin chops

—————— For the spice mixture ——————

1 teaspoon cumin seeds	1 teaspoon salt
1 teaspoon coriander seeds	2 tablespoons roughly chopped coriander
1 cm (½ in) piece fresh root ginger, chopped	¼ teaspoon ground turmeric
1–2 red chillies, seeded and chopped	1 tablespoon freshly squeezed lime juice
2 garlic cloves, chopped	4 large tablespoons Greek yoghurt
1 small shallot, chopped	

Dry-fry the cumin and coriander seeds over a high heat in a small frying pan. Once they begin to jump, tip them out, let them cool, then grind to a powder. Pound the ginger root, chillies, garlic and shallot in a mortar with the salt to form a paste. Gradually work in the coriander, then mix in the spices, turmeric, lime juice and finally the yoghurt. Smear the mixture thickly over the lamb chops and leave for as long as possible. It'll take some 3–4 hours to begin to work well, but they will get much better with time. 1–2 days, covered, in the fridge, is best.

Take the chops out of the fridge, if that's where they've been, at least half an hour before cooking so that they are at room temperature. Either grill the chops under a high heat until crusty and brown – about 4–5 minutes on each side. Or heat a little oil in a non-stick frying pan and fry until browned and just cooked to your liking. Again, 4 minutes per side should be adequate.

Lamb

MOUSSAKA

When it is made with care and high-quality ingredients, moussaka becomes one of the most delicious lamb dishes around. If you've been put off by tired, greasy restaurant slabs of moussaka, then I urge you to try your hand at home. It's not a dish to be rushed — the three elements take some time to prepare, but both sauces can quite happily be made a day in advance.

To cut down on the oil content, I bake the aubergine slices, brushed with just enough oil to keep them moist and add a little flavour (the traditional way is to fry them). You could do away with the oil on the aubergines altogether by steaming them, but I think you then lose out on too much flavour. As is so often the case, compromise is the best option. Whichever way you cook them, do it on the day the moussaka is to be eaten.

Try to get proper Greek kefalotyri cheese if you can (most Greek food stores stock it), as its rich twang suits this production to a T. If you don't have the right-sized dish, use one that is slightly smaller, so that you still get a decent thickness.

SERVES 6

3 large or 4 medium aubergines, sliced lengthways	50 g (2 oz) kefalotyri cheese, or a mixture of Gruyère and Parmesan
Olive oil	A generous ½ teaspoon ground cinnamon
	Salt and freshly ground black pepper

—— *For the meat sauce* ——

1 large onion, chopped	450 g (1 lb) tomatoes, skinned
2 garlic cloves, chopped	and roughly chopped
3 tablespoons olive oil	1 teaspoon sugar
450 g (1 lb) minced lamb	1½ teaspoons ground cinnamon
1 generous glass dry white wine	1 tablespoon dried oregano
2 tablespoons tomato purée	3 tablespoons chopped parsley

—— *For the white sauce* ——

55 g (2 oz) butter	50 g (2 oz) grated kefalotyri cheese,
55 g (2 oz) flour	or mixed Parmesan and Gruyère
570 ml (1 pint) milk	1 egg
	1 egg yolk

To make the meat sauce, cook the onion and garlic gently in the olive oil until tender, without browning. Add the lamb and stir until it loses its raw look. Now add all the remaining meat sauce ingredients except the parsley and season with salt and pepper. Simmer for 20–30 minutes until thick. Stir in the parsley.

Lamb

Next, make the white sauce. Melt the butter and stir in the flour. Keep stirring for about 1 minute. Draw the pan off the heat and add the milk gradually, stirring in well between sploshes. Once you've incorporated about one third of it, increase the amount you add each time. Return to a gentle heat and let it simmer for a good 10–15 minutes, stirring frequently, until it is fairly thick. Remove from the heat, stir in the cheese and salt and pepper. If not using immediately, spear a knob of butter on a fork and rub over the surface to prevent a skin forming. Re-heat the white sauce gently when needed. Just before using, beat the egg and yolk into the sauce.

Sprinkle the slices of aubergine with salt and leave for at least half an hour, preferably a full hour. Wipe clean and steam if you wish, or lay them on oiled baking sheets, brush quite generously with olive oil and bake in the oven at 190°C/375°F/Gas Mark 5 for about 20 minutes until tender and patched with brown.

Take a rectangular or square baking dish, about 30 x 20 cm (12 x 8 in) or 25 x 25 cm (10 x 10 in) and brush lightly with oil. Lay half the aubergine slices on the base, overlapping if necessary, then spread half the meat sauce on top. Repeat these layers, then spoon over the white sauce, covering the meat entirely. Sprinkle over the grated cheese and the cinnamon. Bake at 180°C/350°F/Gas Mark 4 for 50–60 minutes until nicely browned. Let it settle, out of the oven, for 5 minutes before cutting into squares and serving.

Lamb

LEG OF MUTTON STEAKS (OR LAMB) IN THE ARDENNES STYLE

This recipe is adapted from Elizabeth David, whose recipe for venison prepared this way was something my mother cooked fairly regularly when I was a child (it was years before I realized where it came from originally). When I was experimenting with mutton for the first time, I found that this was an excellent way to cook it, as long as you have the patience to brown the diced vegetables properly so as to develop all their sweetness.

SERVES 4

4 thick leg of mutton or lamb steaks	85 ml (3 fl oz) vermouth or dry white wine
Juice of ½ lemon	85 ml (3 fl oz) water
12 juniper berries, crushed	2 slices of cooked ham, finely chopped
1 teaspoon dried thyme or marjoram	75 g (3 oz) breadcrumbs
75 g (3 oz) butter	3 tablespoons chopped parsley
1 small onion, chopped	Salt and freshly ground black pepper
2 carrots, finely diced	

Pre-heat the oven to 170°C/325°F/Gas Mark 3 for mutton (or 180°C/350°F/Gas Mark 4 for lamb). Lay the mutton or lamb out flat and pour over the lemon juice. Mix the juniper berries with the thyme or marjoram and salt and pepper and rub into the meat. If possible do this an hour or two before cooking.

Melt 50 g (2 oz) of the butter in a frying pan. Add the onion and carrots and fry until patched with brown. Add the meat and brown on both sides. Pour over the vermouth or wine and let it sizzle and bubble until reduced to a thin glaze. Now add the water, stir and draw off the heat. Transfer chops, vegetables and pan juices to a shallow oven-proof dish.

Divide the ham between each piece of meat, spreading it out on top. Mix the breadcrumbs and parsley and cover each steak with them. Dot the remaining butter over the crumbs. Place in the oven, and bake for 40–60 minutes until the meat is tender and the breadcrumbs are crisp. Serve immediately.

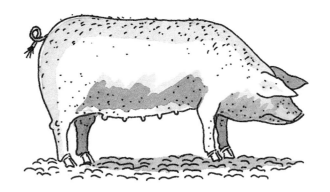

Pork,
Bacon & Ham

Pork,
Bacon & Ham

The household pig has played an enormous and unsung role in our history. It was first domesticated in China over 5000 years ago and for centuries has been the one reliable, affordable source of meat for the world's poor. It was fattened on kitchen slops and trimmings. It could rootle around in scrubby woodland, but would settle quite happily for the back yard. All in all, it was an undemanding and easy domestic animal. Though few of us in this country now keep a pig in the back yard, there are still many parts of rural Europe, Asia and South America where no household is complete without a pig snuffling around nearby. A happy life for the most part with a swift ending and a noble destiny.

By tradition, fresh pork is a late-autumn meat in this country, though nowadays supplies are plentiful year round. In the past, spring-time piglets were fattened in summer and early autumn until they were transformed into plump, hefty porkers, just as fodder dwindled with the onset of cold weather. The timings shift from one country to another in line with the weather. In southern Spain, for instance, the *matanza*, the slaughter of the pig, takes place in late January or February. What isn't eaten fresh is pickled, brined, dried, smoked, or cured as hams, sausages and bacon to preserve the meat for the ensuing months.

Fresh pork can – and should – be a superbly flavoured juicy meat and if you've ever been disappointed by it, as most of us have, then the reason is very simple. What you were eating was probably from an animal that had been intensively raised, with scant room to manoeuvre let alone rootle. At best it may have had access to some jostled space in an enclosed shed. It will probably have been from some modern breed, developed specifically to be lean and 'healthy', regardless of the effect this has on eating quality. It will have been fed a concentrated diet to hasten growth, and slaughtered young. This kind of modern regime affects the flavour of pork more, I think, than it does any other meat. The end result tastes of precious little and is often tough and stringy.

I can still remember the first time I cooked a piece of free-range pork. Actually, that is not quite true. I can't remember what cut it was, I can't remember how I cooked it, but I do remember the taste and my reaction. Here, at last, was a piece of pork that set the tastebuds alight. It was the taste of childhood memory. Nothing tough or dry or stringy about it. It was tender, succulent and true. It was precisely what pork should be.

Many of our older breeds of pig, such as Saddlebacks, Gloucester Old Spots and Tamworths, faced near extinction in this century, ousted by more productive, leaner, modern animals. Luckily, wise individuals realized their worth and safeguarded the last of these animals, breeding them gently and happily in the best circumstances. Now our old breeds are enjoying something of a fashionable revival, just in the nick of time. Crossbred with more modern pigs, raised in the right circumstances, their meat is again becoming available, albeit slowly. Good butchers all around the country now have access to marvellous, humanely raised pork, if only they care to take advantage of it.

CHOOSING PORK

Pork,
Bacon & Ham

Wherever you buy your pork, these are the things to look out for. First the colour of the meat itself. It should be an enticing velvety mid-pink, neither dark nor pallid. The fat (and any pork worth its salt will be blessed with a generous layer of fat) should be firm and white. The pig is the only four-legged animal whose skin we eat (mainly but not exclusively in the form of crackling), so its appearance is very important. It should be dry and silky to the touch. It certainly shouldn't feel slimy or damp, though you may come across some that does. This may reflect poor storage and is best avoided.

IN PRAISE OF FAT

Though fat is unfashionable these days, it should never be sneered at. For a start it is what makes good pork marvellously succulent and juicy. It brings flavour with it but, just as important, it keeps the meat moist as it cooks. One of the great joys of roasting pork is that the fat turns it into a virtually self-basting joint so you need not lift a finger as it cooks. It is also what makes crackling crackle.

But that is not all. Pork fat has a major role to play in cooking other meats as well. The back fat, for instance – firm, supple fat, solid enough to be cut into thin sheets and strips (get the butcher to slice it for you) – is often used to line moulds for pâtés, holding the meat in place and preventing it drying out. Long thin strips of it can be used to lard lean meat that might otherwise dry out in the heat of the oven. Lean game birds can also be kept tender with a jacket of back fat, tied over the breasts.

Flair fat (also known as body fat) is softer, more tender and may be minced with other meats for pâtés to keep them from drying out. It also goes into black puddings, haggis and other sausages. Pork rind or skin, which itself has a more gelatinous texture, backed with a thin layer of fat, makes a rib-sticking, lip-smacking addition to long-cooked stews of all sorts, but particularly those with lots of beans and vegetables in them.

Finally, there is the beautiful, fine, lacy caul fat which stretches out and out into a thin gauzy veil (it may need to be soaked in tepid water first). It is sensational stuff, a culinary secret that has so many uses. It can replace back fat for a finer, glossier casing for pâtés, but I tend to use it more for making small patties of sausagemeat (*crépinettes* is the French name) or holding other small bundles of meat and stuffing together as they cook.

All of these forms of fat freeze very well, which is handy as your butcher may insist that you buy them in greater quantity than you are likely to need at one go (particularly true of caul fat). Divide them into small, practical-sized portions before freezing and then you can use them as you need them.

91

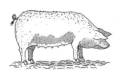

Pork,
Bacon & Ham

Cuts and Cooking

To begin with, two small but essential general tips about cooking pork. The first is that you should never rush it. Slow, gentle measured cooking always produces the best results. Hurry things along and the pork is likely to end up stringy and dry and, of course, may burn. Secondly, pork must always, always be cooked right through and never be served rare. To test it, plunge a skewer into the heart of the thickest part. If the juices run clear, then it is done. If they look at all pink, then carry on cooking.

ROASTING

The brilliant thing about pork is that practically every cut is tender enough to roast, from chops to belly to leg to whatever else you care to mention. Exceptions, and there are always one or two, are some of the extremities, like trotters and tail, which need to be boiled.

The loin, on the bone or boned and rolled, is one of the best small joints for roasting, with plenty of rind for crackling. The leg, in its entirety, makes a magnificent joint, big enough to feed an army. Given that armies are in short supply, it is usually divided into smaller joints. The fillet end is very tender, while the knuckle has oodles of crackling.

The tenderloin or fillet can be speedily roasted (see the recipe on page 109), but since it is so very lean will need to be basted regularly, frequently and efficiently. It looks terrible when it comes out of the oven, so slice it up before you present it to your co-diners, if you want to avoid the scatological jokes.

Another great favourite of mine for big Sunday lunches is a crown roast of pork. Big and bold, it stands proud on the table. It is made from two loins, and will need to be ordered from your butcher well in advance.

Other roasting joints are spare rib, blade, belly, hand and spring.

GRILLING, BARBECUING AND FRYING

Pork is ideal for all these snappy methods of cooking, though you should still avoid rushing the cooking. Loin chops (which if you are lucky may come with a decicious slice of kidney attached) and chump chops are obvious candidates (though, to be honest, I prefer to bake them slowly in the oven). Before you pop them into the pan or on the grill rack, trim off as much of the outer layer of fat as you please. Fat tends to shrink as it is heated, forcing the chops to buckle and twist. To prevent this happening, make incisions in what remains of the fat, cutting from the outside edge in towards the meat.

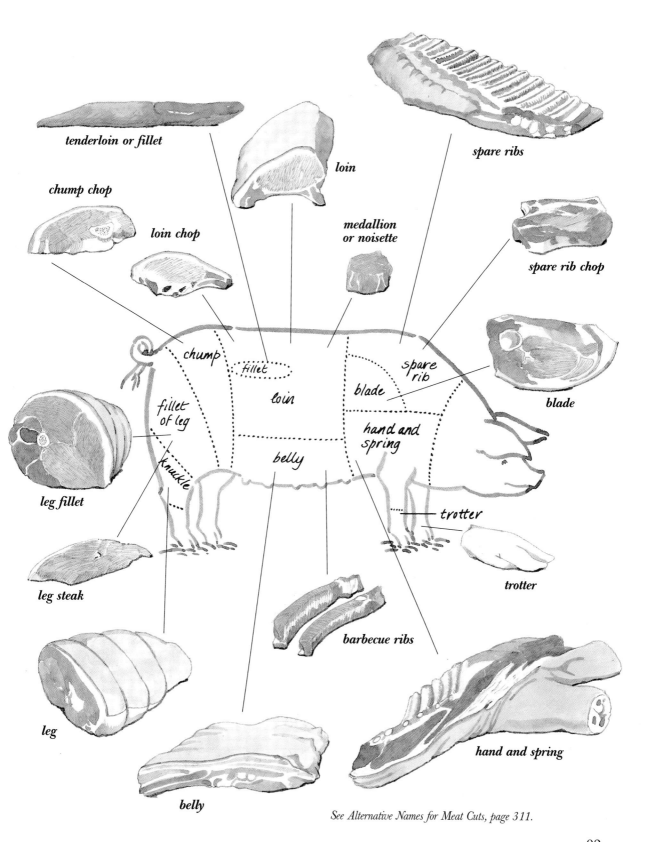

tenderloin or fillet

chump chop

loin chop

loin

medallion or noisette

spare ribs

spare rib chop

blade

chump

fillet

fillet of leg

loin

spare rib

blade

knuckle

belly

hand and spring

leg fillet

leg steak

trotter

trotter

leg

barbecue ribs

belly

hand and spring

See Alternative Names for Meat Cuts, page 311.

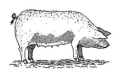

Tenderloin or fillet is a gem for quick, rather luxurious pan-fried dishes. Sliced into medallions, it takes only minutes to cook. It can also be grilled or barbecued, but needs regular basting to keep it moist.

American or Chinese-style spare ribs are not be confused with our British spare rib. The former come from the belly of the animal, the latter from the shoulder. If you want to make barbecued spare ribs, be sure to tell the butcher what you want the ribs for, so that he doesn't get confused either.

Other good cuts are sliced belly of pork, leg steaks, spare rib chops and best end cutlets.

BRAISING AND CASSEROLING

Everything, and that includes the trotters (which add a lovely gelatinous texture to all kinds of stews) and tail. Some of the bigger, leaner joints benefit enormously from being braised as the liquid content does away with the need for basting.

ROASTING PORK JOINTS

Every single reference book I own gives a different temperature and roasting time for roasting pork. Confusing, or what? On the whole, I think that long and slow gives the best results, particularly for larger joints. To me that means 180°–190°C/350°–375°F/Gas Mark 4–5 for 33 minutes per 500 g (30 minutes per lb) plus an extra 30 minutes to be on the safe side. Always, always test that the meat is fully cooked through. A meat thermometer should register 75°C/170°F when the meat is taken out of the oven, rising to 80°C/180°F as it rests. When you poke a thin skewer right into the centre of the meat, the juices that emerge when the skewer is pulled out should be clear. Traces of pink indicate a slightly bloody interior. Put the joint back in the oven, even if it means delaying the meal.

To ensure extra crisp crackling, you can give the joint an initial blast of heat in a high oven (around 230–240°C/450–475°F/Gas Mark 8–9) for 20 minutes, then reduce the heat for the rest of the cooking time. I'm not entirely convinced that this is necessary, but it won't hurt either.

CRACKLING

Any butcher will prepare the skin on a joint for crackling, but it isn't at all difficult to do for yourself at home. All you need is a really sharp knife or, better still, a Stanley knife- or even a scalpel. Holding the joint firmly, score deep parallel lines down one side of the skin. They should be about 5 mm (¼ in) apart and they should cut through the rind itself, down into the layer of fat, though not penetrating right into the meat. When you have scored one side, turn the joint round so that you can tackle the other.

What this does is to allow the fat underneath to bubble up in the heat of the oven, almost frying the skin to a crisp. A joint with a good layer of fat between the skin and the flesh will yield better results than one with a mean negligible layer.

Damp is the deadly enemy of crunchy crackling. This is what really makes it leathery and tough. Avoiding it is not too traumatic, though. Don't let your meat sweat inside a plastic bag or wrap. As soon as you get home, uncover it and wipe it dry, if necessary, place in a shallow dish and then cover it again if you are not using it immediately, allowing an airhole or two so that the meat can breathe. Return it to the fridge, taking great care that juices from the pork do not escape to contaminate other items.

If you want to marinate the pork, remove the rind in one large layer (after it has been scored) and set it aside. Tie it back on before roasting the meat, having dried the joint, or roast it separately, above the joint.

Literally just before you pop the fully prepared joint into the oven, wipe the skin dry with the greatest of care, using several pieces of kitchen paper. Don't bother to oil it – there's quite enough fat there already. The only other thing you need to do is to rub a generous amount of salt into the skin, and whizz it into the heat. Don't be tempted to baste it as it cooks.

Pork,
Bacon & Ham

Scoring pork crackling

Using a very sharp knife or even a Stanley knife, make parallel cuts through the skin about 5 mm (¼ in) apart. Cut right through into the fat, being careful not to score the meat itself.

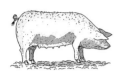

Pork,
Bacon & Ham

Boning and tying a loin of pork

1. *To bone the loin, cut the meat from the bone, using the bone as your guide and stroking the blade of the knife firmly along it.*

2. *When you reach the edge of the bone, ease and lift it away from the meat, then turn and cut the meat from the bone along the other side.*

3. *The boned loin can now be prepared for stuffing (see below).*

4. *After stuffing, roll the meat up and tie firmly with string at regular intervals.*

Preparing a boned loin for stuffing

Cutting a pocket

Making a flap

If the loin comes from the fillet end, cut a pocket in the fattest part of the meat, inserting the tip of the knife in the centre and working it carefully to and fro to open up the cavity.

If the loin has been cut from the rump end, there may not be enough flesh to make a decent-sized pocket. A straight flap will be more successful. Slice the meat horizontally through the centre, open it out like a book, then spread with the stuffing and roll up.

POT-ROASTING

We used to spend a quarter of the year in a tiny house in France when I was a child. The cooking facilities were decidedly basic, and our stove came from the camping shop. It was really a jumped-up two-ring burner with a tin box of an oven underneath. It's still there and I still use it, despite the unerring unreliability of the oven. Roasting meat is not easy in such a contraption and as a result my mother tended to pot-roast larger joints of meat on one of the gas rings. They were always delicious, well-flavoured, juicy and very tender, with small amounts of intensely flavoured thin pan-juices that could be soaked up by mashing boiled potatoes into them or with hunks of French bread.

Pot-roasting is roughly what it says it is, though it is a damper method of cooking than straight oven roasting. In essence, what you are doing is turning your heat-proof casserole into a kind of mini-oven, where the heat comes only from the bottom. I find that pork, particularly the leaner cuts, is extremely good when cooked this way, though other meats such as beef or lamb can be pot-roasted equally successfully.

Usually, the meat is browned in a little fat first, to give it some colour and to flavour the juices. Then it is laid on a bed of chopped vegetables (carrot, onion, celery, for instance) in a heavy flame-proof casserole (a tinny saucepan won't do half so well – it's liable to burn and won't hold the heat so well). A bouquet garni and other flavourings may be added, salt and pepper go in and so too may a small amount of liquid (for instance a glass of wine), though it is not absolutely necessary as the meat will yield up its own juices. The casserole is then covered tightly and placed over a low heat where it can 'roast' gently until the meat is tender.

MAKING PÂTÉS

Technically speaking, a pâté should be cooked in pastry (both words come from the same linguistic root), while a terrine should be cooked in a china, earthenware or metal mould. In reality, the terms have merged and for all intents and purposes they are interchangeable. Anything wrapped in pastry usually carries the tag *en croûte*, in a crust.

Pâtés can be anything from the simple and rustic to the immensely sophisticated, light and rich, studded with truffles and other expensive delicacies. At home I tend to stick to making the more rustic sort. They are very easy to tackle and make excellent additions to buffets, summer lunches and children's lunch boxes.

The backbone of all the less fancy pâtés is pork in one form or another. It brings flavour and texture, it gives supporting substance, its fat stops the mixture from drying

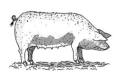

Pork,
Bacon & Ham

out in the oven (never try to reduce quantities drastically) and in the form of bacon, back fat or caul fat, it often encloses the pâté, keeping it neatly in shape. I give a recipe for a favourite pâté de campagne, a country pâté, on page 122, but here are some extra guidelines.

INGREDIENTS

Virtually 50 per cent of the meat content in a pâté should be from fat meat as opposed to lean. A good deal of fat will seep out during the cooking so it can be avoided but, when it comes down to it, pâtés are not meant for dieters. Try to order the meat in advance (it makes life easier for your butcher), and ask if he can mince it all for you, keeping the mixture on the coarse side.

If this isn't possible (say if you are buying the meat from a supermarket, or the butcher's mincer is too large to handle small amounts), then you have a choice between mincing the meat yourself (if you have an old-fashioned mincer), chopping it finely by hand (the best solution but rather tedious and time consuming), and chopping it in the food processor. This last option needs some care and attention. If you just let it whizz freely, you'll end up with a pappy mush, rather than the little tiny bits that you want. Process the meats in very short bursts, scraping down the sides frequently, until they are chopped to your liking. Whichever way it is done, the degree of mincing or chopping dictates the finished texture of the pâté. You may wish to deliberately leave some pieces of meat larger than others. Experiment when you make pâtés and see what you like best. There is endless room for variation and this is what makes pâté-making such fun.

Additions of egg and flour will help to hold the pâté together when it is cooked. Flavourings and seasonings should be on the vigorous side. To test, fry a small knob of the mixture and have a taste, then adjust the seasonings accordingly.

THE MOULD

Purpose-made 'terrines', china or earthenware pâté moulds, are perhaps the prettiest way to present a pâté, and they dispose of the need to unmould it before serving. Still, if you only make pâté once in a blue moon, then a plain old loaf tin is probably your best bet while a china soufflé dish makes a rather more presentable alternative.

Lining and filling the mould
If you are intending to serve the pâté straight from its mould then you can just pack the mixture straight in. Usually, though, the mould is lined, the mixture packed tightly in

and the trailing ends of the lining flipped over to cover. This makes for a neater presentation both in the mould and out of it.

There are three common options for the lining. Easiest to lay your hands on (but most expensive) is streaky bacon. You'll need a fair amount to line the mould completely. The main disadvantage, though, is the powerful flavour it contributes, which may well overwhelm the pâté itself. If you have a passion for bacon this won't matter too much and you can mute the flavour by blanching the bacon for a minute or two in boiling water before using it.

Thin sheets and strips of plain pork fat are a good option and have the advantage of a neutral flavour. You'll have to ask your butcher to slice the strips as thin as possible, then you can flatten them further at home by beating them with a meat mallet. For a pretty finish, lay a lattice of narrow strips of pork fat on top of the pâté before it goes into the oven.

By far the best option, in my opinion, since it is easy to handle and looks coolly professional, is a veil of caul fat (see page 91) which stretches thinly and elegantly to line the mould. Flip the ends over the pâté mixture, covering it neatly. As it cooks the caul fat melts into the pâté, giving the top surface a neat, glossy, webbed look.

The pâté mixture should always be packed into the mould tightly and mounded up neatly above the rim, as the mixture will shrink as it cooks. For this reason it is always better to use a mould that seems slightly too small than one that is on the roomy side.

COOKING

Pâtés are usually cooked in a bain-marie. In other words, the mould is placed in a roasting tin which is then half-filled with hot water and they go into the oven together. If necessary, the water level should be topped up as the pâté cooks. This is another measure to keep the pâté from drying out. The oven temperature is usually slow to moderate. Cooking time depends a great deal on the depth of the dish – if you bake your pâté in a small but deep dish it will take longer than the same amount baked in a wider but shallower dish. Keep checking it as it cooks.

Cover the pâté with foil or a lid, in the oven. If it is to be served from its mould, remove the cover half an hour or so before the pâté is done, so that the top can brown.

To test the pâté, first have a good look at it. If it has shrunk away from the sides and is surrounded by liquid fat, then it is time to go for the conclusive test. For this, treat the pâté like a cake! Plunge a skewer into its heart. If it comes out clean then the pâté is done. Take it out of the oven and let it cool, then cover again with foil, weigh down with tins (this compacts the pâté so that it will be easier to slice) and leave overnight in the fridge or in a cool place.

The flavour will certainly be better the day after it has been made, and will improve

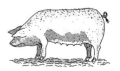

Pork,
Bacon & Ham

further over the next two days or so. If you wish to turn the pâté out, dip the mould in warm water for a minute or so to loosen it, then invert it onto a serving plate and wipe away unsightly fat.

BACON, HAM AND GAMMON

In pre-refrigeration days, the only way to preserve the meat of the plump household pig through the cold damp winter months was to cure it – straight drying was a bit dicey in our climate. Salt worked as a cheap preservative, enhancing and changing the taste of the meat, producing, with the help of various additions, bacon and hams.

In this century, now that we no longer *have* to preserve pork in that way, the old slow-curing methods have all too often been pushed aside in favour of snappy, fast-working, modern techniques that give something of the original taste but produce an inferior product. Bite into a bacon sarnie made with traditionally cured bacon and you'll never want to go back to the mass-produced stuff that oozes white gunge and shrinks pitifully in the pan.

To make bacon, pork is either 'dry-cured' by rubbing in a mixture of salt and flavourings such as sugar, spices, molasses or honey, or 'wet-cured' in brine (usually injected right into the meat) and god knows what else. Ask for dry-cured whenever you have the choice. Bacon that has only been cured is known as 'green' bacon. It may then be smoked which also helps to preserve the meat and adds a different tinge to the taste.

Traditionally, the side of a pig was cured, the hind legs having first been removed for separate treatment to turn them into hams. Hams get a slower curing process than straight bacon. On the continent, many types of ham are then dried slowly and eaten raw in thin slices (Parma ham is the most famous, but the Spanish *jamón serrano* at its best can be every bit as good). In this country hams are made to be cooked. Shoulder may also be given the same treatment.

Commercially cured bacon is made with a whole side, legs and shoulder *in situ*, known as the 'Wiltshire side', presumably named for the first bacon factory, in Calne in Wiltshire. The leg meat, with its lighter cure, is then known as gammon and is sold in joints or steaks and rashers. Gammon, like bacon, must always be cooked.

Whole raw hams and bacon and gammon joints are cooked in much the same way. They will usually need pre-soaking (soaking time depends on the cure – gammon usually needs no more than an overnight soak, but always ask your supplier for his advice on this) and can then can be simmered or baked, wrapped in foil. If you don't own an enormous ham kettle, baking will be the only option for the larger ham.

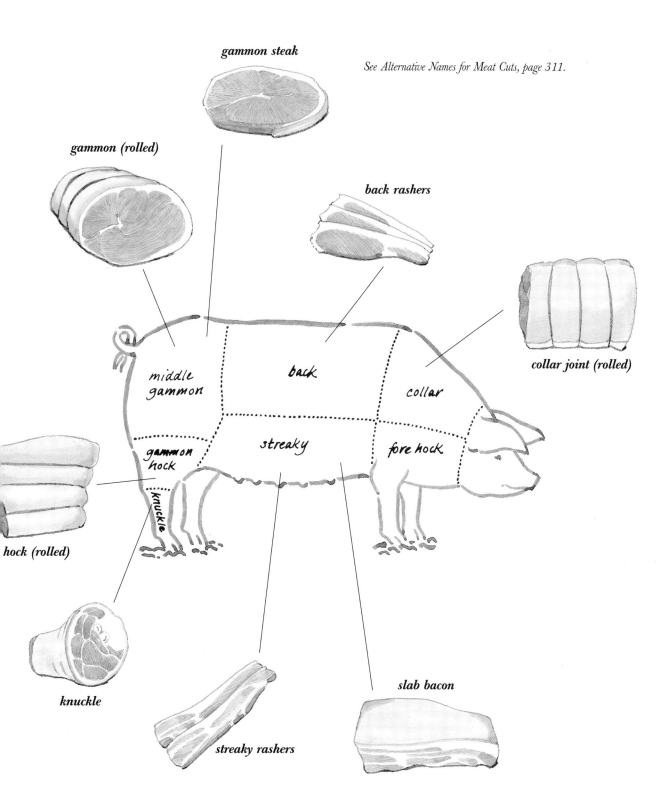

gammon steak

See Alternative Names for Meat Cuts, page 311.

gammon (rolled)

back rashers

collar joint (rolled)

middle gammon

back

collar

gammon hock

streaky

fore hock

knuckle

hock (rolled)

knuckle

slab bacon

streaky rashers

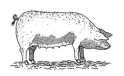

If you choose to simmer a gammon or bacon joint, put it into a pan with a quartered onion, a quartered carrot, a celery stick maybe, and a few bay leaves. Cover with water and bring to barely simmering point. Don't let the water boil. Then allow 22–28 minutes per 500 g (20–25 minutes per lb) plus an extra 20 minutes, for joints up to 4.5 kg (10 lb) in weight. Smaller joints (say around 1.5 kg or 3 lb) should be simmered for 1½ hours. Huge joints over 4.5 kg (10 lb) need only 17–22 minutes per 500 g (15–20 minutes per lb) plus an extra 15 minutes.

To bake gammon or ham, wrap it well in foil, keeping it slightly loose and baggy and bake for 22 minutes per 500 g (20 minutes per lb) at 170°C/325°F/Gas Mark 3 for a large joint of over 2.7 kg (6 lb). Smaller joints will require 28–33 minutes per 500 g (25–30 minutes per lb). Drain off the juices and rest for 20–40 minutes, if serving hot.

Cooked ham, bacon or gammon joints, whether they are to be served hot or cold, are lovely skinned and finished with a baked glaze – see the recipe for Glazed Gammon on page 136, increasing the quantities of mustard and demerara sugar appropriately.

LARDONS

Lardons are thick batons or cubes of bacon, much used in French cooking to flavour casseroles and stews. They are quite the best way to introduce a background bacony resonance and actually have some substance to them, which is what gives them the edge over chopped-up sliced bacon. It is not impossible to buy lardons in Britain, but they are still not widely available. I often bring a packet of high-quality lardons back with me from France, where you can pick them up in the meanest of grocery stores.

To make your own, you will need to buy slab bacon, in other words a whole chunk of bacon that has not been sliced, preferably traditionally cured, green or smoked, as you wish, or as the recipe dictates. Cut off the rind, then slice the bacon about 5 mm (¼ in) thick. Cut into strips.

French recipes often suggest that you blanch the bacon before using it to reduce the salt. For very mild, white sauced stews this can be a good idea or if your bacon is excessively salty but by and large I find it unnecessary, since today's bacon is not nearly as salty as it once was.

CROWN ROAST OF PORK WITH SPICED PRUNE AND APRICOT STUFFING

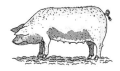

This is one of the most impressive joints you can serve, but do give your butcher ample notice as the pork will have to be cut from the carcase in a way that is slightly different from the norm (the rib bones are cut longer than usual). Allow plenty of time for cooking, too. Mine took a full 4½ hours!

The joint produces a fair amount of its own juices, but if you want to extend them just deglaze the pan (as in the Roast Loin of Pork with Apple, Ginger and Orange Stuffing, see page 104) with wine, stock or even cider. You can't fit a huge amount of stuffing inside the crown so, if you wish, double the quantity and bake the extra alongside the joint for the final 40 minutes.

SERVES 8 GREEDY PEOPLE OR 10 MORE ABSTEMIOUS ONES

1 prepared crown roast of pork weighing about 3–3.5 kg (7–8 lb)

——— *For the stuffing* ———

6 prunes	1 teaspoon coriander seeds, coarsely crushed
6 dried apricots	1 level teaspoon aniseeds
1 onion, chopped	225 g (8 oz) pork sausagemeat
25 g (1 oz) butter	75 g (3 oz) soft brown breadcrumbs
1½ teaspoons black mustard seeds	Salt and freshly ground black pepper

Pre-heat the oven to 230°C/450°F/Gas Mark 8. To make the stuffing, soak the prunes and apricots until soft, if necessary, then dry and chop them. Soften the onion in the butter until tender, then add the spices. Sauté until the mustard seeds begin to jump. Draw off the heat and mix with the dried fruit, sausagemeat, breadcrumbs, salt and pepper.

Weigh a roasting tin (you'll see why in a minute). Now grease and stand the crown roast on it. Fill the central cavity with the stuffing, doming it up in the centre and gently pushing the meat into a nice circular crown. Weigh on the tin, then deduct the weight of the tin to get the weight of the stuffed crown. Calculate the roasting time by allowing 33 minutes per 500 g (30 minutes per lb) and 20 minutes extra. Protect the tips of the bones with twists of silver foil. After it has had 1½–2 hours in the oven you will also need to protect the stuffing from burning with a circle of foil.

Roast the crown at the pre-heated oven temperature for the first 15 minutes, then reduce it to 180°C/350°F/Gas Mark 4 for the remainder of the cooking time. Test to make sure the meat is cooked, then turn off the oven, open the door and leave the roast to relax for 25–30 minutes before carving.

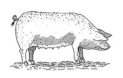

ROAST LOIN OF PORK WITH APPLE, GINGER AND ORANGE STUFFING

❧

This is a smaller roast for a family meal, boned and rolled so that it is as easy as pie to carve. It's not an onerous task to bone and roll the loin at home and scoring the crackling is great fun, but if you want to save time, ask your butcher to prepare it for you.

The best way to stuff the loin depends rather on which end of the animal it comes from (see page 96). Whether you smear it over the flap or push it into the pocket, this stuffing is perfect for pork. The apple and orange provide the fruitiness that goes so well with it and the ginger adds a high note without dominating.

To be honest, I'm not a great gravy fan – I far prefer to serve roast pork with an apple sauce, like the two which follow. But if you do want to extend the pan juices to moisten the meat, the easiest way is to boil them up with a generous slug of cider and a pinch of sugar (or two) to soften the acidity.

SERVES 6

1 boned loin of pork, weighing about 1.25–1.5 kg (3–3½ lb)	1 big glass cider, optional
Salt	A pinch of sugar, optional

——— *For the stuffing* ———

1 small onion, finely chopped	2 tablespoons chopped parsley
1 small eating apple, cored and finely chopped	50 g (2 oz) fresh white breadcrumbs
1–2 spheres preserved stem ginger, finely chopped	1 egg, lightly beaten
Finely grated zest and juice of ½ orange	Salt and freshly ground black pepper

Pre-heat the oven to 190°C/375°F/Gas Mark 5. If you've bought the joint ready boned and rolled, snip off the strings and unroll the pork carefully. If you've bought a whole untouched piece, score the crackling (see page 95), then bone as per the diagrams on page 96. If the joint comes from the upper fillet end, make a pocket for the stuffing. Otherwise, make a flap (see page 96).

Mix the stuffing ingredients, adding just enough egg to bind, and push into the pocket or spread over the cut sides of the meat. Either way don't cram it all in or it will expand as it cooks, oozing out in an unsightly way. Far better to save the excess to make little stuffing balls. Roll up the meat and tie it firmly in place with string, making sure that the skin which will become the crackling is back on top of the joint. Weigh the joint and calculate the cooking time, allowing 33 minutes per 500 g (30 minutes per lb) plus 30 minutes.

Set the rolled joint on a rack over a roasting tin. Dry the skin thoroughly, then rub plenty of fine salt into it. Roast in the oven.

Roll any left-over stuffing into walnut-sized balls and pop them into the roasting tin about half an hour before the joint is done so that they have time to brown and cook through. Check occasionally and remove when they seem nicely browned.

Test the meat to see if it is done; the juices should run clear when a skewer is inserted. Transfer to a serving plate and let it relax in a warm place for 15–20 minutes while you make a simple gravy, if you want to.

Spoon any excess fat out of the roasting tin then place it over the hob and add the cider and a pinch of sugar. Bring up to the boil, stirring and scraping in the meaty residues. Let it bubble for a few minutes before tasting and adjusting the seasonings, adding a little more sugar if it is on the sharp side. Strain and serve alongside the meat and crackling.

French Canadian Roast Apple Sauce

This is one of the best of all versions of apple sauce, with the added bonus of a crisp, caramelized crust on top. It comes from Nicola Cox's Game Cookery *– a marvellous book – published by Gollancz. Serve the sauce with roast pork, goose or any fatty meat. If you add just a little more sugar, it also makes a most delicious pudding!*

SERVES 4 – 6

675 g (1½ lb) tart cooking apples	1 tablespoon dark rum, optional
2 cloves	A pinch of ground cloves
Demerara sugar	¼ teaspoon ground cinnamon
Finely grated zest and juice of 1 lemon	

Pre-heat the oven to 180°C/350°F/Gas Mark 4. Peel, core and slice the apples thickly. Cram into a baking dish, adding the cloves, about 3 tablespoons of demerara sugar and the lemon zest as you go. Pour over the lemon juice and a tablespoon or so of water. Bake in the oven for 45 minutes or until tender (if you like, it can go into the same oven as the pork, in which case it will need a little less time).

Now splash on the rum, if using, and sprinkle with cloves and cinnamon and an even layer of demerara sugar. Whip under a pre-heated grill and cook until the sugar caramelizes. Mash up the softened apple as you serve so that it becomes more sauce-like.

SPICED APPLE SAUCE

This is a more conventional apple sauce, perked up with a few spices, but nothing more fancy than that. If you wish to serve the sauce cold, leave out the butter.

SERVES 6

675 g (1½ lb) cooking apples	3 allspice berries, bruised
1 large cinnamon stick	40 g (1½ oz) butter
3 cloves	Sugar, to taste
1 blade of mace	Freshly ground black pepper

Peel and core the apples, then chop roughly. Put into a heavy-based pan with the spices and enough water to dampen the base. Cover and place over a low–medium heat until the juices begin to run. Raise the heat a little and cook until the apples have collapsed to a purée, stirring once or twice to make sure it isn't catching on the base. If it threatens to burn, lower the heat and add another spoonful of water.

Fish out the spices if you can find them, then add the butter, pepper and a couple of spoonfuls of sugar. Beat with a wooden spoon to smooth out and mix. Taste and add more sugar if needed. Serve warm or cold with the roast pork.

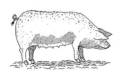

ROAST PORK IN THE FLORENTINE STYLE
(Arista alla Fiorentina)

'Florentine' when it appears in the name of a recipe usually implies that there is spinach some-where in it. Not in this case, though. Arista alla Fiorentina, which one might well translate as Florentine roast, is entirely spinach free, unless you care to accompany it with some spinach on the side. Not a bad idea in fact, as you will need some kind of green vegetable to serve with the pork and the freshness of lightly cooked spinach would be just the ticket.

By rights, Arista alla Fiorentina is a joint of pork cooked on a spit, turned constantly in the heat, with, maybe, a dish of potatoes underneath to catch the juices that drip down. I don't have the set-up for spit-roasting and nor do most people, so I cook my pork in the oven instead.

SERVES 5 - 6

1.5 kg (3 lb) rolled boned loin of pork (see page 96)

2 garlic cloves

1 sprig of rosemary or ½ tablespoon fennel seeds

A little olive oil

900 g (2 lb) potatoes, peeled and cut into 5 cm (2 in) chunks

Salt and freshly ground black pepper

Pre-heat the oven to 220°C/425°F/Gas Mark 7. Score the rind for crackling (see page 95), if it hasn't already been done. Snip off the strings and carefully cut the rind off the pork in one piece so that it can be replaced. Chop the garlic finely with the rosemary leaves, if using, or chop and mix with the fennel seeds. Using a thin-bladed, sharp knife, make slits all over the pork and push the garlic and rosemary or fennel mixture right down into the meat.

Tie the rind back into place, brush with oil and sprinkle generously with salt. Place in a roasting tin and roast in the oven for 20 minutes, then place potatoes all around the pork, turning them in the fat. Season with salt and pepper. Reduce the heat to 170°C/325°F/Gas Mark 3 and roast for a further 1 hour 25 minutes, basting the potatoes occasionally.

ROAST FILLET OF PORK WITH PEACHES

Since fillet is long and lean, it can take, indeed benefits from, fast roasting at a high temperature. Here it is lightly spiced, but what makes this dish is the accompanying baked peaches. Use firm, all-but-ripe peaches that won't collapse in the heat of the oven.

SERVES 6

¼ teaspoon ground coriander

¼ teaspoon ground cinnamon

¼ teaspoon freshly ground black pepper

2 pork fillets

2 tablespoons oil

3 tablespoons honey

3 peaches, halved and pitted (but not skinned)

Salt

Pre-heat the oven to 220°C/425°F/Gas Mark 7. Mix the coriander, cinnamon and pepper. Oil a roasting tin or oven-proof dish which is just large enough to take the fillets and later on the peach halves. Lay the pork in the dish and sprinkle over the mixed spices. Spoon over the oil. Bake in the oven for 20 minutes. Meanwhile, put the honey and 2 tablespoons of water in a small pan and warm very gently, stirring, until the honey has dissolved.

After the first 20 minutes, place peach halves, cut side up, around the pork. Pour the honey mixture over the fillet and peaches and season the pork with salt. Cook for a further 20 minutes, basting occasionally. Turn off the oven, prop the door slightly ajar and leave to rest for 5 minutes. Slice the fillets and serve with the peaches and pan juices.

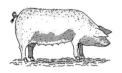

CHAR SIU

(Chinese Honey-roast Pork)

This has to be one of my all-time favourite ways of cooking pork. Char Siu is the stuff you see hanging up in the windows of Chinese restaurants, and this recipe, from Yan-Kit So's Classic Food of China *(Macmillan) is a marvellous home version. The best cuts of pork to use are best chump end, neck end and shoulder blade. Serve it thinly sliced with rice and maybe some stir-fried greens fragrant with ginger and garlic.*

Many supermarkets now sell hoisin sauce and yellow bean sauce. For the red beancurd you'll have to head for an oriental food store. You could leave it out, but the flavour wouldn't be so superb. If possible, use an ordinary oven and not a fan oven, to prevent the meat from drying out.

SERVES 4–6

1–1.25 kg (2¼–2½ lb) pork (see above for cuts), boned and rinded but with the fat left on

About 3 tablespoons clear honey

———— *For the marinade* ————

1 teaspoon salt	1 teaspoon very finely chopped garlic
8 tablespoons sugar	4 tablespoons light soy sauce
2 tablespoons hoisin sauce	1 tablespoon Shaoxing wine
2 tablespoons ground yellow bean sauce	or medium dry sherry
1 tablespoon mashed red beancurd cheese	

Cut the pork into three strips. Make 3 diagonal cuts in opposite directions on each strip, cutting three-quarters through the thickness. Mix all the marinade ingredients then pour over the pork. Turn the pieces so that they are all thoroughly coated. Leave for 4–8 hours, turning the pieces frequently.

Pre-heat the oven to 180°C/350°F/Gas Mark 4. Place the pork, fat side up, on a wire cake rack in the top of the oven, over a roasting tin containing 1 cm (½ in) water. Roast for about 50 minutes. Half-way through the roasting time, brush the pork with marinade and turn over. After 50 minutes, test that the pork is cooked through. If the fat does not yet have a caramelized, almost burnt colour (mine is usually way off at this stage), turn the pieces fat-side up and roast at the highest possible temperature for a final 5–10 minutes.

Take the meat out of the oven, still on its rack and brush all over with honey, making sure it gets right down into the crevices. Let excess honey drip off through the rack.

Pour the remaining marinade into a pan and simmer for about 1 minute, then pour into saucers for use as a dipping sauce. Transfer the pork to a serving plate and carve into slices. Serve immediately. Left-overs can be served cold, or re-heated in the oven.

MEMORIES OF SILESIAN HEAVEN

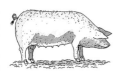

Many years ago I tried a dish called Silesian Heaven, pot-roasted pork with dried fruit. It was simplicity itself and quite delicious. When I tried to find the recipe recently, all I could dig up in German cook books were much more complicated, though no doubt far more authentic, versions. I let memory guide me instead and luckily, it worked.

The tartness of the fruit (apples and apricots are particularly important here) sets off the richness of pork perfectly. If your fruit is of the old-fashioned, bone-dry leather variety, then let it soak in the wine and water for 4 hours or so.

SERVES 4-6

450 g (1 lb) mixed dried fruit such as apricots, prunes, apples and pears	4 cloves
1 generous glass dry white wine	1 onion
1 rolled, boned joint pork, weighing about 1.3–1.75 kg (3–4 lb)	1 cinnamon stick
	25 g (1 oz) flour
	Salt and freshly ground black pepper

Pre-heat the oven to 170°C/325°F/Gas Mark 3. Mix the dried fruit with the wine and enough water to cover. Place the pork in a casserole and surround with the fruit and liquid. Stick the cloves into the onion and add to the casserole along with the cinnamon stick. Sprinkle with the flour and season with salt and pepper. Cover tightly and cook in the oven for 2 hours. Turn the pork a couple of times as it cooks.

Jerked Pork Fillet with Fresh Pineapple Chutney

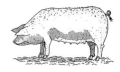

The key ingredient in Jamaican jerked pork, apart from the pork itself, is the allspice berries, toasted to bring out the full aroma. The fresh pineapple chutney is not an authentic Jamaican accompaniment, but it does add an appropriate balancing note of sweetness. The fillet can be either barbecued, which gives a lovely smoky flavour, or grilled.

SERVES 6

2 pork fillets, weighing about 675 g (1½ lb) in all	A little sunflower or vegetable oil Salt and freshly ground black pepper

—— *For the spice paste* ——

2 heaped tablespoons allspice berries	½ Scotch Bonnet chilli or 1 red chilli,
1 teaspoon cinnamon	seeded and roughly chopped
½ teaspoon grated nutmeg	1 bay leaf, chopped
4 spring onions, chopped	1 tablespoon dark rum

—— *For the pineapple chutney* ——

1 ripe pineapple, peeled, cored and finely diced	4 spring onions, sliced
	½ Scotch Bonnet chilli or 1 red chilli,
Juice of 1 lime	seeded and finely chopped
1 cm (½ in) piece fresh root ginger, grated	2 tablespoons chopped coriander

To make the paste, dry-fry the allspice berries in a small heavy pan over a high heat until they give off a delicious scent. Grind or pound to a powder with the other dry spices. Either pound or process with the spring onions, chilli, bay leaf, rum, salt and pepper to make a paste. Rub this over the pork fillets and leave for an hour at room temperature (or longer in the fridge, in which case they should be brought back to room temperature before cooking).

To make the chutney, just mix all the ingredients, cover and leave for an hour before using. Taste and adjust the seasonings.

Brush the fillets with oil and barbecue or grill at a high heat until lightly browned, then move to a medium heat (or turn down the grill) and continue cooking for 15–20 minutes until cooked through. Rest for 5 minutes on a plate by the side of the barbecue, or in a warm place, before slicing. Serve with the fresh pineapple chutney.

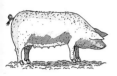

PORC AUX PRUNEAUX DE TOURS

The area around Tours in Western France was once famed for its prunes, though now prune drying is history. Prunes, however, linger on in the local repertoire. The classier pâtisseries make wicked pruneaux fourrés, *stuffed with apricot and almond pastes and glazed with apricot gel, then there's the unlikely sounding but absolutely delicious* matelote d'anguilles *— prune and eel stew — and this dish of pork cooked with prunes, the local wine and lots of cream.*

When I was a child we spent every summer in this area and on highdays and holidays my mother would often make us Porc aux Pruneaux de Tours. Though it can be made with cheaper cuts of pork and is all too often drowned in a floury wine sauce, the best recipe and by far the easiest is this one, largely my mother's version though with a few more prunes (I love them!) and a little less cream. It is a fabulous dish for a dinner party, particularly mid-week when cooking and preparation time is at a premium. If you remember, put the prunes to soak the night before, even if they are of the soft, no-soak, ready-to-eat variety.

SERVES 6

24 prunes	Seasoned flour, for dusting
300 ml (10 fl oz) Vouvray or other	1 level tablespoon redcurrant jelly
dry white wine	300 ml (10 fl oz) whipping cream
2 pork fillets	A squeeze of lemon juice
50 g (2 oz) butter	Salt and freshly ground black pepper

Soak the prunes in the wine for as long as possible — at least an hour — but if you have time, leave them overnight. Slit open the prunes and remove their stones. Reserve the prunes and don't throw out the wine!

Slice each tenderloin thickly into 9 discs (that's 18 altogether). Heat the butter in a wide frying pan until it is foaming, dust the pieces of pork with flour and fry over a moderate heat until just tender. If necessary, do this in two batches so as not to overcrowd the pan. Slices of fillet don't take very long — about 4 minutes on each side. Remove from the pan, arrange on a serving dish and keep warm.

Pour any excess fat from the pan, return to the heat and pour in the wine from soaking the prunes. Bring up to the boil, scraping in all the meaty residues. Stir in the redcurrant jelly, then boil hard over a high heat until reduced to a syrupy consistency.

Now stir in the cream and reduce the sauce until nicely thickened. When it is almost done, pop in the prunes to warm through. Finally add a splash of lemon juice to heighten the flavours and season with salt and pepper. Dot the prunes around the pork and pour over the sauce. Serve at once.

MACEDONIAN PORK SMOTHERED IN LEEKS

This is a robust, countryish family sort of stew, not the thing for smart dinner parties. It has a full flavour, surprisingly intense for something that is basically so simple. This, I think, is as much down to the cut of meat, the shoulder, as it is to the method. I came across the recipe when I was judging an American cookery book competition. We had to test two recipes from each of the seven books that made it to the final. This one comes from Paula Wolfert's The Cooking of the Eastern Mediterranean, *which is full of such homely but often unexpected recipes.*

SERVES 4 – 6

750 g (1¾ lb) boned, trimmed shoulder of pork, cut into 2.5 cm (1 in) cubes	1 x 400 g (14 oz) tin chopped tomatoes
1 tablespoon olive oil	1 celery stick, chopped
1 medium onion, grated	9–12 leeks, depending on size
	Salt and freshly ground black pepper

Brown the pieces of pork lightly in the oil in a wide, covered frying pan (the pieces should form a single layer) over a moderately high heat. Turn them over after about 8 minutes and let the other side colour. Uncover, boil down the juices and pour off most of the fat.

Add the onion and fry until browned. Now add the tomatoes, 450 ml (15 fl oz) water, the celery, salt and pepper. Cover and simmer for 30 minutes.

Wash the leeks thoroughly and cut into 5 cm (2 in) lengths. Place in a pan, cover with water, bring up to the boil and simmer for 5 minutes. Drain thoroughly and add to the pork. Half cover the pan and cook for a further 45–60 minutes or until the meat is very tender and almost all the liquid has been absorbed. Serve with a good sprinkling of freshly ground pepper.

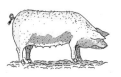

SPICED CHINESE SPARE RIBS

I love sticky, grilled spare ribs. You can't possibly eat them tidily and neatly and half the fun would be lost if you tried. The only refinement to introduce to the table is plentiful fingerbowls. I prefer to grill the ribs in groups of 3 or 4 – easier to handle than large sheets, but not as fiddly as individual ribs – and I always blanch them first to ensure that the meat stays meltingly tender. Although they are nicest grilled (particularly over an outdoor barbecue, in which case I'd suggest you double the quantities as there's nothing like fresh air to sharpen the appetite), they can also be roasted in the oven if it makes life easier.

SERVES 4 AS A FIRST COURSE

1.5 kg (3 lb) pork spare ribs

——— *Marinade* ———

1 heaped teaspoon Szechuan peppercorns or black peppercorns	3 garlic cloves, crushed
7 tablespoons hoisin sauce	2 tablespoons rice wine or dry sherry
1½ tablespoons clear honey	1 tablespoon Chinese black vinegar or red wine vinegar

Divide the sheets of spare ribs into small clumps of 3 or 4 ribs, for easy handling. Blanch them in boiling water for 15 minutes.

Dry-fry the peppercorns (either sort) over a high heat until they start to smell aromatic. Cool and grind them to a powder. Mix with the remaining marinade ingredients and slather thickly over the spare ribs. Set aside for at least 1 hour and preferably 3–4 hours or even overnight (in the fridge).

To grill the ribs, pre-heat the grill (or barbecue) thoroughly. Grill them fairly slowly, about 15 cm (6 in) away from the heat, turning frequently, until they are crisp and catching at the edges. This should take a good 15 minutes, so if necessary move the ribs further away from the heat so that they don't get burnt to a crisp.

If you prefer, you can cook them in the oven pre-heated to 220°C/425°F/Gas Mark 7. Place the ribs on a wire rack over a roasting tin and roast for 20–25 minutes until crisp and slightly frazzled.

RILLETTES AND RILLONS

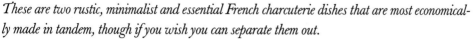

These are two rustic, minimalist and essential French charcuterie dishes that are most economically made in tandem, though if you wish you can separate them out.

Rillons are slow-baked cubes of belly of pork, gently roasted until deep brown and meltingly tender. They can be eaten cold, sliced and served with cornichons or chutney and a tomato salad, though many people may, I suspect, find them a little too greasy. I've always preferred them hot (when I was a child, they were a regular mid-week treat when we were in France), simply re-heated in the oven then dished up with mashed potatoes and fried slices of apple.

Rillettes (always in the plural) are also made from belly of pork, but they demand a little more application and patience on the part of the cook. The cooked meat is torn into fine, fine shreds (a processor makes them too smooth) and potted down with the fat from cooking. When we walked back from school in France, we all looked forward to our goûter — tea-time snack — of a hunk of baguette smeared with rillettes. Many of our neighbours made their own, not only from pork, but often with mixtures of pork and rabbit or pork and goose. I remember M. Deroin's massive black cauldron that came out every year for the creation of rillettes. It was so big that it had to simmer over an outdoor fire, frequently stirred, sending its rich fragrance wafting across the village. Again, cornichons and other pickles go well with rillettes.

This is my version of my mother's recipe for the pair, taken from her very first book, Charcuterie *(Macmillan).*

675 g (1½ lb) belly of pork, cut into 10 cm (4 in) cubes	350 g (12 oz) flair fat, cut into smallish pieces
675 g (1½ lb) belly of pork, cut into small strips about 2.5 cm (1 in) long and 5 mm (¼ in) wide	1 teaspoon quatre épices (see page 120)
	4 sprigs of thyme
	1 bay leaf
	Salt

Pre-heat the oven to 140°C/275°F/Gas Mark 1. Put all of the meats and fat into a shallow, heavy oven-proof dish, adding about 4 tablespoons of water to prevent them from sticking. Cover with foil and bake for about 4 hours. Remove from the oven and increase the temperature to about 200°C/400°F/Gas Mark 6. Pick out the large chunks of meat (these will make the rillons) and place them in a dish in the hot oven, uncovered, turning occasionally until they are richly browned. Once cooked, they can be eaten hot or cold.

The rest of the meat and fat will make the rillettes. Strain the meat, pressing through all the liquid fat. Save it and put it in the fridge to solidify. Transfer the strained meat (including small pieces of fat) to a mortar and pound to break down into a fibrous mush (unless you have a massive mortar, you'll have to do this in several batches). Return

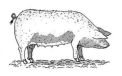
the rillettes to the dish and use a pair of forks to shred any lumps that remain – if you've pounded vigorously enough, there won't be many. Mix in the spices, herbs and plenty of salt. Place over a low heat and cook gently for a further 10–15 minutes, stirring now and then to meld in the flavourings. Discard the bay leaf and thyme. Taste and adjust the seasoning, then pack the meat into small ramekins.

Lift the solidified fat out of the bowl in the fridge, leaving behind the juice. Melt and pour over enough to cover the meat shreds. Leave to cool, cover with foil or clingfilm and store in the fridge. Eat within 5 days.

QUATRE ÉPICES

2 tablespoons black peppercorns	1 teaspoon ground cloves
1 teaspoon freshly grated nutmeg	1 teaspoon ground cinnamon

Grind the peppercorns to a powder and mix with the remaining spices. Store in an airtight jar.

PORK CHOPS WITH MARSALA

A recipe for a quick supper with a touch of class. The sweetness of the Marsala reduces down to a lovely sauce.

SERVES 4

4 pork chops	4 strips of lemon zest
2 tablespoons olive oil	1 tablespoon lemon juice
A sprig of rosemary	Salt and freshly ground black pepper
200 ml (7 fl oz) medium-sweet Marsala	

Pat the chops dry with kitchen paper then brown slowly on both sides in the olive oil in a frying pan that the chops fit into snugly. Pour off the excess fat, turn the heat down and add all the remaining ingredients. Simmer, half-covered, for 20 minutes, turning the chops once. Discard the lemon zest and rosemary. Remove the chops from the pan and keep warm. Boil the juices remaining in the pan until they are reduced to a thin layer on the base. Taste and adjust the seasonings, pour over the chops and serve.

HUNTER'S STEW

(Bigos)

Bigos is almost the national Polish dish — well, it's certainly one of the best known and best loved. It's a tremendous, filling, hearty 'stew' of sauerkraut and pork, flavoured with mushrooms and wine. Though it tastes great when it is first made, those in the know will prefer it re-heated the next day, or even the day after, allowing time for the flavours to mellow and mature. Do store it carefully in the fridge, however, and re-heat it thoroughly each time, adding a little extra stock and/or butter to lubricate it.

This recipe for Bigos (and there are many variations on the theme) comes from the Magical Buska restaurant in north London.

SERVES 8-10

25 g (1 oz) dried porcini	225–450 g (8 oz–1 lb) smoked boiling sausage, or garlic sausage, sliced
1.25 kg (2½ lb) sauerkraut	
675 g (1½ lb) white cabbage	8 prunes, pitted and chopped
100–225 g (4–8 oz) smoked streaky bacon, diced	300 ml (10 fl oz) stock or water
	300 ml (10 fl oz) red wine
25 g (1 oz) butter or oil	1 bay leaf
1 large onion, chopped	1 tablespoon sugar
225–450 g (8 oz–1 lb) boneless pork chops, cubed	Salt and freshly ground black pepper

Cover the porcini with hot water and soak for half an hour. Pick out the mushrooms and chop. Then strain and reserve the soaking liquid. Rinse the sauerkraut in cold water. Shred the cabbage finely, discarding the tough stalks. Put the sauerkraut into a large pan with the cabbage and add 300 ml (10 fl oz) water and some pepper. Simmer for 40 minutes.

Meanwhile, cook the bacon in a large frying pan, adding a little of the butter or oil if needed, until lightly browned. Scoop out and reserve. Fry the onion in the fat, adding the remaining butter or oil, until tender and translucent but not browned. Now add the cubed pork and cook gently until lightly coloured. Add the soaked mushrooms and their soaking liquid, bacon, onion, cooked meat and all the remaining ingredients to the sauerkraut and cabbage. Cook gently, covered, simmering quietly for 40 minutes. Taste and adjust the seasonings, then serve.

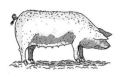

PÂTÉ DE CAMPAGNE

This is about the easiest of pâtés to make, with a fine robust flavour. If you wish you can embell-
ish it by lining the terrine with strips of bacon, though I think it's nicer without. Too much salty
bacon can be overwhelming.

SERVES 8-10

450 g (1 lb) belly of pork	1 large egg
350 g (12 oz) raw, boned chicken or veal	¼ teaspoon ground allspice
225 g (8 oz) pork liver	1 teaspoon thyme leaves
225 g (8 oz) flair fat or back fat	1½ tablespoons chopped parsley
2 garlic cloves, crushed	Caul fat, to line the mould
85 ml (3 fl oz) dry white wine	4 bay leaves, optional
2 tablespoons brandy	Salt and freshly ground black pepper
1 tablespoon flour	

If you have a helpful butcher, ask him to mince the belly of pork *coarsely* with the chicken or veal, liver and flair or back fat. If you don't and you are landed with the work, either chop them all very finely, or chop roughly and process in brief spurts so that the mixture is lumpily minced – continuous processing risks producing a smooth paste, which is not what you want.

Mix the minced meats with all the remaining ingredients except the bay leaves and caul fat. To check the seasoning, fry a small knob and taste, then adjust the salt and pepper etc. accordingly. If you have time, leave the mixture to sit for an hour or two then mix again with your hands.

Line a 1.2 litre (2 pint) or two 500 ml (1 pint) terrines or loaf tins with caul fat, leaving the ends trailing over the sides. Pack the pâté mixture into the moulds and, if you wish, lay a few decorative bay leaves on top. Fold the trailing caul fat neatly over the pâté. Cover the terrines with their lid or foil.

Stand the terrines in a roasting tin of hot water, which should come about half-way up each terrine. Bake at 170°C/325°F/Gas Mark 3 for 1½–2 hours, uncovering the pâté for the last 30 minutes so that it can brown. The pâté is done when it has shrunk well away from the sides of the dish and the juices run clear and yellow-white, rather than pink.

Cool the pâté for an hour, cover with a layer of foil, then weigh it down with tins or whatever is handy and leave until completely cool before slicing. The pâté will taste even better if left in the fridge for a day or two.

If you want to make the pâté look a little neater and less gappy around the edges, melt half a pack of concentrated butter, or clarify 100 g (4 oz) ordinary butter and pour it round the pâté, filling in all the holes.

PORK WITH CHEESE AND MUSHROOM CRUST

The cheese and mustard topping on these pork chops bakes to a delicious brown in the heat of the oven, while the meat stays tender and moist.

SERVES 2

2 pork chops, about 2 cm (¾ in) thick	Salt and freshly
A little oil	ground black pepper

——— *For the crust* ———

25 g (1 oz) breadcrumbs	1 tablespoon Dijon mustard
25 g (1 oz) grated Cheddar	2 teaspoons oil

Pre-heat the oven to 170°C/325°F/Gas Mark 3. First, prepare the chops by trimming off excess fat. Next, make the crust by mixing all the ingredients thoroughly with your hands to form a thick paste. Brush the chops with oil and season with salt and pepper. Place them in an oven-proof dish and bake for 15 minutes. Whip out of the oven, turn them over and spread the top side thickly with the crust mixture. Return to the oven for 10–15 minutes until browned.

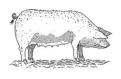

PORK CHOPS WITH AROMATIC HERBS

This recipe is a wonderfully simple way to inject life into plain pork chops. The original comes from Elizabeth David's Spices, Salt and Aromatics in the English Kitchen *(Penguin). Like all Mrs David's books, this is one that I flick through regularly for new ideas and inspiration, always finding something interesting that I'd missed before or that I'd forgotten.*

I've adapted the recipe slightly — in the original, fennel stalks are used rather than the seeds which I've substituted. Fresh thyme and rosemary will give more flavour than dried, but dried is better than nothing in this case.

SERVES 2

2 thick pork chops	4 sprigs of rosemary
1 garlic clove	or 2 teaspoons dried rosemary
Olive oil	3 bay leaves
6 sprigs of thyme or 1 tablespoon	½ tablespoon fennel seeds
dried thyme leaves	Salt and freshly ground black pepper

Pre-heat the oven to 170°C/325°F/Gas Mark 3. Score the chops lightly on both sides. Cut the clove of garlic in half and rub the cut surfaces over the meat on both sides. Season lightly with salt and pepper, pressing it in. Brush both sides of the chops with olive oil.

Mix the herbs and fennel seeds and spread out in a shallow, heat-proof dish, just large enough to take the two chops without overlapping. Lay the chops on top. If possible, do this several hours in advance so that the meat has time to absorb some of the flavours of the herbs.

Brown the chops lightly on both sides under the grill, on their bed of herbs. Cover with foil and transfer to the oven. Bake for 40–45 minutes. Pour off the excess fat and serve the chops with their herbs.

AUSTRIAN PORK WITH PEARS AND POTATOES

This is a heavenly simple dish that requires only a few minutes of preparation time. The real work happens in the oven, untended by human hand, as the pork, potatoes and pears cook gently together to a melting tenderness. It's not grand cuisine, but it does make a perfect (and very cheap) family supper, and I bet there won't be any left-overs.

SERVES 4

450 g (1 lb) belly of pork, cut into 5 cm (2 in) cubes
450 g (1 lb) potatoes, peeled and thickly sliced
450 g (1 lb) pears, cored and quartered
1 stick cinnamon

2 teaspoons caraway seeds
½ tablespoon sugar
600 ml (1 pint) meat or chicken stock
Salt and freshly ground black pepper

Pre-heat the oven to 190°C/375°F/Gas Mark 5. Mix the pork, potatoes and pears together in a lightly greased roasting tin. Tuck the cinnamon down amongst the pork cubes. Sprinkle with the caraway seeds, sugar, salt and pepper. Pour over the stock. Cover with foil and bake for 2 hours.

Pork,
Bacon & Ham

CÔTES DE PORC SAUCE CHARCUTIÈRE

Sauce Charcutière is one of the great French sauces for pork; it takes its name from the wife of the charcutier, the pork butcher and traiteur found in every town throughout the country. It is a lovely way to jazz up plain grilled pork chops, though if you get a taste for it you may well want to dish it up with sausages and other pork products as well.

Some recipes for Sauce Charcutière include tomato but others don't. I quite like it in there, but if you want to simplify matters, leave it out.

SERVES 4

4 pork chops	Salt and freshly
A little oil	ground black pepper

———— For the sauce charcutière ————

90 g (3½ oz) shallots, finely chopped	1 teaspoon sugar, optional
25 g (1 oz) butter or lard	4 cornichons or gherkins, chopped
1 tablespoon flour	1 heaped tablespoon Dijon
50 ml (2 fl oz) dry white wine	or coarse-grained mustard
50 ml (2 fl oz) white wine vinegar	1 tablespoon chopped parsley
450 ml (15 fl oz) pork or chicken stock	1 teaspoon chopped tarragon
225 g (8 oz) tomatoes, skinned, seeded and	½ tablespoon chopped chives
roughly chopped, optional	

To make the sauce, sweat the shallots gently in the butter or lard until tender. Sprinkle over the flour and stir over a medium heat until the roux turns a nice hazelnut brown. Stir in the wine, then the vinegar and finally the stock. Let it simmer quietly for half an hour or so until about the thickness of single cream (or a little thicker if you prefer). Meanwhile, if using the tomatoes, put them into a small pan with the sugar and cook them down to a thick mush over a high heat. Sieve into the main sauce. Finally stir in all the remaining ingredients, then taste and adjust the seasoning. If you intend to re-heat the sauce, leave this last stage until the sauce is hot again or the re-heating process will damage the flavours of the mustard and herbs.

Meanwhile, brush the chops with oil and grill gently until cooked through, then season. Serve with the sauce.

SAUSAGES COOKED IN RED WINE

A straightforward upgrading for good butcher's sausages. Serve piping hot with plenty of mashed potato and mustard.

SERVES 4

8 good-quality meaty sausages	150 ml (5 fl oz) red wine
25 g (1 oz) butter	Salt and freshly ground black pepper
1 bay leaf	

Pre-heat the oven to 190°C/375°F/Gas Mark 5. Prick the sausages all over, then fry briskly in the butter to brown them. Transfer to an oven-proof dish which is only just big enough to take them all in a single layer. Tuck the bay leaf down amongst them. Pour the wine into the frying pan in which the sausages were browned, bring up to the boil, stirring, and pour over the sausages. Season with salt and pepper, then cover with foil and bake for 20–30 minutes.

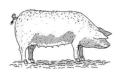

SAUSAGE AND PORCINI RISOTTO

This is one of my favourite risottos, perfect for a cold winter's evening when you need something powerfully full of flavour and comfort to shore you up.

Though you could use any good, meaty pork sausages, it's worth a trip to an Italian deli to get the proper luganega sausages. For a plainer sausage risotto, omit the mushrooms and use white wine instead of red.

SERVES 4 – 6

15 g (½ oz) dried porcini mushrooms

225 g (8 oz) luganega sausages (see above)

1.2 litres (2 pints) chicken, meat or vegetable stock

1 onion, chopped

2 garlic cloves, chopped

25 g (1 oz) butter

1 tablespoon sunflower oil

275 g (10 oz) arborio or other risotto rice

4 sage leaves

1 glass dry red wine

3 tablespoons freshly grated Parmesan

Salt and freshly ground black pepper

Cover the porcini with hot water, leave to soak for 15 minutes, then pick out the pieces and chop roughly. Leave the soaking water in the bowl to settle. Cut the sausages into pieces about 1 cm (½ in) thick.

Heat the stock until it boils, then reduce the heat as low as possible so that it stays hot as you cook.

In a separate, large, heavy-based pan, cook the onion and garlic gently in 15 g (½ oz) of the butter and the oil until tender, without browning. Raise the heat, add the sausages and fry until browned. Add the rice, sage, and soaked mushrooms and stir for 1 minute until the rice is translucent. Add salt and pepper, and pour in the wine and soaking liquid from the mushrooms, taking care to stop before you reach the grit at the bottom. Simmer until it has almost all been absorbed, stirring constantly.

Now add a generous ladleful of the hot stock and stir until it has all been absorbed. Repeat until the rice is just cooked, without being soggy. Ideally at this point the risotto should be damp, slightly moist but not swimming in liquid. Draw off the heat and beat in the remaining butter and the Parmesan. Adjust the seasonings and serve with extra Parmesan for those who want it.

HERBED CRÉPINETTES WITH RED WINE SAUCE

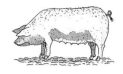

These crépinettes are really just grown-up versions of cheeseburgers. They rely heavily on good-quality sausagemeat and lots of fresh herbs (be generous and add as many as looks right to you — tastes differ enormously). The caul fat is essential to keep the cheese in place and to gloss the surface.

SERVES 4

675 g (1½ lb) good-quality pork sausagemeat	2 garlic cloves, very finely chopped
Lots of herbs, chopped	4 slices Gruyère
(e.g. parsley, a little sage, chervil, chives,	100–175 g (4–6 oz) caul fat
basil, oregano, marjoram)	Salt and freshly ground black pepper
2 shallots, very finely chopped	

For the sauce

2 shallots, chopped	1 glass red wine
450 g (1 lb) tomatoes, skinned,	½ tablespoon red wine vinegar or
seeded and chopped	sherry vinegar
1 bay leaf	1 tablespoon caster sugar

Pre-heat the oven to 200°C/400°F/Gas Mark 6. Mix the sausagemeat with the herbs, shallots, garlic, salt and pepper. Divide into four and shape each portion into a flat round patty, about 2 cm (¾ in) thick. Lay a slice of Gruyère on top of each one, trimming it to fit. Meanwhile, soak the caul fat in water to soften it, if necessary, then squeeze dry. Carefully pull it out to make one large lacy sheet. Cut out four squares, each one large enough to wrap up one patty. Wrap the patties, or crépinettes, up neatly, cheese on top, with the edges tucked away tidily underneath.

Make a bed of the shallots, chopped tomatoes and bay leaf in a shallow tin just large enough to take the four crépinettes. Sit them on top and pour the wine around them. Roast in the oven for 35–40 minutes until cooked through. Transfer the crépinettes to a shallow serving dish and keep warm while you finish the sauce.

Add the vinegar and sugar to the juices in the tin and boil hard, stirring frequently, on the hob, until reduced to a nice sauce. Spoon a little around the crépinettes and serve the rest alongside.

Pork,
Bacon & Ham

SAUSAGE AND APPLE PIE

This is the kind of homely, countryish pie that I love. It tastes best hot or warm from the oven, though I suspect that any cold left-overs won't be hanging around for long.

SERVES 6-8

450 g (1 lb) puff pastry

450 g (1 lb) good-quality pork sausagemeat

3–4 sage leaves, chopped

A little freshly ground nutmeg

2 large eating apples, peeled, cored and sliced

1 egg yolk

Salt and freshly ground black pepper

Roll out half the pastry and line a 21–23 cm (8½–9 in) round pie plate. Using your hands, spread out the sausagemeat over the base. Scatter the sage leaves over it and season lightly with salt, pepper and nutmeg. Now cover with the apple slices and sprinkle again with salt, pepper and nutmeg. Roll out the remaining pastry to form a lid. Beat the egg yolk lightly with 1 tablespoon of cold water. Brush the edges of the pie pastry with this egg wash and lay the lid on top. Press the edges together to seal and trim off any excess pastry, then make a hole in the centre of the lid so the steam can escape. Chill in the fridge for 30 minutes.

Put a baking tray in the oven and pre-heat the oven to 220°C/425°F/Gas Mark 7.

Brush the pastry with the egg wash and pop it into the oven on top of the baking tray so that the base gets an instant blast of heat. After 15 minutes, reduce the heat to 180°C/350°F/Gas Mark 4 and cook for a further 30–40 minutes. Test with a skewer to make sure that the apple is tender.

HAM WITH SAUCE ROBERT

Sauce Robert is a white wine sauce with a hint of mustard that goes particularly well with ham. Sometimes it is made with vinegar as well as wine to sharpen it up. I prefer it without, but you can if you wish replace 25 ml (1 fl oz) of the wine with white wine vinegar for a tarter flavour. The sauce can be made in advance and kept in the fridge for a day or two.

When ham is to be served hot like this, you will need the best cooked ham possible, cut thick to give substance. If no one near you sells good ham, cut freshly as you like it, then partner the sauce with thin gammon steaks, or pork chops. It also goes well with poached eggs, or grilled pork and herb sausages.

The sauce dates back a good 400 years…but who, you may wonder, was Robert? The invention of the sauce is often credited to a cook called Robert Vinot who plied his trade towards the end of the sixteenth century. Larousse Gastronomique *tells us that this is wrong. Rabelais mentioned 'Robert, the inventor of Sauce Robert' in 1552, years before M Vinot came on the scene. Who Rabelais' Robert was remains a mystery, though he was obviously a fine cook.*

SERVES 4

15 g (½ oz) butter	4 thick slices of cooked ham
1 tablespoon sunflower oil	

—— *For the sauce* ——

1 large onion, finely chopped	300 ml (10 fl oz) pork or chicken stock
25 g (1 oz) butter	1 tablespoon Dijon mustard
1 tablespoon flour	1 teaspoon sugar
200 ml (7 fl oz) dry white wine	Salt and freshly ground black pepper

First make the sauce. Cook the onion slowly in the butter in a fairly large pan until golden – a good 10 minutes or more. Sprinkle with the flour and stir until hazelnut brown. Gradually stir in the wine as if making a white sauce. Then stir in the stock. Bring up to the boil and simmer, stirring occasionally, until the sauce has reduced by about one third. (If you are making the sauce in advance, stop at this point and re-heat it when needed.) Mix a tablespoon or two of the sauce into the mustard, then stir back into the sauce with the sugar, salt and pepper to taste. Keep warm.

Heat the butter and oil in a wide frying pan and fry the ham briefly to heat through and brown lightly. Serve the hot ham with the sauce.

JAMBON PERSILLÉ

On the whole I'm not keen on bits and bobs set in aspic, but Jambon Persillé is a glorious exception. It makes a stunning centrepiece for a buffet, but should be made at least a day in advance (it keeps for several days in the fridge). A classic Jambon Persillé does not need gelatine. A calf's foot is simmered with the meat and that is quite enough to gel the liquid, as well as giving extra flavour. I find this method simpler since it saves hunting down calves' feet.

SERVES 8

1.75 kg (4 lb) gammon joint, soaked overnight and drained	1 bouquet garni (see page 33)
1 large onion, quartered	6 black peppercorns
1 leek, cut into 5 cm (2 in) lengths	300 ml (10 fl oz) dry white wine
1 celery stick, cut into 4	300 ml (10 fl oz) chicken or veal stock
1 large carrot, thickly sliced	2 sachets powdered gelatine
	25 g (1 oz) chopped parsley

Place the gammon in a pan and cover with water. Bring up to the boil and simmer for 10 minutes. Drain and rinse under cold water. Rinse the pan, and return the gammon to it. Add the vegetables, bouquet garni, peppercorns, wine, stock and enough water to cover. Bring up to the boil and skim, then simmer for 2–3 hours until the gammon is very tender. Frequently skim off any scum and fat as it simmers. If necessary, top up with boiling water so that the meat is always covered.

Remove the meat and boil the liquid hard to concentrate the flavour. Taste frequently and remove from the heat before it becomes too salty. Strain through a sieve lined with muslin or kitchen paper. Measure out 900 ml (1½ pints). If you don't have quite enough, top up with stock or water. Place 6 tablespoons of the cooking liquid into a small pan and sprinkle over the gelatine. Leave for 4–5 minutes then heat very gently, stirring, until completely dissolved. Mix in another 6 tablespoons of the warm liquid one at a time then tip the mixture back into the liquid, stirring well. Leave to cool, then transfer it to the fridge until it begins to thicken.

Using two forks, tear the meat into pieces around 2.5 cm (1 in) thick and mix with the chopped parsley. Spread a third of the meat and parsley mixture in a single layer in a 2 litre (3½ pint) bowl and pour over enough of the stock to barely cover it. Chill until just set. Repeat twice more, pouring over all the remaining stock the last time round. Cover and chill for at least 5 hours or overnight.

To turn out, loosen the edges with a sharp knife, then invert the Jambon Persillé onto a serving dish and shake gently until it slips out. If it clings stubbornly, dip into hot water for a few seconds, then try again.

BOILED SMOKED BACON KNUCKLE
WITH SAVOY CABBAGE

A modern way of cooking a traditional Irish favourite. Instead of boiling the cabbage to death with the bacon, the two just come together at the last minute. It's a remarkably economical dish too, though you'll have to go to an old-fashioned butcher for the bacon knuckle. Serve with boiled potatoes (main-crop not new) and soda bread. Save the second lot of cooking water for making split pea or lentil soup.

SERVES 4

1 smoked bacon knuckle	50 g (2 oz) butter
1 onion, halved	½ Savoy cabbage, thickly shredded
1 carrot, quartered	3 juniper berries, crushed
2 garlic cloves	A few shakes of balsamic or sherry vinegar
1 bay leaf	Freshly ground black pepper

Cover the knuckle with water and bring up to the boil. Simmer for 5 minutes, then drain. Cover with clean water and add the onion, carrot, garlic and the bay leaf. Bring up to the boil and simmer until the meat is tender – about 1 hour – skimming off any scum as it cooks. When cooked, leave the meat to cool in the broth. This can all be done up to a day ahead.

Skin the knuckle, then strip the meat off in biggish chunks and strain the broth. Measure 300 ml (10 fl oz) of it into a pan large enough to take the cabbage and add 15 g (½ oz) of the butter. Bring up to the boil, cram in the cabbage and the juniper berries, then bring back to the boil and let it simmer for about 2 minutes. Add the meat to the pan and simmer for a final 3–5 minutes until the cabbage is tender but not smelly. Draw off the heat. Stir in the remaining butter, the vinegar and plenty of pepper and serve immediately.

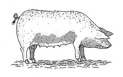

GLAZED GAMMON

A large joint of glazed gammon looks pretty impressive and, as long as you allow plenty of time, it is very easy to cook. It will need to be soaked first, then boiled (well, simmered really) and then gets a final spell in the oven to gloss the glaze.

SERVES 8–10

1 gammon joint, weighing	1 carrot
around 2.75 kg (6 lb)	1 bay leaf
1 onion	A few sprigs of parsley

——— *For the glaze* ———

2 tablespoons Dijon or English mustard	Whole cloves, to decorate
2 tablespoons demerara sugar	

Soak the gammon joint overnight in cold water then drain well. If you don't have time to do this you can accelerate the process by putting the joint into a pan of cold water, bringing it to the boil and letting it simmer for 5 minutes. Then throw out the water, which will take a fair amount of salt with it.

Put the soaked or blanched joint into a large pan with the onion, carrot, bay leaf and parsley. Cover with cold water and bring slowly to the boil. Cover and simmer lazily for 2 hours, topping up the water level regularly with more hot water. Leave the joint to cool for half an hour in its cooking liquid if you plan to serve it hot, or longer at your convenience if you wish to serve it cold.

Lift the joint out of the liquid onto a board and wipe it dry. Carefully peel off the skin: start by making a couple of cuts just through the skin itself, not the fat underneath, so that you can get a hold of it, then pull it off, without removing the fat. While you are at it, taste the stock. If it isn't too salty, save it for making soup – it's especially good for a dried pea soup.

Pre-heat the oven to 220°C/425°F/Gas Mark 7.

Transfer the joint to a roasting tin. Smear the fat with the mustard, then press the sugar firmly and evenly all over it. Using the tip of a sharp knife, score the fat with parallel lines, first in one direction, then at an angle, to form diamonds. Finally, press a clove into the centre of each diamond. Roast the joint for about 25 minutes until nicely browned and glazed.

If you are serving the joint hot, let it rest for 20 minutes before carving. Otherwise leave it to cool slowly in its own time.

Veal

Veal

The issue of veal has loomed large of late, with protests to match the heyday of Greenham Common against the live export of calves to countries where 'crating' (rearing in barbarically small cages on a deficient diet that guarantees white flesh) is still permitted. This practice is no longer allowed in Britain, but for most of our farmers, raising veal is simply uneconomical anyway. In fact, as consumers, we must shoulder a large portion of the blame for the fate of these unhappy creatures ourselves. Why? Because most of us drink milk and don't eat veal; calves are a by-product of the dairying system, a means of keeping the cow in milk. But although veal is by and large unwanted here, calf's meat is highly rated on the continent.

For years I mistakenly avoided cooking and printing recipes for veal. What I should have been doing was to encourage readers to buy and eat home-grown veal. As things stand, there is so little demand for it that most butchers don't even bother to buy it in, but with luck that should begin to change. It is not difficult to pick out veal that has been decently raised. The colour gives it away instantly. The new fashionable word is 'rose veal', in other words, meat with a clean, sweet rosy hue to it. If an animal has had room to move and a tolerable diet, then there is no way his flesh will be pallid and white.

Rose veal still has the delicate flavour that makes veal so popular in other countries, though as you'd expect it is a mite more pronounced than white veal. When cooking veal, you should bear in mind that it will need something tart to set it off. This can be no more than a squeeze of fresh lemon juice as it is served, or may perhaps entail adding capers, white wine, tomatoes, or other ingredients with an edge to them, to the pan as the meat cooks.

CHOOSING VEAL

Avoid very pale veal and very red veal. What you are after is something in between, a pretty rosy pink, clear and clean. What little fat there is, and that's not a lot, should be ivory white and firm.

CUTS AND COOKING

ROASTING

Since veal is a lean, young meat, great care must be paid to it as it cooks to prevent drying out. It is tender, though, and makes a superb roast, as long as it is cosseted all the time in the oven. Barding, larding and frequent basting all help, as does a day or two in a bath of marinade. Veal is usually served cooked through, but not overcooked. Good cuts for roasting include the leg, loin, boned rolled shoulder or breast and best end of neck.

Either brown the joint over direct heat first, or start it off at a high temperature (230°C/450°F/Gas Mark 8) for 20 minutes. Then roast at 180°C/350°F/Gas Mark 4, allowing 28 minutes per 500 g (25 minutes per lb). The internal temperature should read 70°C/160°F on a meat thermometer, rising to 75°C/170°F as the meat rests.

FRYING

Escalopes of course, loin chops, best end cutlets, rump and cushion (fillet).

GRILLING

Grilled veal is all too often tough and dry. You can just about get away with grilling a meaty, chunky chop as long as you brush it several times with oil as it cooks and leave salting until it is on the plate. It's worth marinating the chops first, too, as a precaution.

POT-ROASTING AND BRAISING

Pot-roasting and braising are brilliant methods for cooking veal. I prefer it to roasting for choicer pieces like boned leg, loin, or boned rolled shoulder. It keeps the meat perfectly moist and tender, you can add plenty of invigorating flavourings and the veal will be as good hot as cold.

CASSEROLING

Practically any bit will do. This is the way to use the cheaper cuts, which may be too awkward or bitty for other methods. Shin (particularly for Osso Buco), scrag end, middle neck and flank all fit the bill nicely.

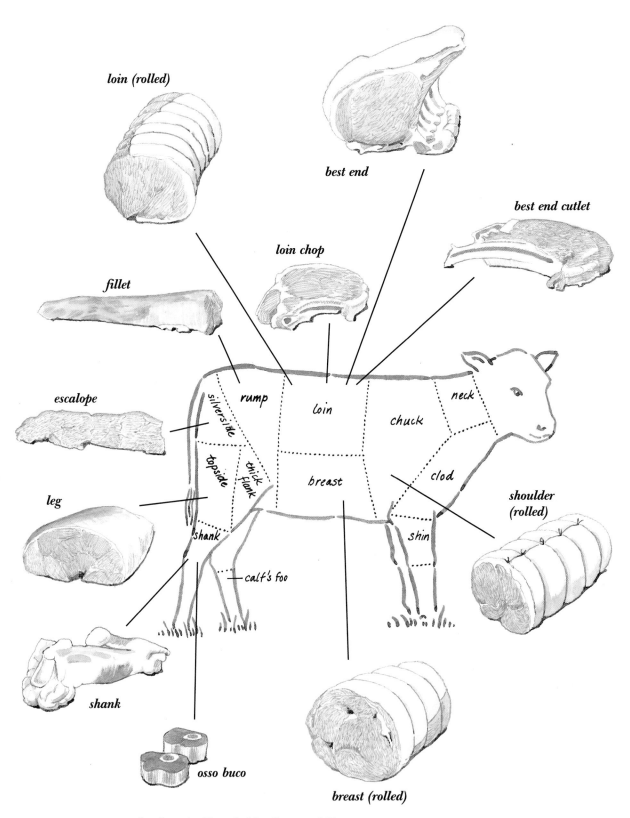

loin (rolled)

best end

best end cutlet

loin chop

fillet

escalope

rump

silverside

loin

neck

chuck

topside

thick flank

breast

clod

shoulder
(rolled)

leg

shank

shin

calf's foo

shank

osso buco

breast (rolled)

See Alternative Names for Meat Cuts, page 311.

SALTIMBOCCA ALLA ROMANA

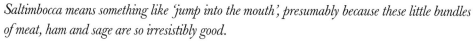

Saltimbocca means something like 'jump into the mouth', presumably because these little bundles of meat, ham and sage are so irresistibly good.

The rolls can be made in advance, but they should be cooked only at the last minute as they don't benefit from being re-heated once they are done. If you temporarily store the uncooked rolls in the fridge, make sure they are brought back to room temperature before they go into the pan.

SERVES 4

8 thin slices veal or turkey breast steaks	25 g (1 oz) butter
8 slices Parma ham	120 ml (4 fl oz) Marsala
8 sage leaves	Salt and freshly ground black pepper

Sandwich each slice of veal or turkey between two sheets of greaseproof paper and flatten them out using a rolling pin. A bit of bashing is fine, but not too much as it can make them holey. It is simpler to just roll them out like pastry.

Lay a piece of Parma ham on each slice of veal, trimming it to fit. Grind over a little pepper. Perch a sage leaf in the centre, flip the sides in over the sage leaf, then roll up neatly and skewer each one in place with a wooden cocktail stick.

Brown the rolls in the butter, then pour in the Marsala and season with salt and pepper. Cover and simmer for about 10 minutes, until cooked through. Serve immediately.

Veal

VITELLO TONNATO

Vitello Tonnato, veal with a tuna fish mayonnaise, is an Italian dish that I love to make for large summer buffets. It comes as a welcome change from endless Coronation Chicken and is every bit as good, quite apart from being rather more unusual.

If you've not come across it before, it may sound a rather bizarre combination, but in fact it turns out to be a marriage made in heaven. If needs be, a large turkey breast joint can be substituted for the veal, though the meat tends to be rather drier and less interesting.

Cook the veal in advance and blend the mayonnaise ahead of time, but leave the final arranging on the plates until as late as possible. Ideally you will be making your own mayonnaise, but actually it works just fine with high-quality, bought mayonnaise. To be honest, if I've a large party of people coming to eat, the last thing I want to do is to spend ages whisking.

SERVES 8-10

1 carrot, diced	250 ml (8 fl oz) dry white wine
1 onion, chopped	120 ml (4 fl oz) olive oil
2 celery sticks, chopped	Salt and freshly ground black pepper
1 bay leaf	A few sprigs of parsley
1 sprig of thyme	A few capers
1.5 kg (3 lb) joint of veal, rolled and tied	

——— *For the tuna mayonnaise* ———

450 ml (15 fl oz) mayonnaise	1 teaspoon capers
200 g (7 oz) drained, tinned tuna	A squeeze of lemon juice
5 tinned anchovy fillets, roughly chopped	

Make a bed of the carrot, onion, celery, bay leaf and thyme in the bottom of a flame-proof casserole which will take the veal snugly. Lay the veal on top and pour over the wine and olive oil. Bring to a simmer, then reduce the heat, cover and cook gently for about 1½ hours or until tender. Turn the veal once or twice during the cooking time so that it cooks evenly. Cool in its own juices and when cold strain off the juices and discard the vegetables and herbs.

For the sauce, put a little of the mayonnaise into the bowl of the processor with the tuna, anchovy and capers and whizz until smooth. Mix in the rest of the mayonnaise and enough of the cooking juices from the veal to thin the sauce down to the consistency of double cream. Taste and adjust the seasoning, sharpening the sauce with a little lemon juice.

To serve, slice the veal thinly and arrange on a serving plate. Spoon over the sauce (leave this until the last possible minute, as it tends to form a skin) and decorate with sprigs of parsley and a few capers.

VEAL POJARSKI

Veal Pojarski are light, delicate, but rich rissoles. They are particularly good served on a bed of spinach, or a sorrel purée, with a poached egg perched atop each one. Accompanying lemon wedges are essential to sharpen their mildness.

The classic Veal Pojarski is made with the ingredients listed below, but the meat is taken from a veal chop and once mixed is re-shaped against the bone in its original form. Try it for fun one day, but in the meantime stick with this simpler version.

SERVES 6

100 g (4 oz) slightly stale breadcrumbs	100 g (4 oz) butter, softened
Milk	A good grinding of nutmeg
450 g (1 lb) lean veal (loin is ideal), minced	Salt and freshly ground black pepper

—— *To coat* ——

1 egg, lightly beaten	Clarified butter (see page 156),
Fine breadcrumbs	or butter and oil for frying

—— *To serve* ——

Lemon wedges	6 poached eggs, optional

Soak the breadcrumbs in milk for 10 minutes, then drain and squeeze out the excess milk. Mix thoroughly with the veal and butter, then season generously with salt, pepper and nutmeg. Divide into 6 portions (if the mixture is too soft to hold its shape, chill in the fridge for 20 minutes or so). Roll each one into a ball, then flatten slightly to a thickness of about 2 cm (¾ in). Dip each one into the egg, then coat in breadcrumbs. Leave in the fridge for an hour or so, to set.

Bring the rissoles back to room temperature, then fry in clarified butter, or half butter half oil, over a medium heat, turning once or twice until they are a rich golden brown. Serve immediately with lemon wedges and a poached egg on top of each one, if you wish.

Veal

BLANQUETTE DE VEAU

Blanquette de Veau is a pale veal and mushroom stew that is widely made in France. I've had a couple of totally insipid versions, made worse with gluey sauces, but a blanquette doesn't have to be like that. At its best it should be smooth and well flavoured, though not the kind of thing that will knock your tastebuds for six.

To get the best flavour, it is important, I think, to use the right cuts of veal and that means a plentiful chunk of breast or neck with bones and cartilage thrown in to give the sauce a velvety texture. This is backed up with bone-free shoulder to add substance. In smarter restaurants, the bits of bone will be removed before the stew is served. Unless you are very finickety and have plenty of time, this is quite unnecessary at home.

SERVES 6

900 g (2 lb) breast or neck of veal, including bones and cartilage, cut into 5 cm (2 in) chunks
450 g (1 lb) boned shoulder of veal, cut into 5 cm (2 in) pieces
1 onion, quartered
4 cloves
1 large carrot, quartered
1 celery stick, quartered
1 garlic clove, peeled but left whole
300 ml (10 fl oz) dry white wine
2 bay leaves

2 sprigs of thyme
4 sprigs of parsley
1 sprig of tarragon (optional)
24 pearl onions, skinned
8 oz (225g) button mushrooms, quartered if on the large side
40 g (1½ oz) butter
1½ tablespoons flour
2 egg yolks
150 ml (5 fl oz) crème fraîche, or double cream
A squeeze of lemon juice
Salt and freshly ground black pepper

Put the meat into a large pan and add enough water to cover. Bring slowly to the boil, skimming off any scum as it rises. Add the onion, each quarter studded with a clove, the carrot, celery, garlic and white wine. Tie the herbs together with a piece of string to make a bouquet garni and pop that in too. Season with salt and pepper (use white pepper if you are aiming for a truly pale, unsullied, stew). Cover and leave to simmer for 1¼–1½ hours until the meat is tender. Pick out the onion, carrot, celery, garlic and bouquet garni and discard.

Add the pearl onions and the mushrooms and continue to simmer, uncovered, until the onions and mushrooms are tender – another 15–20 minutes. Transfer the solids to a bowl and strain the cooking juices.

Melt the butter in a large pan and sprinkle over the flour. Stir for a minute without letting it brown. Gradually whisk in the reserved cooking stock from the veal, adding just a splash or two at first, then building up to a steady flow. Bring up to the boil and simmer for about 20 minutes until the sauce is reduced to a rich, creamy consistency. Stir every now and then to prevent burning. If you are making the stew in advance, stop at this point, spear an extra knob of butter on a fork and rub it over the surface of the sauce to prevent a skin from forming. Re-heat it later when you are almost ready to eat.

Return the veal and vegetables to the hot sauce and simmer for a few more minutes to heat through thoroughly. Reduce the heat to low. Beat the egg yolks lightly into the cream, then gradually whisk in a few spoonfuls of the hot sauce, one at a time. Tip this back into the pan, and stir for a minute or two without letting it boil, until the sauce thickens slightly. Draw off the heat, add a squeeze of lemon juice (two if you used double cream), then taste and adjust the seasoning.

Serve with rice or new potatoes. I like to sprinkle over a little chopped parsley, though of course, this means that the whole ensemble loses a little of its characteristic ghostly pallor.

Veal

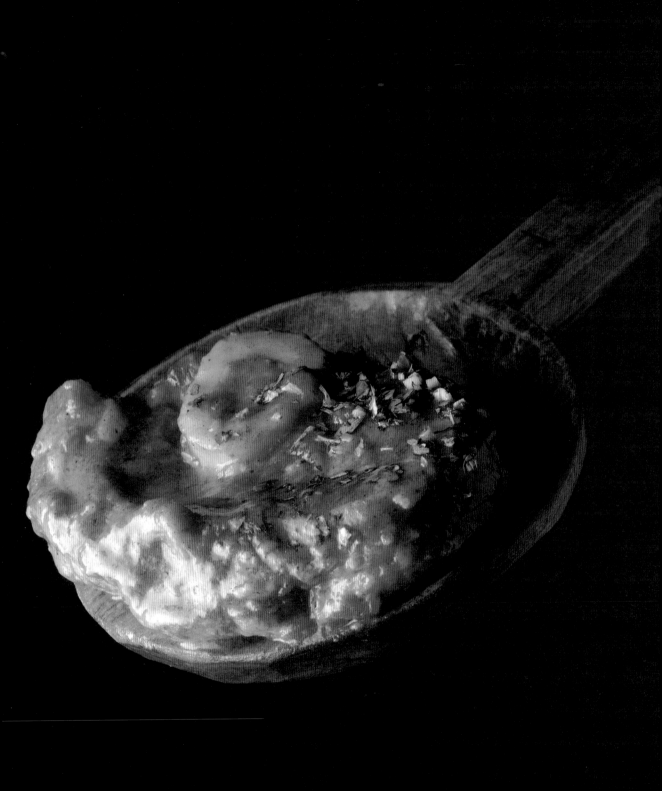

OSSO BUCO ALLA MILANESE

Osso buco refers directly to the piece of meat used for this stew. It comes from the shin, cut across into steaks with the bone sitting squat in the centre. Ask for the slices to be cut from the upper, thicker part of the shin, so that there's plenty of meat on them.

There is some debate about the proper way to make Osso Buco alla Milanese. Tomatoes are at the crux of the matter, though tomato-less versions are often given a different name. To me, they are what make the stew so good, invigorating what might otherwise be rather a mild dish. However, what really injects vitality into the stew is the final addition – the gremolata, an uncomplicated mixture of very finely chopped garlic, parsley and lemon zest. If you are not keen on raw garlic, then you can sprinkle over the gremolata five minutes or so before the stew is finished so that some of the rawness is lost in the heat, but it really isn't half as good.

SERVES 4

4 slices of shin of veal, 4–5 cm (1½–2 in) thick, cut with the marrow bone

Seasoned flour, for dusting

50 g (2 oz) butter

1 garlic clove, quartered

150 ml (5 fl oz) dry white wine

350 g (12 oz) tomatoes, skinned, seeded and chopped

150 ml (5 fl oz) chicken, veal or vegetable stock

Salt and freshly ground black pepper

——— For the gremolata ———

Finely grated zest of 1 lemon

2–3 tablespoons chopped parsley

1–2 garlic cloves, chopped

Dust the veal with flour and fry in the butter in a wide frying pan over a brisk heat until browned on both sides. Add the quartered garlic clove to the pan when the meat is half done, so that it has time to flavour the butter without burning. Scoop out and discard the garlic when the veal is browned.

Reduce the heat and add the wine to the pan. Let the *ossi buchi* simmer gently for 10 minutes. Next add the tomatoes and cook for another 10 minutes or so until they begin to collapse to a purée. Add enough stock to barely cover the meat and season with salt and pepper. Bring to a quiet simmer, cover tightly (use foil or a tin tray if there is no proper lid for your frying pan) and leave to simmer for 1½–2 hours or until the meat is very tender. Check every now and then, turning the meat once or twice and adding a little water if the liquid level seems to be dropping perilously low. By the end of the cooking time the sauce should be fairly thick. If it is on the watery side, uncover and let it boil down for another 10–15 minutes or so until it has thickened. Taste and adjust the seasoning.

Veal

While the *ossi buchi* are cooking, make the gremolata. Mix the zest with the parsley and garlic, then chop the whole lot together very finely. Once the stew is done, sprinkle this mixture over it and serve with Risotto Milanese (see page 306) if you want to be truly authentic – and a marvellous combination it is too – or lots of mashed potato that has had plenty of butter and freshly grated Parmesan beaten into it.

WIENER SCHNITZEL

Wiener Schnitzel is just a grand name for breaded veal escalopes. Proper Wiener Schnitzel are fried in lard. You could, if you preferred, use butter or even olive oil, but technically you'd be making something quite different. For such a delicate meat, you really do need fine breadcrumbs, not large lumpy ones.

SERVES 4

4 veal escalopes	Fine breadcrumbs, to coat
Lard, for frying	Salt and freshly ground black pepper
Seasoned flour, for dusting	Lemon wedges, to serve
1 egg, lightly beaten	

Snip the edges of the escalopes here and there to prevent them from curling in the pan when they are fried. Sandwich each one between two sheets of greaseproof paper and beat lightly with a rolling pin until they are slightly thinner and larger. Don't be too energetic or you'll end up with unsightly holes in the schnitzels.

Melt enough lard in a frying pan to give a depth of about 1 cm (½ in). While it is heating, flour the escalopes on both sides, shaking off the excess, then dip them into egg, shake off the excess, and finally, coat each one evenly in breadcrumbs, pressing them into place. Fry until golden brown on both sides, turning once. This should only take 4–5 minutes. Drain briefly on kitchen paper, season with salt and pepper and serve immediately with lemon wedges.

BRAISED VEAL SHANKS

Veal

Veal shanks, like lamb shanks, are an underrated cut of meat. They are superb slowly braised until the meat is so tender that it falls off the bone. In this recipe, they sit on a bed of vegetables, sharpened with a few capers and scented with citrus zests and herbs.

SERVES 4 – 6

4 veal shanks	2 strips dried orange zest
3 tablespoons olive oil	2 strips lemon zest
1 onion, chopped	3 sprigs of thyme
1 large carrot, finely diced	1 small sprig of rosemary
1 celery stick, sliced	3 sprigs of parsley
1 head of garlic, separated into cloves	300 ml (10 fl oz) dry white wine
and peeled, but not chopped	A squeeze of lemon juice
3 tablespoons capers	Salt and freshly ground black pepper

Brown the veal shanks in the olive oil, then set aside. Fry the onion, carrot and celery in the oil until browned. Transfer to a heat-proof casserole. Pour boiling water over the garlic, leave for 1 minute, then drain and add to the vegetables. Scatter over the capers. Tie the orange and lemon zest, thyme, rosemary and parsley together with a piece of string to make a bouquet garni and bed it down amongst the vegetables. Snuggle the veal shanks on top, pour over the white wine and season with salt and pepper.

Bring up to the boil, then reduce the heat to as low as possible and cover tightly (if the lid is slightly loose, lay a sheet of foil over the pan first, then clamp the lid on). Leave to cook gently for about 2 hours, turning the meat every now and then, until it is meltingly tender. Put the meat onto a serving dish, skim what fat you can from the juices and taste. Sharpen if necessary with a dash or two of lemon juice and adjust the seasoning. Spoon the vegetables around the veal and moisten with a little of the sauce. Strain and serve the rest separately.

Veal

GRILLED VEAL CHOPS WITH DEEP-FRIED SAGE LEAVES

Simple though this may sound, the combination of tender, grilled chops and crisply deep-fried sage leaves is superb. It is an idea I came across some years ago at the Pont de la Tour restaurant in London, and it made a deep and lasting impression on me.

The sage leaves take only a couple of seconds to deep-fry. If you've never deep-fried herbs before, it would be sensible to have a few extra leaves to hand so you can experiment with one or two first. There's nothing particularly tricky about it, but timing is crucial. The fried leaves should be translucent and crispish, but not burnt! They can be quite addictive, so once you get the knack, you may even want to cook a few more than I suggest in the recipe.

SERVES 4

20–24 sage leaves	2 tablespoons olive oil
Oil, for frying	1 tablespoon lemon juice
4 veal chops	Salt and freshly ground black pepper

Wash and dry the sage leaves thoroughly. Heat a small pan of oil until a cube of bread dropped in fizzes gently. Drop in about a third of the sage leaves and, as soon as they stop sizzling, scoop them out and drain them on kitchen paper. Cook the rest in two more batches.

Brush the veal chops with a little oil then season with pepper. Grill them under a moderately hot grill, turning occasionally, until crusty and just cooked through. When they are almost done, warm the olive oil with the lemon juice in a small pan, taking care not to overheat it. Place the veal chops on plates, season with salt and spoon over the oil. Place the deep-fried sage leaves on top and serve at once.

Veal

VITELLO AL ALBESE

One of the best dishes I've ever eaten was Vitello al Albese in a restaurant in the hills above Turin. The veal (eaten raw, which is every bit as safe as, say, eating a steak tartare; it is, after all, only the junior version of the same animal) was a rosy pink and cut so thin that you could read the emblem of the restaurant, stamped on the plate, through it. The meat was dressed very simply with sensational olive oil, salt, pepper, Parmesan and, the crowning glory (this was late autumn), shavings of white truffle.

If you happen to be feeling very flush and can lay your hands on a truffle, then I can think of few better ways to use it. Most of the time, however, most of us will have to do without, but even so, Vitello al Albese is an elegant, delicious and simple starter. Exact quantities are really up to you. I happen to like quite a lot of Parmesan, cut into paper-thin shavings with a potato peeler and a lively squeeze of lemon juice. The one essential thing is to cut the veal inordinately thinly. Make sure your knife is well sharpened.

SERVES 4

175 g (6 oz) veal fillet	Shavings of Parmesan
A drizzle of top-quality extra virgin olive oil	Salt and plenty of freshly ground black
Lemon juice	pepper

Put the fillet into the freezer for 20 minutes or so until it is fairly firm. Don't forget that it is there. You're not aiming to freeze the meat, but to stiffen it up so that it is easier to slice paper thin.

Now slice the fillet as thinly as you can. You should almost be able to see through the slices, but if you can't quite manage that, you can flatten them further by sandwiching between sheets of greaseproof paper and beating them lightly with a wooden rolling pin. Keep covered until ready to eat.

Just before serving, lay the slices of meat on 4 serving plates, barely overlapping. Season with salt and pepper, drizzle over the olive oil, then squeeze over a little lemon juice. Scatter with shavings of fresh Parmesan and serve up immediately.

Escalope de Veau aux Fines Herbes

A snappy way to cook veal escalopes, with a creamy, luxurious sauce laden with fresh herbs.

SERVES 2

2 veal or turkey escalopes	1 teaspoon finely chopped parsley
Seasoned flour, for dusting	1 teaspoon finely chopped chives
25 g (1 oz) butter	1 teaspoon finely chopped chervil
2 tablespoons vermouth	A squeeze of lemon juice, optional
5 tablespoons crème fraîche or double cream	Salt and freshly ground black pepper

Make a few snips round the edges of the escalopes to prevent them from curling up as they fry. Sandwich each one between two sheets of greaseproof paper and use a rolling pin to roll and beat them out lightly until they are about half their original thickness. Don't go overboard – you are not aiming for a web of meat but for tender, hole-free, escalopes of an even thickness. Dust with seasoned flour.

Melt the butter in a wide frying pan over a medium-high heat. As soon as it is foaming, add the escalopes and fry for about 3–4 minutes on each side, until they are lightly browned and just cooked through. Transfer to a warm serving dish, cover and keep warm.

Pour off the excess fat, return the pan to the heat and add the vermouth. Bring up to the boil, scraping in the brown residues stuck to the bottom of the pan, and boil until reduced to a scant tablespoonful. Stir in the crème fraîche or double cream and bring up to the boil. Draw off the heat, stir in the herbs, salt and pepper and, if you used double cream, a squeeze of lemon juice. Taste and adjust the seasoning, then pour over the escalopes. Serve immediately.

Veal

PORTUGUESE-STYLE VEAL CHOPS

Like Wiener Schnitzel, these chops are also breaded, but first they are rubbed with garlic and marinated in wine. The crumb coating is a little different too, enlivened with coriander (a herb that is characteristic of Portuguese cooking, though it is rare in most other traditional European cuisines) and lemon zest.

SERVES 4

4 veal chops	Olive oil or lard, for frying
2 garlic cloves	1 lemon cut into wedges, to serve
1 large glass dry white wine	Salt and freshly ground black pepper

—— *To coat* ——

25–50 g (1–2 oz) dry breadcrumbs	Finely grated zest of 1 lemon
2 tablespoons finely chopped coriander	1 egg, lightly beaten

A few hours or the day before cooking, beat the chops lightly with a rolling pin to flatten them slightly. Season with salt and pepper. Halve the cloves of garlic and rub the cut sides over the meat. Put the chops into a shallow dish, add the garlic and pour over the wine. Leave to marinate for as long as possible – at least a couple of hours and preferably overnight. Turn the chops occasionally so that they marinate evenly.

Shortly before serving, drain and dry the chops. Mix the breadcrumbs with the coriander, lemon zest, salt and pepper. Dip the chops into the beaten egg and shake off the excess, then coat them in the breadcrumb mixture, patting the crumbs evenly over the chops. Heat enough olive oil or lard to form a layer about 5 mm (¼ in) deep (or even a little more), over a moderate heat and brown the chops gently on both sides. Drain briefly on kitchen paper and serve with lemon wedges.

HORTOBAGYI PALACSINTA

(Hungarian Pancakes with Veal and Soured Cream)

Hortobagyi Palacsinta seem to be an essential dish on the majority of Hungarian restaurant menus, and when they are good, you can see why. Invariably served as a first course, the pancakes are filled with a creamy minced veal mixture and napped with soured cream. Both pancakes and filling can be made well in advance.

SERVES 6

──────── *For the pancakes* ────────

175 g (6 oz) flour	250 ml (8 fl oz) milk
A pinch of salt	250 ml (8 fl oz) sparkling mineral water
3 eggs	Clarified butter, for frying (see below)

──────── *For the filling* ────────

1 tablespoon lard	300 ml (10 fl oz) crème fraîche or soured
2 onions, grated or finely chopped	cream mixed with double cream
450 g (1 lb) veal, cut into 1 cm (½ in) cubes	15–25 g (½–1 oz) butter
1 tablespoon paprika	Salt and freshly ground black pepper

Sift the flour with the salt. Make a well in the centre and break in the eggs. Add about half of the milk. Stir, gradually drawing in the flour and adding the remaining milk slowly to form a smooth batter. Leave to rest for half an hour. Just before using, stir in enough of the mineral water to make a thin batter with the consistency of runny single cream.

Brush a heavy-based frying pan, about 20–23 cm (8–9 inch) in diameter, with clarified butter and heat thoroughly. Stir the batter, then add a small amount to the pan and cook as usual, brushing the pan with butter between pancakes. You should have enough batter to make 12 pancakes, allowing for one or two disasters.

For the filling, melt the lard in a frying pan and add the onions and veal. Fry for about 5 minutes, then sprinkle with the paprika, cover and stew gently for a further 30 minutes until the meat is tender. Drain off most of the juices and reserve. Mince the meat or chop it very finely and return it to the pan along with 2 tablespoons of the crème fraîche and some salt and pepper. Simmer for 5 minutes until thick and pulpy.

Pre-heat the oven to 180°C/350°F/Gas Mark 4.

Veal

Fill the pancakes with the veal mixture and roll up, tucking in the ends as you go. Arrange them neatly and snugly in a heat-proof serving dish. Dot with the butter, then cover and pop into the oven to heat through. Meanwhile, boil the reserved juices from cooking the veal until reduced by about half. Add the remaining cream and boil until reduced by about one third. Season, and pour over the pancakes. Serve immediately.

Note: To clarify butter, melt some butter in a pan and heat through, skimming off any scum that rises to the surface. Leave to stand, off the heat, for a few minutes until the white sediment has settled at the bottom. Carefully pour off the melted, clarified butter, leaving the sediment behind.

Chicken

& Poultry

Chicken
& Poultry

We eat more chicken in this country than any other meat, red or white. Chicken is cheap, plentiful, unlikely to offend the most cautious of palates, can be cooked in all sorts of ways and takes kindly to an infinite range of flavourings. No doubt it is because of all these attributes that we allow chicken to eclipse other forms of poultry in the popularity stakes.

But while the average chicken makes an undemanding and undemonstrative everyday meat, its brethren fowl can do much more in the way of tickling and treating the taste-buds. The first amongst these is also chicken, but fully free-range chicken with a distinct taste and a firm texture, closely followed by guinea fowl which make something of a halfway house between chicken and pheasant. Duck and goose are fattier birds, darker fleshed, richer and more obviously fit for special occasions. Poussin and turkey make the special-occasion grade too, not so much for their gustatory merit, as for their sizes: poussin cute and petite at one end of the scale, turkey hefty and ungainly but impressive at the other.

CHICKEN

First let me make it plain that I am not a fan of mass-produced chickens. When it comes down to the morality of raising birds in crowded confinement, everyone must make up his or her own mind. What is undoubtedly true is that it takes its toll in terms of taste. Pappy and damp as cotton wool, the flesh tastes of almost nothing at all. It may satisfy the desire for meat of some sort for precious little outlay, it may be improved upon by clever spicing and vigorous use of herbs, but I can't think of much more to be said in its favour.

A genuinely free-range bird is quite another matter. I use the word genuine quite deliberately, as the term free-range is often (and I'm afraid quite legally) applied to birds raised in a form of semi-intensive regime that most of us would not recognize as free-range. Some freedom is better than none and the more exercise a bird gets and the more it can peck around at liberty, the better it will taste. No chicken will ever have as pronounced a flavour as, say, duck, but at best it can be quite distinct and delicious. A fully free-range bird, fed a good grain-heavy diet, will be blessed with a relatively firm texture. In other words, there's something to get your teeth into, though it will by no means be tough. With a genuine free-range bird, straight roast chicken regains all its glory, becoming a centrepiece worthy of any occasion.

POUSSINS

Technically there is a slight difference between a poussin and a spring chicken, though in general the terms are used interchangeably. A poussin is 4–6 weeks old and weighs around 450–675 g (1–1½ lb), while a spring chicken can be a smidgen older and heftier. Certainly when it comes to cooking they are much of a muchness.

There's no getting round the fact that poussins taste of precious little at all or, if you want to be polite about it, that they are 'delicately flavoured'. Hardly surprising given their immaturity and size. However, they do score well on other counts. The main one, as you might well expect, is tenderness. They've barely had time to flex their muscles, so the meat is pale as ivory, soft and moist.

They're small so they don't take that much time to cook, but big enough to furnish a more than generous main course for one, or a light bite for two. They look quite glamorous enough to grace a smart dinner plate, and they do away with the need for carving, a plus for those of us who are less than proficient in this sphere.

Poussins are excellent roasted and easier than chicken to fry or grill evenly. Naturally you can casserole them, but it's a bit pointless as they usually emerge in a bedraggled state. You might just as well use chicken joints and save a few pence.

There are two ways to approach the cooking of poussins. If you think their flavour is 'delicate', then you'll want to tread lightly, not adding any other ingredients that could overwhelm, which cuts out rather a lot of options. Still, all those classic chicken with cream sauce recipes, flavoured mutedly with mushroom, tarragon or mustard are easily adapted to poussins. In the same restrained vein, you could do far worse than roast them with a few fresh sweet herbs slipped under the skin snug against the flesh, rubbed with lemon juice, seasoned well and buttered copiously.

On the other hand, if you consider poussins bland-tasting, then you've a great deal more latitude for play. With a jot of imagination, blandness becomes a virtue – here you have the poultry equivalent of a blank sheet of paper, waiting to be writ large upon, in whatever colours and script take your fancy.

GUINEA FOWL

These pretty speckled black and white birds are native to the Guinea coast of West Africa. They were domesticated centuries ago and have long been known in Europe. When I was a child, guinea fowl was a great rarity in Britain, a treat that came only with

Chicken
& Poultry

our annual trips to France, where it was more widely reared and greatly appreciated. The situation hasn't changed that much, except that guinea fowl is gradually making itself a small niche in this country, sold now by good poulterers and in a few select larger supermarkets.

When it comes to cooking, the first thing to note is that guinea fowl are smaller and more meagrely fleshed than chicken. One plump bird is just about enough to stretch around four at a pinch (accompanied by plenty of vegetables) as long as you are not serving rapacious meat-eaters. If you are, or if you are determined to have enough cold left-over meat for the next day's sandwiches, then you'd better double up and cook two of them.

Though they can be cooked in any way that you might cook chicken or pheasant (and indeed, vice versa; chicken or, later on in the year, pheasant could be substituted for guinea fowl in any of the recipes given in this chapter) the flesh has a tendency to be dry. If roasting, make sure that the breast is well protected from the heat – barded (see page 218) with thin sheets of pork fat or at least covered with rashers of streaky bacon – and frequently basted as it cooks. As a rule, though, I usually opt for pot-roasting, casseroling or poaching guinea fowl, by far the best ways to keep it moist.

DUCK

Most of what we buy in the shops is duckling, though it is often – usually, even – referred to as duck. A duckling becomes a duck at about two months old, at the point when it reaches its second feather stage. Despite their youth, they can grow to as much as 3 kg (7 lb) in weight (when plucked and drawn), though smaller ducklings are more common fare.

Many people by-pass duck for the simple reason that it seems to be a bird made up almost entirely of fat, with a mean layer of muscle hidden underneath. This is a shame and not at all accurate. True, duck is gifted with a chunky layer of fat, but the meat is all the more succulent and well-flavoured for that. It is a rich meat, but you'll find that a great deal of the fat melts out during cooking, leaving the skin irresistibly crisp and brown. There is something very luxurious about straight roast duck, particularly if it is accompanied by a fruity sauce (Duck à l'Orange, for instance, when properly made, is a sensational dish and so too is Duck with Marmalade, my quick version on page 196).

Chicken
& Poultry

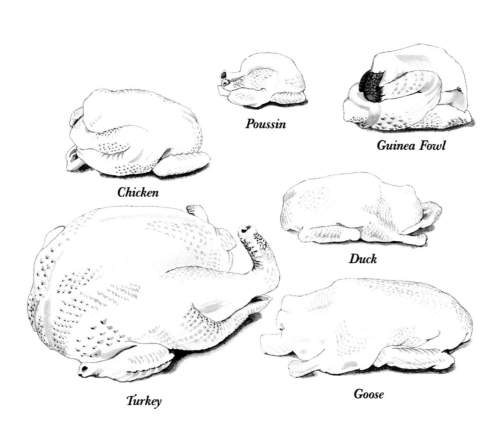

Poussin

Guinea Fowl

Chicken

Duck

Turkey

Goose

Duck can also be more economical than you might think. With a bit of forethought, a brace of duck will provide one quick but classy main course for four (the breasts alone), one more homely meal again for four (a stew of the legs and wings), plenty of stock for soup and if you can be bothered to render it down, beautiful pure white fat which will transform sautéd potatoes into something so good that you're bound to overindulge.

GOOSE

Goose has always been a bird for the autumn and winter months. The first goose of the year was eaten on Michaelmas Day on the 29 September, when the young birds had just reached plump maturity. By Christmas time, the geese were fat and large and took pride of place in the traditional Christmas lunch (far more interesting, if truth be told, than a bland turkey).

These days goose elicits much the same reaction as duck, but on a larger scale. It can't be denied that a big bird shrinks down in size in the oven as the fat melts off, but as long as it is not overcooked, goose is a wonderful treat for a celebratory autumn meal. Nature

Chicken
& Poultry

has worked out her schedule in the most amiable way, bringing in the new season's apples, pears and quinces, not to mention the first dried fruit from the summer months, just in time to go with the goose. Even if you don't want to make a fully blown stuffing (a lively home-made sage and onion stuffing is an old favourite), chop up fresh tree-fruit and dried fruit and half-fill the stomach cavity with them. During the long cooking time, they will soften and blend to form a perfect accompaniment.

If you happen to have some plums or frozen gooseberries around, then a simple, sharpish plum or gooseberry compote will stand well with goose, as will cranberry sauce or Cumberland sauce.

TURKEY

The all-American bird that has made itself thoroughly at home here. In its wild state it was what the early settlers dined upon and was dished up at the very first Thanksgiving meal in 1621. Though turkeys have been raised in Britain for centuries, it is only in the past 100 years or less that the turkey has become the Christmas bird – before that a fine fat goose took pride of place.

Like chicken, mass-produced turkey tends to be bland and also has a tendency towards dryness. As a festive offering its only real qualification is its enormous size. If you want more than that, then you will have to order in a traditionally raised fresh turkey that has been well-hung to bring out the full flavour.

In a bid to make year-round sales, turkey producers now sell many cuts of turkey that are small enough to fit day-to-day demand. Since turkey is hardly an electrifying meat, this seems a very sound idea. Rolled turkey breast joints can be roast, or better pot-roast with lots of invigorating herbs and vegetables and other flavourings, plus a good shot of wine or brandy to liven matters up. Turkey breast steaks take only a few shakes to cook, but best of all, I think, are the boned thighs. Darker fleshed, they have more substance to them and, with a good stuffing, make a lovely small, easy-to-carve roasting joint.

Techniques

HEALTH AND HYGIENE

A word about handling chicken and poussins in particular, though the same precautions should become second nature when preparing any pale-fleshed domestic fowl.

Chicken can carry a form of salmonella, a bacteria which causes most unpleasant food poisoning and can be dangerous for elderly people, children, invalids and pregnant women. Salmonella is destroyed by high heat and as long as chicken is thoroughly cooked, with no trace of rawness left, there is no cause for worry. Where you must take enormous care, however, is in the storage, handling and preparation of uncooked chicken. Make sure the chicken is stored in the fridge, in such a way that its juices cannot possibly drip onto other foods and contaminate them. Nor should it brush up against anything else. After handling and preparing raw chicken always, always wash your hands and every single bit of equipment (including that chopping board) immediately in hot soapy water. Rinse well and throw the water out.

JOINTING AND CUTTING

Armed with a strong, sharp knife, or a sturdy pair of poultry shears, cutting up poultry is a doddle. For the sake of a few minutes of your time, you can save yourself more than a few pence (whole birds tend to be cheaper than packaged joints). Though free-range chicken portions are sometimes available these days, they're not that common, so if you want to concoct a casserole with star quality, then it's as well to know how to joint your own bird.

These methods can all be used for chicken, duck or guinea fowl, not to mention game birds such as pheasant.

Dividing a bird into four pieces

First of all a neat butcher's trick: grab the tips of the thigh bones firmly in one hand, the wings in the other, and give the bird a sharp yank, to stretch it out. Besides being good for a laugh, it also loosens the joints of the bird.

Cut the skin between the thigh and the main body on one side. With the tip of your knife, feel out the choice little nugget of meat known as the oyster that lies just behind the thigh close up against the backbone and carefully loosen and cut it out so that it remains connected to the thigh. Now bend the thigh back to snap the thigh joint and simply slice through to release the thigh. If you wish, cut through the joint that attaches the

Chicken
& Poultry

1. Cut down between each thigh and the body. Loosen the oyster, leaving it connected to the thigh. Snap the thigh joint and cut it off.

2. Cut down one side of the breastbone to loosen the meat, then cut right through the breastbone.

3. Turn the bird over and cut the backbone and ribcage away from the breast portions.

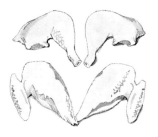

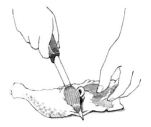

4. Make a few more cuts in order to divide the breasts in half.

5. You will now have 4 pieces: 2 leg portions and 2 breast portions with the wings attached.

6. Take each leg and cut through the joint between the drumstick and the thigh.

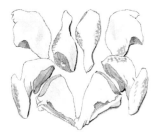

7. You will now have 6 pieces: 2 thighs, 2 drumsticks, and the breast portions as before.

8. Halve each breast portion along the rib bones, leaving some of the breast meat attached to the wing.

9. You will now have eight pieces.

scaly bony tip of the drumstick and save the tip for the stockpot. Repeat the whole process on the other side.

Cut down one side of the breastbone, to loosen the meat. Cut through the breastbone with a knife or shears. Turn the bird over and cut the backbone and ribcage away from the breast in one large piece. Make the last few cuts to divide the breast pieces (which will have the wings attached) into two and Bob's your uncle.

The wing tips, by the way, have very little meat on them, so you might just as well cut them off too while you are at it and throw them into the stockpot along with the backbone.

Dividing a bird into six pieces

Cut the bird into four as above. Take each thigh in turn and use your fingers to feel for the joint between the thigh proper and the drumstick. Slice through it firmly and you'll end up with six bits altogether.

Dividing a bird into eight pieces

Cut the bird into six, as above. This time it is the breast portions that get the chop. Cut each one in half on the diagonal cutting along the rib-bones to the breast, so that a portion of breast meat stays with the wing, but a slightly larger chunk is cut free. And that's it. Eight pieces, perfect for a stew or casserole.

Cutting boneless breast and leg portion

If you want to use the breasts of a chicken or duck for one dish and the legs for another, then this is the way to tackle it. Save the raw carcase to boil up a pot of the best stock.

First cut off the thighs as if you were cutting the bird into four. Bend back the wings

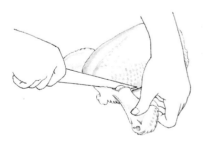

1. *After removing the thighs (see previous page), bend back the wings to snap open the joints, then cut them off.*

2. *Cut the meat from the breastbone along one side, then gently slice the breast from the ribs in one piece; repeat for the other side.*

to snap open their joint and cut them off. Using a sharp knife, cut the meat from the breastbone along one side. Keeping the blade flat against the carcase, gently slice the breast from the ribs in one piece. Repeat on the other side and you are done; two breasts, two thighs, and the carcase and wings for the stockpot.

BONING A CHICKEN OR DUCK

It was years before I plucked up the courage to bone a bird myself and then I discovered that, although it requires a modicum of patience at first, it is in fact a most straightforward and logical process and so very satisfying, too! A semi-boned bird is one where leg and wing bones are left *in situ*, but I like to see a task right through, and usually work on to a fully-boned bird. Either way, the boned-out flesh can then be stuffed with a fat sausage of stuffing, sewed back up and roasted or poached, to make a joint that is simplicity itself to carve.

Semi-boning

Begin by cutting off the wing-tips and the scaly tips of the drumsticks.. Turn the bird over and slit through the meat along the backbone from one end to the other. Cut out the wishbone.

Now it gets fun. Stroke the blade of the knife along the backbone to loosen the flesh. Work one side at a time. With the tip of the knife, feel out the oyster that nestles close to each thigh, and cut away from the bone. Now continue cutting patiently, close to the bone, pulling back the thighbone to expose and loosen the joint so that it can be severed, still keeping the thigh attached to the meat. Do the same with the wingbone. Keep going until you reach the breastbone, then repeat on the other side. Now the only place where flesh and carcase meet is along the edge of the breastbone. Ease the bone away from the flesh, taking great care not to tear the skin. Your chicken is now semi-boned

Full-boning

Take one semi-boned chicken. All there is left to do is bone the thighs and wings. Piece of cake. Lay the boned chicken flat, cut side up, on the table before you. Locate the first thigh bone, and with a small sharp knife, scrape the flesh from the bone in short strokes, pushing the meat back as you work to expose the bare bone and cutting through tough tendons (if you can, cut them out without piercing the flesh). When you reach the joint, snap it open and cut out the bone. Repeat with the bone of the drumstick, then turn the meat round and bone the other thigh. Use exactly the same procedure with the wing bones. Push the boned wings and thighs through to the cut side before stuffing, as if you were turning a cardigan inside out. *Finito.*

Semi-boning

 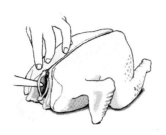 

Chicken
& Poultry

1. *After trimming the wings and drumsticks, turn the bird over and cut through the meat along the backbone.*

2. *Carefully cut the meat away from the wishbone and take out the bone.*

3. *Loosen the flesh from the back-bone along one side. Cut the oyster of flesh away from the bone. Pull back the thighbone to loosen the joint. Do the same with the wingbone.*

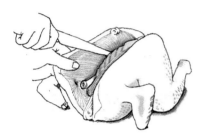 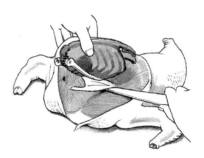

4. *Keep cutting the flesh carefully and patiently away from the carcase until you reach the breastbone, then repeat steps 3 and 4 on the other side of the bird.*

5. *Ease the breastbone gently away from the flesh, being careful not to tear the skin.*

Full-boning

1. *Semi-bone the bird as above. Lay it out flat and scrape the flesh away from the thigh bone in short strokes. Repeat with the second thigh and the wings.*

2. *Push the boned wings and thighs through to the cut side before stuffing the bird.*

Chicken
& Poultry

The various types of poultry all require their own individual methods of roasting, which are given in the recipes that follow. The only generality that I can think of applies to the white-fleshed birds – chicken, turkey, poussins, guinea fowl and even goose. All of them should be thoroughly cooked through (but not overcooked, please note), not only for safety's sake, but also because the semi-cooked flesh tastes horrid.

Duck breasts are best cooked rare or medium-rare like a steak, but awkwardly enough the thighs are better cooked through. You can either semi-roast the bird, cut off the breasts to eat first, then return the remainder of the bird to the oven for another 10 minutes or eat the whole lot well cooked.

As with any meat, roast poultry should be left to rest in a warm place for a good 10–15 minutes before carving, which gives you plenty of time to make gravy, or finish off the vegetables.

TESTING CHICKEN, POUSSIN, GUINEA FOWL OR TURKEY FOR DONENESS

The same tests apply to all these birds. First of all the legs and wings should wobble loosely. The more accurate test, though, is to plunge a skewer right down into the thickest part of the thigh, where it snuggles close to the breast. If the juices run pink, then the bird is not yet cooked through, and should be returned to the oven. When the juices run clear, it is ready to be rested and then served. The internal temperature should reach 85°C/185°F on a meat thermometer, rising to 90°C/190°F as the meat rests.

CHICKEN STOCK

Making chicken stock is a doddle and a quick, virtually foolproof one if you have a microwave. Chicken stock also happens to be the most universally useful of stocks, because although it has plenty of flavour, it is a potentially neutral flavour that enhances rather than overwhelms whatever it is added to. As a result it can form the basis of umpteen sauces and endless soups. You can use the bones left after you've roasted a chicken, but a raw carcase makes the best stock of all. It may well be worth asking your butcher to save a few carcases for you next time he's cutting up chickens and then to make a double batch. If you can get the giblets as well, so much the better, though the liver is best saved for something else.

I use exactly the same method for making stock from all sorts of birds – anything from duck, through to game birds such as pheasant, partridge or mallard.

Chicken
& Poultry

MAKES ABOUT 1.2 LITRES (2 PINTS)

1 chicken carcase and,	1 bay leaf
if available, giblets (not liver) and skin	3 sprigs of parsley
1 onion, quartered	2 sprigs of thyme
1 carrot, sliced	6 black peppercorns
2 celery sticks, sliced	

Put all the ingredients in a pan and cover generously with water. Bring up to the boil, then simmer gently for 2–3 hours, occasionally skimming off any scum that rises to the top. Add more boiling water if the liquid level drops too low. Strain and cool. If you have time, chill overnight in the fridge and lift off the congealed fat from the surface the next day. If not, then skim off as much fat as you can.

To microwave, put all the ingredients in the largest microwaveable bowl that you own. Cover with boiling water, then cover tightly with clingfilm. Microwave on full power for 25 minutes, then let it stand for half an hour before straining.

TO FREEZE STOCK

Measure the amount of stock you have and make a note of it. Pour into a wide frying pan and boil hard until reduced right down to a few spoonfuls. Cool slightly, then pour into ice-cube trays and freeze. Divide the amount of stock you started off with by the number of ice-cubes (i.e. if you started off with 1.5 litres (3 pints) and you have 6 cubes worth, then each cube is the equivalent of 250 ml (½ pint) of stock). Then you'll know how much diluted stock each ice-cube represents. Once frozen, drop the ice-cubes into a freezer bag and label.

When needed, take the required number of ice-cubes, place in a measuring jug and top up with enough hot water to make up to the original quantity.

POULET À L'ESTRAGON

(Chicken with Tarragon)

Tarragon-scented roast chicken with a creamy sauce makes a perfect Sunday lunch main-piece. To enjoy it at its best you will need a real free-range bird, with flesh that has some flavour and resistance to it. The tarragon, stuffed into its body cavity and in the sauce, has such a strong affinity with chicken that it is surprising we don't use them together more. However, that doesn't mean you should go overboard with the herb. It's fairly powerful and a little goes a fair old way. The amount I've added to the sauce seems about right to me, though since all herbs vary in intensity, you may want to add a little more. Keep tasting (no problem in this case, as long as you don't guzzle more than your fair share) to get it right.

SERVES 4

1.75 kg (4 lb) free-range chicken	300 ml (10 fl oz) crème fraîche
½ lemon	or double cream
4 branches of tarragon	Lemon juice
50 g (2 oz) unsalted butter	Salt and freshly
50 ml (2 fl oz) vermouth, or	ground black pepper
a small glass dry white wine	

Pre-heat the oven to 200°C/400°F/Gas Mark 6. Rub the skin of the chicken all over with the lemon half. Stuff the spent lemon half into the stomach cavity of the chicken along with 3 of the branches of tarragon. Chop the leaves of the remaining tarragon, discarding the stalk. Sit the bird in a roasting tin, smear the butter thickly over its skin and season generously with salt and pepper. Roast for 1–1¼ hours until cooked through. Transfer the bird to a serving dish and let it rest in the oven with the heat turned off and the door ajar, while you make the sauce.

Skim off as much fat as you can from the roasting tin, leaving behind the roasting juices. Put the tin on the hob and pour in the vermouth or wine. Bring up to the boil, scraping in any residues from roasting, and boil until reduced to a few spoonfuls. Now add the cream and stir, and let it return to the boil. Continue to cook hard until reduced to a good consistency. Draw off the heat and add 2–3 teaspoons of the chopped tarragon. Season with salt and pepper and a dash of lemon juice. Taste and adjust the seasoning, then serve the sauce with the chicken.

ROAST CHICKEN WITH PORCINI

This is a nifty way of lifting ordinary roast chicken right out of the ordinary…and keeping it moist while it cooks. Butter, flavoured with dried porcini mushrooms, parsley and lemon, is smeared between the flesh and the skin before the chicken goes into the oven. And that's all there is to it.

Even if you don't have the porcini mushrooms, plain unadulterated butter smeared under the skin will effectively create a more or less self-basting extra-juicy chicken.

SERVES 4

1.5–2 kg (3½–4 lb) free-range chicken

15 g (½ oz) dried porcini mushrooms, soaked

2 tablespoons chopped parsley

1 garlic clove, roughly chopped

Finely grated zest of 1 lemon

Juice of ½ a lemon

50 g (2 oz) butter, softened

1 small onion, quartered

Salt and freshly ground black pepper

Pre-heat the oven to 220°C/425°F/Gas Mark 7. Place the porcini in a small bowl and cover with hot water. Leave for at least 20 minutes to soak and soften. Pick the pieces out carefully and pat dry on kitchen paper or a clean tea towel. Strain the soaking water and save to use as mushroom stock in a soup or sauce. It freezes well.

Chop the porcini, parsley, garlic and lemon zest together very finely. Mash with the lemon juice, butter, salt and pepper.

Gently wiggle your fingers under the skin of the chicken, easing it away from the flesh on the breast and upper thighs without pulling it right off. Now – and I find this easiest with fingers, but you may prefer to use a spoon as well or instead – push the flavoured butter between the skin and flesh, smearing it around as evenly as possible. Put the onion quarters inside the cavity of the chicken.

Weigh the chicken and calculate the roasting time. Allow 17 minutes per 500 g (15 minutes per lb), adding 10 minutes extra on top. Roast in the oven, basting frequently with the juices. If it threatens to burn, cover with foil.

African Chicken in Peanut Sauce

Chicken
& Poultry

Ground peanuts (plain, not salted or dry-roasted, please) are what thicken the sauce of this African chicken stew. It's the kind of dish that will please both children (as long as you keep the cayenne pepper to a minimum) and adults. The original recipe I was given called for the chicken to be cut into four, though I prefer smaller pieces – say eight altogether. I leave the choice to you.

SERVES 4

100 g (4 oz) raw, shelled peanuts (unsalted)	1 tablespoon tomato purée
1.5–1.75 kg (3–4 lb) chicken, jointed (see page 163)	½–1 teaspoon cayenne pepper
	1 tablespoon paprika
2 tablespoons oil	½ teaspoon each ground ginger,
1 onion, finely chopped	cinnamon and coriander
100 g (4 oz) tomatoes, skinned and roughly chopped	Salt
	450 ml (15 fl oz) chicken stock

Spread the peanuts out on a baking tray and toast in a hot oven (around 200°C/400°F/Gas Mark 6) for 5–8 minutes until lightly browned, shaking and checking frequently. Cool, then grind to a powdery paste.

Brown the chicken in the oil and transfer to a flame-proof casserole. Cook the onion gently in the same oil until golden. Add the tomatoes, tomato purée, spices and salt. Stir for about 3 minutes, then add the stock. Bring up to the boil, stirring, then pour over the chicken. Cover, reduce the heat and simmer for 30 minutes.

Stir in the ground peanuts, breaking up the larger lumps (the small ones will dissolve as the sauce simmers). Continue to simmer, covered, for a further 10–15 minutes, until the chicken is tender and the sauce has thickened. Skim the fat from the surface, then taste and adjust the seasonings before serving.

COQ AU VIN

❦

A dinner-party favourite of the seventies, now sadly and foolishly neglected, though I suspect it is on the brink of returning to fashionable plates. It is certainly a dish worth mastering.

SERVES 4 – 5

225 g (8 oz) small pickling or pearl onions

40 g (1½ oz) butter

1 tablespoon sunflower oil

100 g (4 oz) lardons or slab bacon (see page 102)

1 x 1.75 kg (4 lb) chicken, cut into 8 pieces (see page 165)

Seasoned flour

3 tablespoons brandy

450 ml (15 fl oz) red wine

600 ml (1 pint) chicken stock

1 bouquet garni (see page 33)

2 garlic cloves, finely chopped

½ tablespoon tomato purée

225 g (8 oz) button mushrooms, halved or quartered if large

Salt and freshly ground black pepper

—— For the beurre manié ——

25 g (1 oz) butter 25 g (1 oz) flour

To skin the onions, top and tail them, then cover with boiling water. Leave for a couple of minutes, then drain. The skins should now slip off easily. Heat 15 g (½ oz) of the butter with the oil and fry the lardons or bacon until lightly browned. Scoop out and transfer to a flame-proof casserole. Brown the pickling onions in the same fat, turning them so that they fry to a rich and more or less even brown colour all over. Put into the casserole. Add a little more butter to the pan. Dust the chicken with flour and brown briskly all over. Pour over the brandy, swirl the pan around, then set light to it with a match if you have an electric hob, or by tilting the pan toward the flame if you cook on gas. Once the flames have died down, put the chicken and juices into the casserole.

Return the frying pan to the heat and pour in the wine. Bring up to the boil, scraping in the residues from frying, then let it boil down until reduced by half. Pour over the chicken. Bring the stock to the boil in the frying pan, then pour that over the chicken too. Season with salt and pepper, add the bouquet garni, garlic and tomato purée. Simmer gently, covered, for about 40 minutes until the chicken is tender.

Meanwhile, fry the mushrooms in the remaining butter. Mash the butter and flour for the beurre manié together evenly.

Once the chicken is cooked, lift out with as many of the onions and lardons as you can locate. Boil the sauce down, uncovered, until reduced by half. Throw away the bouquet garni. Stir in about half the beurre manié, in small knobs and let it cook, without letting it boil hard, for a few minutes to thicken slightly. If necessary add a little more, though the sauce is not meant to be heavily thickened, just given a little more substance. Taste and adjust the seasoning. Return the chicken, onions and lardons to the pan along with the mushrooms and let them heat through for a few minutes.

Serve with boiled buttered potatoes, sprinkled with parsley and green peas.

CHICKEN MARENGO

The battle of Marengo took place in June 1800. Napoleon, ravenous after a hard day's slaughter and tactics, asked his chef, Dunand, for a good, satisfying supper. All that Dunand could lay his hands on was a chicken, a bottle of white wine, tomatoes, garlic and mushrooms (not bad going, if you ask me), and with these ingredients he created Poulet à la Marengo.

SERVES 4

1.5–2 kg (3½–4 lb) chicken, cut into 8 pieces (see page 165)	1 x 400 g (14 oz) tin chopped tomatoes
50 g (2 oz) butter	2 garlic cloves, chopped
2 tablespoons sunflower oil	1 bouquet garni (see page 33)
1 onion, chopped	175 g (6 oz) button mushrooms, halved or quartered if large
1 tablespoon flour	Salt and freshly ground black pepper
1 generous glass white wine	

Brown the chicken briskly in half the butter and oil then set aside. Add the onion to the pan and fry gently until tender. Sprinkle over the flour, stir for a few seconds then add the wine. Bring up to the boil, stirring and scraping in all the residues stuck to the bottom of the pan. Now add the tomatoes, garlic, bouquet garni, salt and pepper and return the chicken to the pan. Add enough hot water just to cover the chicken then bring up to the boil and simmer for 40–60 minutes, half-covered, until the chicken is cooked through and the sauce is reduced to a rich consistency. If it seems watery, remove the lid towards the end of the cooking time and let the sauce boil down.

Meanwhile, sauté the mushrooms in the remaining butter and oil then drain briefly on kitchen paper. When the chicken is done, stir in the mushrooms, simmer for a minute or two longer, then taste and adjust the seasoning.

SOY SAUCE CHICKEN

❦

In this Chinese recipe the chicken is cooked whole in an intense, spiced sauce made largely with soy sauce. The chicken, sitting in its pond of inky liquid, is half poached, half steamed. It needs to be turned and basted frequently to ensure that it is evenly cooked and that every part has time and occasion to soak up the flavours. Though it is good hot, it really tastes far better cold. Either way the sauce is powerfully salty and should be treated as a dipping sauce, not ladled over like a Western gravy.

SERVES 4-6

1.5–1.75 kg (3–4 lb) chicken	1 teaspoon salt
4 slices unpeeled fresh root ginger	1 teaspoon coarsely crushed
6 spring onions, trimmed	black peppercorns

—— *For the sauce* ——

3 whole star anise	150 ml (5 fl oz) Shaoxing wine
2 cinnamon sticks	or dry sherry
2 strips dried orange peel	5 tablespoons light muscovado sugar
300 ml (10 fl oz) dark soy sauce	600 ml (1 pint) water

Stuff the cavity of the chicken with the ginger, spring onions, salt and pepper. Put all the ingredients for the sauce into a large pan or flame-proof casserole, just big enough to take the chicken. Bring up to the boil slowly, stirring until the sugar has dissolved.

Now put the chicken into the pan, breast side down and baste a few times with the sauce. Reduce the heat to low, cover tightly and leave to simmer for 20 minutes, basting frequently. Turn the chicken onto its side, baste, then cover and cook for a further 10 minutes, basting once or twice. Now turn onto the other side and repeat. Finally, sit the chicken breast side up, cover and cook for a final 20 minutes, again basting frequently. Test for doneness by pushing a skewer into the thickest part of the chicken. If the juices run clear then it is done. If they are pinkish, cook for a further 10 minutes or so and then test again.

To serve hot, carefully lift the chicken out of the pan, tilting it so that the juices trapped inside can pour out and back into the sauce. Carve the chicken and place bowls of sauce strategically around the table.

To serve cold, leave the chicken in the pan, in its sauce, still covered, for at least an hour or until cold, basting every now and then. Lift out, draining off the sauce from the cavity, then cut into suitable pieces. Skim any fat from the sauce, then spoon a little over the chicken to keep it moist.

Spatchcocked Poussins with Orange and Lemon

In this recipe, two methods are employed to enhance the taste of young poussins and to keep them tender and juicy. First they are marinated, then given a protective smear of butter flavoured with ground coriander, orange and lemon.

With all that to keep them from drying out, they can be quickly roasted in a hot oven, to emerge glistening and brown.

SERVES 2 GENEROUSLY

25 g (1 oz) butter, softened

Finely grated zest and juice of 1 orange

Finely grated zest and juice of 1 lemon

½ teaspoon ground coriander

1 tablespoon finely chopped parsley

2 poussins, spatchcocked (see page 220)

1 tablespoon honey

Salt and freshly ground black pepper

Process or beat the butter with the zest of the orange and lemon, 1 tablespoon of lemon juice, the coriander, parsley and some pepper. Place the poussins in a shallow dish. Warm the orange juice with the remaining lemon juice and the honey very gently, without letting it get anywhere near boiling, stirring until the honey has dissolved. Add salt and pepper, cool, then pour over the poussins. Leave to marinate, basting and turning occasionally, for at least 1 hour and up to 8 hours.

Pre-heat the oven to 200°C/400°F/Gas Mark 6.

If you've kept the flavoured butter in the fridge, bring it out and let it warm up to room temperature. Now the messy bit. Using your fingers, loosen the skin of the poussins without detaching it completely. Smear the butter between the flesh and the skin, making sure that the breast is evenly coated. Pat the skin back into shape.

Set the poussins flat in a roasting tin and pour over the remaining marinade. Bake for 20–25 minutes until browned and cooked through. Baste occasionally with the pan juices as they cook.

BURMESE DRY CHICKEN CURRY

(Kyetha See Byan)

This 'dry' curry, i.e. one that's not swilling in sauce, is a fragrant affair, scented right at the end of the cooking time with freshly ground cardamom and green coriander leaves. I can't claim to be at all knowledgeable about Burmese cooking, but the two Burmese meals I have eaten, in a small restaurant in Greenwich (then the Mandalay, though now that it has moved to Herne Hill, the name has changed to the Maymyo), were altogether different in flavour and style from the food of neighbouring countries such as Thailand or India, though many of the same ingredients are used.

SERVES 4–6

2 onions, roughly chopped	4 tablespoons vegetable oil
5 garlic cloves, roughly chopped	1.5–1.75 kg (3–4 lb) chicken, cut into
1 cm (½ in) piece root ginger, chopped	8 pieces (see page 165)
2 sticks lemon grass, roughly chopped	4 green cardamom pods
1–2 red chillies, seeded and roughly chopped	2 tablespoons roughly chopped
1 tablespoon fish sauce (*nam pla*)	coriander leaves
1 teaspoon turmeric	Salt and freshly ground black pepper

Process the first 7 ingredients together to form a smooth paste. Heat the oil in a wide frying pan and add the paste. Stir until all the moisture has evaporated and the paste begins to brown.

Now add the chicken pieces, stirring well to ensure that they are all coated evenly. As you stir, scrape the base of the pan to prevent burning. Cover tightly and simmer for 35–45 minutes – the juices from the chicken will provide enough liquid for this type of curry. When the chicken is nearly cooked, stir occasionally.

While it cooks, slit open the cardamom pods, extract the black seeds and crush. Once the chicken is just about cooked through, stir in the cardamom and the coriander leaves. Cover again for a minute or so, then taste and adjust the seasoning. Serve with rice.

GALANTINE OF CHICKEN WITH APRICOTS AND PISTACHIOS

A galantine of chicken is nothing more than a stuffed boned chicken, though technically it is one that is often served cold, and may be cosseted in a coating of clear aspic. My version comes without the aspic and, though you can eat it hot, it is much nicer cold (when it will slice more neatly), served in decent-sized slices, with maybe a fruit chutney or Cumberland or cranberry sauce.

You will need a sturdy long needle and some white cotton thread to sew the stuffed bird up. A square of muslin, or a J-cloth that's been boiled for 5 minutes, wrapped around the galantine as it cooks, ensures that it doesn't burst open and collapse in the water.

SERVES 6-8

1 fully boned chicken (see page 166)   25 g (1 oz) butter

——— *For the stock* ———

Bones from the chicken   1 onion, quartered

1 carrot, quartered   1 bouquet garni (see page 33)

1 celery stick, quartered

——— *For the stuffing* ———

50 g (2 oz) shelled pistachios   2 shallots, very finely chopped

100 g (4 oz) chicken livers, chopped   ½ teaspoon thyme leaves

225 g (8 oz) minced veal   2½ tablespoons brandy

50 g (2 oz) pork back fat, minced   75 g (3 oz) dried apricots, chopped

1 garlic clove, crushed   1 egg, beaten

2 tablespoons chopped parsley   Salt and freshly ground black pepper

Put all the ingredients for the stock into a pan with 1.2 litres (2 pints) of water. Bring up to the boil, then simmer, skimming off any scum, for at least as long as it takes you to prepare all the ingredients for the stuffing or a couple of hours if you have the time. Strain the stock and cool slightly before using.

Mix all the stuffing ingredients with your hands, adding just enough egg to bind. Lay the chicken out flat, skin side down. Make a fat sausage of the stuffing down the middle, then bring the sides and ends up around the stuffing and sew up with strong thread. Don't pull the chicken round too tightly, as the stuffing will swell slightly as it cooks.

Melt the butter in a frying pan and brown the chicken thoroughly all over. Wrap it up in a large square of muslin and tie the ends securely with string. Put it into a flame-proof casserole or a large pan and pour the stock over it, adding extra cold water to cover as needed. Bring gently to the boil, then reduce the heat right down low, cover and cook slowly for 2 hours, turning once. If you prefer, you can cook it in the oven – once it has come to the boil, transfer to the oven, pre-heated to 140°C/275°F/Gas Mark 1, for the same amount of time. Leave to cool in its stock. To serve, unwrap and slice.

ROAST CHICKEN WITH BANANAS AND ORANGE

Recipes like this one, which require minimal work and emerge from the oven tasting as if you'd slaved for ages over them, are heaven-sent. This recipe came about more by accident than deliberation (you know the scene – what on earth have we got left in the house for supper tonight?) then has been polished by frequent repeats. The alcohol in the rum burns off in the oven, so you can safely offer this to children, who love it, as well as adults.

There's just one slightly technical bit of preparation to do, and that is separating out the orange segments, minus skin. To do this you will need a small but sharp knife. Cut the peel off the orange, taking it right down to the flesh and leaving no bitter white pith behind. Stand the orange upright, then carefully slice down between each orange segment and the white skin that separates it from its next-door neighbour. This way you will be able to ease out the segments neatly skinned and ready to use. Save the juice that is squeezed out of the orange as you do this and add to the roasting tin when you add the fruit.

The chicken is best served with plain rice to soak up the juices, rather than potatoes or noodles.

SERVES 4

1.5–1.75 kg (3–4 lb) chicken, cut into 4	2 oranges
(see pages 163–5) or 4 chicken joints	3 tablespoons rum
25 g (1 oz) butter	Salt and freshly ground black pepper
4 bananas	

Pre-heat the oven to 190°C/375°F/Gas Mark 5. Place the chicken joints in a roasting tin, season with salt and pepper and dot with the butter. Spoon 4 tablespoonfuls of water around them. Roast in the oven for 20 minutes. Meanwhile, peel the bananas and oranges and divide the oranges into skinned segments (see above). Save any orange juice that is squeezed out as you work.

After the first 20 minutes in the oven, add the whole peeled bananas along with the orange segments and their juice. Spoon over the rum. Return to the oven for 15–20 minutes, basting occasionally, until the chicken is cooked through. Serve immediately.

SAUTÉED CHICKEN WITH HERBS

I love this way of cooking chicken. It turns out with such a fresh, lively taste, full of summer and vitality. Take whatever herbs you can get — try to use at least three but be cautious with some of the more pungent ones like tarragon, sage or rosemary. If I had to settle for just a small selection, I'd probably go for plenty of parsley, a fair amount of basil and chives, with some thyme or marjoram to add their warmth, but I usually go for the herbs that are looking perkiest in the garden.

Though this chicken is best served hot from the pan, it makes a more than acceptable picnic piece when cold.

SERVES 4

1 chicken, cut into 8 pieces (see page 165)

2–3 tablespoons olive oil

3 garlic cloves, sliced

2 shallots, finely chopped

3 tablespoons chopped herbs

(e.g. parsley, basil, chives, thyme, oregano, tarragon, marjoram)

Juice of ½ lemon

Salt and freshly ground black pepper

Dry the chicken pieces thoroughly. Heat the oil in a heavy frying pan over a high heat. Brown the chicken pieces in the oil in two batches unless your pan is big enough to accommodate all the bits with ease. When browned, reduce the heat to medium high and return the first batch of chicken to the pan, snuggling the pieces close together in a single layer. Cover the pan and leave to cook for about 10 minutes.

Uncover and turn over the chicken pieces, spooning their juices over them. Sprinkle over the garlic, shallots, half the herbs, salt and pepper. Cover again and cook for a further 8 minutes.

Uncover and turn the pieces again in their juices. Test to see how they are doing. If they need more time, cover again and cook for a final 5 minutes or so.

Lift the chicken pieces out with the cooked shallots, garlic and pan juices. Squeeze over some lemon juice, sprinkle with the remaining herbs and serve.

SOUTHERN-FRIED POUSSIN WITH MILK GRAVY

From the deep South of the US of A…though it's chicken not poussins that get this treatment over there. It adapts particularly well, however, to give deliciously crisp halves of poussin, with a mild sauce. You can adapt the recipe to give a more Mediterranean flavour by replacing half or all the fat with olive oil and slipping some garlic into the pan towards the end of the cooking time. In that case, skip the milk gravy and replace with a tomato salsa or sauce.

SERVES 2 GENEROUSLY

Flour, for dusting	2 poussins, cut in half
Cayenne pepper	Lard or sunflower or vegetable oil for frying

——— *For the gravy* ———

1 tablespoon flour	Salt and freshly ground black pepper
300 ml (10 fl oz) full cream milk	

Season some flour generously with salt, pepper and cayenne pepper, and toss the poussin halves in it until evenly coated. Shake off excess.

Heat enough lard or oil in a heavy-bottomed pan to give a depth of about 2 cm (¾ in) until good and hot. Add the poussin pieces, skin side down (if they won't all fit in comfortably, cook in two batches). As soon as they are browned, reduce the heat, turn them over and cook until the other side is browned. Turn again and continue cooking until cooked through (about 20 minutes in all). Drain the poussins on absorbent paper, then keep warm in the oven while you make the gravy.

Pour off all except about 2 tablespoons of fat. Sprinkle over the flour and mix well, scraping up the nice brown bits on the bottom of the pan. Now gradually stir in the milk, bringing the sauce to the boil and stirring for a few minutes until the gravy has thickened and the taste of raw flour has disappeared. Season with salt and pepper and serve.

GRILLED SPICED CHICKEN WITH MANGO SALSA

❦

SERVES 4

1 chicken, spatchcocked (see page 220)

——— *For the marinade* ———

½ teaspoon cumin seeds

½ teaspoon coriander seeds

¼ teaspoon black peppercorns

Juice of 1 lime or ½ large lemon

3 tablespoons olive oil

——— *For the salsa* ———

2 ripe mangoes, peeled, stoned and finely diced

½ red onion, finely diced

½ red or green chilli, seeded and finely chopped

2 tablespoons chopped coriander

Juice of ½–1 lime

Salt

First make the marinade: mix together the cumin, coriander and peppercorns. Dry-fry over a high heat until they give off a rich aromatic scent. Cool, then crush coarsely. Mix with the lime juice and olive oil. Make a couple of slashes across the thickest parts of the chicken, then lay flat, skin side up, in a shallow dish or tin. Pour over the marinade and smear it over the chicken so that it is fairly evenly distributed. Cover loosely and leave for at least 2 hours and up to 24 hours, turning occasionally.

To make the salsa, mix together all the ingredients. Cover and set aside for at least half an hour and up to 4 hours. Taste and adjust the seasoning, adding a little more lime juice, if necessary. If it is stored in the fridge, remove 20 minutes or so before cooking so that it can come back to room temperature.

Heat up the grill (or better still, barbecue) and grill the chicken, skin side to the heat, keeping it a good 10–12 cm (4–5 in) from the heat so that it doesn't cook too quickly. Turn every now and then and brush with any marinade left in the dish. Take it slowly and don't be tempted to rush. The skill of grilling a chicken is to get it cooked through to the bone without burning the outside and that demands a degree of patience. All in all, it will probably take a good 25–30 minutes to cook. To check whether it's done, plunge a skewer into the thickest part of the thigh, where it nestles up against the breast. If the juices run pink, return it to the heat.

Once it is cooked, cut the chicken up as best you can and serve it immediately with the salsa.

THAI BARBECUED CHICKEN

In Thailand this is cooked out on the streets over open braziers. When you hand over your money, you are given in return a portion of chicken along with a small plastic bag full of sauce. Unless there's an adjacent table or ledge to sit on, it can be a messy business dipping and eating as you walk along the street, but it is worth the sticky fingers and chin.

The only special ingredient you really need is fish sauce or nam pla, *which is available from most oriental food stores and now even from some larger supermarkets. If you really can't find any, use light soy sauce in its place. Fresh red chillies are not always available either, but if needs be, replace them with dried red chillies, crumbled or chopped very finely. The spice paste can also be used for fish and prawns.*

SERVES 4

1 plump chicken, cut into 8 pieces (see page 165)	Coriander leaves for garnishing

—— For the spice paste ——

1 tablespoon black peppercorns	Juice of ½ lemon
1 tablepoon chopped garlic	1 tablespoon fish sauce (*nam pla*)
1 tablespoon chopped coriander root or stem	1 tablespoon oil
½ tablespoon sugar	

—— For the sweet chilli sauce ——

75 g (3 oz) sugar	2 red chillies, seeded and very finely chopped
85 ml (3 fl oz) rice vinegar or cider vinegar	A pinch of salt

To make the spice paste, crush the peppercorns, pound to a paste with the garlic and coriander, then work in the remaining ingredients. Alternatively, process or liquidize with a hand-held blender.

Make a few deep slashes across the fattest portions of the chicken, then rub the spice paste all over the chicken pieces. Leave for at least 1 hour and preferably overnight.

To make the sauce, stir the sugar and vinegar over a moderate heat until the sugar has completely dissolved. Bring up to the boil and simmer for 5 minutes. Draw off the heat, stir in the chillies and salt and cool.

To cook the chicken, grill over a moderately hot barbecue until well-browned and cooked through to the bone, turning occasionally. Be patient and don't rush this, since you want to end up with chicken that is cooked all the way through, not burnt on the outside and raw on the inside. Serve, sprinkled with coriander leaves, with bowls of the chilli sauce for dipping.

DEVILLED DRUMSTICKS

In summertime, devilling sauces are perfect for smearing over chicken that is about to be grilled over the barbecue (or under the kitchen grill if barbecues are out of the question). The anointed drumsticks can also be cooked in the oven – very handy if you are preparing them for a large party of people, though of course you won't get the extra smoky flavour that comes with the barbecue or grill.

SERVES 4

| 8 chicken drumsticks | A little sunflower oil for baking |

—— For the devil sauce ——

1 tablespoon clear honey	2 tablespoons sunflower oil
1 tablespoon Worcestershire sauce	A generous pinch of cayenne pepper
1 tablespoon Dijon mustard	½ teaspoon salt

Pre-heat the oven to 200°C/400°F/Gas Mark 6 if baking. Mix together the sauce ingredients then brush or smear all over the drumsticks.

To bake: Arrange the drumsticks on a lightly oiled shallow baking tray then place in the oven for 30 minutes, turning occasionally, until well browned and cooked right through to the bone. Serve hot or cold.

To grill: Pre-heat the grill thoroughly. Line the grill pan with silver foil, then arrange the drumsticks on the rack and grill, about 10 cm (4 in) from the heat, turning frequently until dark brown and cooked through to the bone. Brush the drumsticks with any left-over sauce as they cook.

To barbecue: Keep the drumsticks about 10–12 cm (4–5 in) away from the glowing charcoal so that they cook through before they burn to a frazzle. Brush with any left-over sauce as they cook.

SAVOY-WRAPPED CHICKEN BREASTS

Steaming keeps chicken moist and tender, but leaves it looking rather pallid. A jacket of green Savoy cabbage covers its nakedness and tastes good too. Interior colour comes in the form of sun-dried tomatoes and chives.

SERVES 4

4 chicken breasts, boned and skinned	2 tablespoons chopped chives
6 sun-dried tomatoes in oil, chopped	8 large Savoy cabbage leaves
100 g (4 oz) goat's cheese	Salt and freshly ground black pepper

Season the chicken breasts lightly. Mash the sun-dried tomatoes with the goat's cheese, chives, plenty of freshly ground pepper and a little salt, if needed. Smear the stuffing between the fillet and the main breast.

Blanch the cabbage leaves in boiling water for about 1 minute until pliable. Drain and run under cold water. Drain again and pat dry. Snip out the thick part of the stem then wrap them around the chicken breasts, enclosing them completely (you may not need all of the leaves).

Steam for 15–20 minutes, until just cooked through.

THAI STIR-FRIED CHICKEN
WITH BASIL

(Gai Paad Ga-Prow)

Chicken
& Poultry

I first tasted this in a market in Northern Thailand where holy basil is cheap enough to use with unfettered abandon. It is cooked in two shakes and makes a marvellously quick lunch with a bowl of rice. If you can't get holy basil, then ordinary sweet basil does just fine as a stand-in.

SERVES 4

50 g (2 oz) basil leaves	3 red chillies, seeded and thinly shredded
4 tablespoons vegetable oil	1 cm (½ in) piece fresh root ginger, finely
450 g (1 lb) boned, skinned chicken, coarsely	chopped
minced or finely chopped	2 tablespoons fish sauce (*nam pla*)
4 shallots, thinly sliced	2 teaspoons dark muscovado sugar
4 garlic cloves, chopped	Salt, if needed

Set aside 5 or 6 basil leaves for a final garnish and tear up the rest roughly. Heat a wok over a high heat for a couple of minutes, then add 2 tablespoons of oil. Wait a few seconds for the oil to get really hot, then add the chicken and stir-fry until just cooked through – this will take no more than a minute or two. Scrape the chicken out into a bowl.

Add the remaining oil to the wok and heat thoroughly. Add the shallots and stir-fry for about 30 seconds. Now add the garlic, chillies and ginger and stir-fry for another minute. Add the torn-up basil leaves and stir-fry for a further 1 minute. Finally, return the chicken and its juices to the pan along with the fish sauce and sugar. Stir-fry briefly to heat the chicken right up again until piping hot. Scoop into a serving dish, top with the reserved basil and serve with rice.

189

V. Good

Chicken
& Poultry

SRI OWEN'S CHICKEN BIRYANI

❦

Indonesian cook Sri Owen admits that her method for making biryani is not authentically Indian, but the result is superb, nonetheless, so I'm afraid I don't care. The recipe comes from her ency-clopaedic Rice Book *(Doubleday).*

The resulting biryani, all gold and white, is fairly mild, though if you wish, you can increase the amount of cayenne a little.

SERVES 4

225–275 g (8–10 oz) Basmati
or long-grain rice, rinsed

2 tablespoons olive oil

2 shallots, chopped

2 garlic cloves chopped

1 teaspoon finely chopped fresh root ginger

4 boneless, skinned chicken breasts,
sliced very thinly

½ teaspoon cayenne pepper

½ teaspoon ground cumin

1 teaspoon ground coriander

A pinch of ground nutmeg

¼ teaspoon ground cinnamon

¼ teaspoon turmeric

175 ml (6 fl oz) natural yoghurt

1 teaspoon sugar

3 tablespoons raisins or sultanas

Salt and freshly ground black pepper

—— *To garnish* ——

1 tablespoon fried shallots

2 tablespoons toasted flaked almonds

Boil the rice in 1.75 litres (3 pints) of water with ½ teaspoon salt for 8 minutes, stirring once and making sure the water stays at a rolling boil. Drain and reserve.

In a large saucepan or casserole with a tight-fitting lid, heat the oil and fry the shallots, garlic and ginger root for 2 minutes, stirring constantly. Add the chicken, raise the heat and stir-fry for 3 minutes. Now add all the ground spices, stir again for a few seconds only, add the yoghurt and continue stirring for 1 minute. Stir in the sugar and raisins or sultanas. Taste and adjust the seasoning. Pile the rice on top.

Cover the saucepan with foil or a tea-towel and clamp the lid on tightly. Reduce the heat to low and leave to cook undisturbed for 10 minutes. Remove from the heat and leave to rest, still undisturbed and tightly covered, for a further 5 minutes. Uncover, sprinkle with the garnishes and serve.

POT-ROASTED GUINEA FOWL WITH ONIONS AND THYME

Terrifically easy and terrifically good. Pot-roasting keeps guinea fowl from drying out and the lengthily cooked onions melt to a soft sweetness, absorbing the flavours of the guinea fowl and thyme.

SERVES 4

1 guinea fowl	1 bouquet garni (see page 33)
1 tablespoon sunflower oil	1½ teaspoons thyme leaves
40 g (1½ oz) butter	Salt and freshly ground black pepper
900 g (2 lb) onions, thinly sliced	

Brown the guinea fowl all over in the oil and 15 g (½ oz) of the butter over a brisk heat. Melt the remaining butter in a flame-proof casserole. Add the onions and stir briefly. Cover and cook over a gentle heat for 10 minutes until they are beginning to soften. Bury the bouquet garni amongst them, then sit the guinea fowl, breast-side down, on top and season with salt and pepper.

Cover the casserole tightly and cook over a low to moderate heat for 30 minutes. Turn the guinea fowl the right way up, sprinkle with the thyme leaves and continue cooking, still tightly covered, for another 20 minutes or so or until cooked through and the onions are meltingly tender. Remove the bouquet garni and serve.

MEXICO MEETS FRANCE
PINTADE AU VINAIGRE

This recipe is an amalgam of two vinegar-heavy recipes, one from France, the other from Mexico, both usually made with chicken rather than guinea fowl. Slow cooking mutes the insistent tartness of the vinegar, leaving just a welcome edge. The mild gaminess of guinea fowl takes particularly well to this treatment.

SERVES 4

1 guinea fowl, cut into 8 pieces (see page 165)

1–2 tablespoons sunflower oil

4 shallots, thinly sliced

4 garlic cloves, thinly sliced

85 ml (3 fl oz) red wine vinegar

300 ml (10 fl oz) chicken stock

¾ teaspoon cumin seeds, bruised

A generous pinch of ground cloves

1 teaspoon dried oregano

1 green chilli, seeded and thinly sliced

2 tablespoons chopped coriander

Salt and freshly ground black pepper

Brown the guinea fowl in the oil over a brisk heat in a wide frying pan in two batches. Remove the guinea fowl and pour out the excess oil. Spread out the shallots and garlic in the pan and snuggle the guinea fowl over them in a single tight layer. Add all the remaining ingredients except the coriander. Bring up to the boil, then cover and cook over a gentle heat for about 40 minutes or until the guinea fowl is very tender, stirring once or twice. Lift out the guinea fowl pieces and keep warm. Boil down the juices in the pan until reduced by half. Taste and adjust the seasoning, then pour over the guinea fowl and serve, sprinkled with the coriander.

GUINEA FOWL WITH GREEN PEPPERCORNS

This takes me straight back to my childhood and to France. My mother cut this recipe, originally for duck, from the local paper. Made with guinea fowl, it quickly became a family favourite. Use green peppercorns preserved in brine rather than freeze-dried ones.

SERVES 3-4

550 g (1¼ lb) pearl onions

1 guinea fowl

50 g (2 oz) butter

1 tablespoon sunflower oil

1 rounded tablespoon green peppercorns
with their juice

1½ tablespoons each of brandy and
Benedictine, or 3 tablespoons of brandy

250 ml (8 fl oz) chicken stock

Salt

To skin the onions, top and tail, then cover with boiling water. Leave for 1–2 minutes, then drain. The skins should now slip off readily. Brown first the guinea fowl and then the onions in the butter and oil, then transfer them to a deep, flame-proof casserole. Add the peppercorns, alcohol and 3–4 tablespoons of the stock. Sprinkle with a little salt, cover and cook gently until the bird is done, turning it occasionally and basting it with more stock – but keep the liquid level low.

After about 45–60 minutes, remove the bird from the casserole and carve, arranging it on a warm shallow serving dish with the onions. Season with salt.

Skim the fat from the pan juices, taste and adjust the seasoning. Add a little more stock, but only enough to lighten the sauce, which should not be copious. Pour over the bird and serve.

POACHED GUINEA FOWL WITH BASIL AND TOMATO VINAIGRETTE

Chicken
& Poultry

If you want to serve guinea fowl cold for a summer lunch, then I'd suggest that you poach it, letting it cool in its poaching liquid so that the flesh stays perfectly juicy. Of course, poached guinea fowl can also be served hot. Either way, this scented basil and tomato vinaigrette makes a fine partner. Save the richly flavoured cooking liquid to make soup.

SERVES 3 - 4

1 guinea fowl	1 onion, quartered
600 ml (1 pint) chicken or vegetable stock	1 carrot, thickly sliced
or 1 generous glass white wine	6 peppercorns
1 bouquet garni (see page 33)	

—— *For the vinaigrette* ——

25 g (1 oz) basil leaves, roughly torn up	350 g (12 oz) tomatoes, skinned, seeded
1 garlic clove, roughly chopped	and finely diced
1 tablespoon lemon juice	A pinch or two of sugar
5 tablespoons olive oil	

Put the guinea fowl into a close-fitting flame-proof casserole or pan with all the ingredients except those for the vinaigrette. Add some water, if necessary, so that the liquid comes about two-thirds of the way up the bird. Bring up to the boil, cover and simmer gently for about 1–1¼ hours or until the guinea fowl is very tender.

To serve hot, lift the guinea fowl out of the poaching water and quickly remove the skin. Carve the bird at the table.

To serve cold, draw the pan off the heat and leave the bird to cool in the cooking liquid. Lift out, drain, skin and cut into pieces.

To make the vinaigrette, put all the ingredients except the tomatoes and sugar into a food processor and whizz until smooth. Stir in the tomatoes, then taste and adjust the seasoning with the sugar. Serve with the hot or cold guinea fowl.

ROAST DUCK WITH MARMALADE

One might call this the 'cheat's Duck à l'Orange', if it weren't for the fact that it is actually rather nicer than nine out of ten versions of that over-exposed restaurant fall-back.

Use one of the high-fruit-content 'extra jams' or better still a completely sugar-free marmalade from a healthfood shop. If you prefer to do without the cream in the sauce, add a little extra stock to soften the flavour.

SERVES 4

2–2.5 kg (4–5 lb) duck	150 ml (5 fl oz) duck or chicken stock
1 orange	1½ teaspoons sugar
175 g (6 oz) fine-cut marmalade	150 ml (5 fl oz) double cream
150 ml (5 fl oz) orange juice	Salt and freshly ground black pepper

Pre-heat the oven to 190°C/375°F/Gas Mark 5. Wipe the duck skin and prick all over with a sharp-pronged fork. Halve the orange and place both halves in the central cavity. Roast the duck breast-side down on a rack over a roasting tin for 40 minutes.

Remove from the oven, turn the duck breast-side up and smear 1 generous tablespoon of the marmalade over the bird. Return to the oven and cook for a further 40–50 minutes until cooked. Check from time to time and if the marmalade is blackening too fast cover with silver foil. Aim to finish up with a very dark brown duck, with the odd piece of orange caught and slightly blackened by the heat.

To make the sauce, bring the remaining marmalade, orange juice, stock and sugar, gently to the boil, stirring occasionally. Simmer together for 10 minutes, checking to make sure it isn't burning on the bottom of the pan (if using a sugar-free jam this is much less likely to happen). When the duck is cooked, re-heat the sauce, if necessary, remove from the heat and allow to cool for a minute or so. Then stir in the cream and season.

ROAST DUCK WITH GINGER AND LEMON STUFFING

Roast duck is, I think, one of life's luxuries, as long as it is not overcooked. Roast duck, brushed with a mixture of honey and brandy as it cooks so that the skin crisps to a crackling sweetness, is even better.

SERVES 4

2–2.5 kg (4–5 lb) duck	1 tablespoon brandy
1 tablespoon honey	

——— For the stuffing ———

25 g (1 oz) currants	2 spheres preserved stem ginger, chopped
½ onion, chopped	1 tablespoon chopped parsley
15 g (½ oz) butter	Leaves of 1 large sprig of thyme
75 g (3 oz) breadcrumbs	½ teaspoon chopped rosemary
Finely grated zest of 1 lemon	1 egg, beaten
2 tablespoons lemon juice	Salt and freshly ground black pepper

Pre-heat the oven to 190°C/375°F/Gas Mark 5. To make the stuffing, soak the currants in water for half an hour to plump them up, then drain. Cook the onion gently in the butter without browning. Mix the breadcrumbs with the onion and butter, currants, and all the remaining ingredients, adding just enough of the egg to bind. Fill the cavity of the duck about two-thirds full with the stuffing. Roll any left-overs into golf-ball-sized balls.

Prick the skin of the duck all over with a fork. Calculate the cooking time of the duck by weighing it, and allowing 22 minutes per 500 g (20 minutes per lb). Roast the duck, breast-side down for two-thirds of the cooking time (if the fat in the roasting pan threatens to burn, add a tablespoon or two of water – carefully, as the fat will spit). Warm the honey and brandy in a small pan until just runny. Brush over the skin of the duck and season with salt and pepper. Return the duck to the oven, right way up this time. Set the extra stuffing balls around it, turning first to coat them in fat, then roast for the final third of the cooking time.

DUCK NOODLE SOUP

A big bowl of lightly spiced duck noodle soup, packed with little bits and bobs, makes a most soothing and satisfying meal, squeezing the last of the goodness out of a duck. This one is more substantial than the quick version on page 205.

SERVES 4

1.2 litres (2 pints) of well-flavoured duck stock (see page 168)

1½ tablespoons soy sauce

1½ tablespoons rice wine or dry sherry

1 tablespoon rice vinegar or cider vinegar

1½ tablespoons demerara sugar

1 star anise

1 clove

5 cm (2 in) cinnamon stick

1 cm (½ in) piece fresh root ginger, cut into matchsticks

1 carrot, cut into fine matchsticks

1 red chilli, seeded and cut into rings

4 spring onions, shredded

1 layer Chinese egg thread noodles

Scraps of duck from the carcase used for stock

100 g (4 oz) bean curd, cubed

Skim or blot as much fat as you can from the surface of the stock, then put it into a pan with the soy sauce, rice wine, vinegar, sugar, star anise, clove, cinnamon and ginger. Bring gently to the boil. Add the carrot and simmer for 2 minutes.

Now add the chilli, spring onions and noodles. Simmer for 2 minutes or so until the noodles are done. Finally, stir in the scraps of duck and the bean curd. Give it one more minute to heat through, then taste and adjust the seasonings. Serve in deep bowls.

TO RENDER DOWN DUCK FAT

Duck or goose fat is a superb medium for sautéing potatoes. A small restaurant near the village I go to every year in France always fries its shoelace chips in goose fat, and they are what make the meal worthwhile. Though you can use the fat that runs off during cooking, the best fat, pale and untainted, is obtained by rendering down raw fat. You may not get enough from the trimmings of one duck for a big load of chips, but there should be plenty for a couple of rounds of sauté potatoes.

Begin by trimming off all the lumps of fat and excess skin. Cut them into small pieces – around the size of a postage stamp. Put into a pan with a glass of water. Cook, uncovered, over the lowest possible heat (use a diffuser mat to even it out) for about 1–1½ hours, until the fat has melted down. Strain and reserve the fat. Store in the fridge.

FAISINJAN

This is an adaptation of a classic Persian dish, where ground walnuts are used to thicken the sauce of a duck stew, though chicken or pheasant could well be used instead. Essential to a real Faisinjan is sour pomegranate syrup, which is very hard to get in this country. Instead, I've used a mixture of fresh, sweet pomegranate juice and lemon juice, as well as the seeds of a second pomegranate to underline the fruitiness.

SERVES 4

2 small pomegranates

2–2.5 kg (4–5 lb) duck, cut into 8 pieces

(see page 165)

3 tablespoons oil

1 onion, chopped

225 g (8 oz) shelled walnuts, coarsely ground

or very finely chopped

450 ml (15 fl oz) light duck or chicken stock,

or water

1 cinnamon stick

2 cloves

Juice of ½ lemon

A pinch of sugar

Salt and freshly ground black pepper

Chopped parsley, to serve

Squeeze the juice from one of the pomegranates (use a lemon squeezer). Extract the seeds of the other one, carefully picking them out and discarding any bitter pithy white bits. Reserve.

Brown the duck pieces briskly in half the oil, in two batches if necessary, so as not to overcrowd the pan. Transfer to a flame-proof casserole. Fry the onion in the same fat until it is tender and translucent, adding a little more oil if necessary. Scoop into the casserole. Now add the walnuts to the pan, again with a little extra oil if needed, and fry until they begin to change colour. Scrape into the casserole.

Return the frying pan to the heat and pour in the stock or water. Bring up to the boil, stirring and scraping up all the nice brown bits on the bottom of the pan. Pour over the contents of the casserole. Add the cinnamon stick, cloves, pomegranate juice, lemon juice, a generous pinch of sugar, salt and pepper. Cover and simmer for 30 minutes. Uncover and continue simmering until the meat is very tender and the sauce is thick – another 15–30 minutes. Taste and adjust the seasonings. Serve sprinkled with pomegranate seeds and parsley.

DUCK, TOMATO AND PEPPER STEW

I happen to like duck legs cooked patiently until the meat is extremely tender, which is exactly what happens here. They are gently stewed in a tomatoey, peppery sauce, but the unusual touch is a final enrichment of chocolate. Don't worry that you'll end up with a duck-flavoured chocolate pud. All this small amount will do is add an unidentifiable depth and richness to the sauce.

SERVES 4

4 duck legs, cut into 2 pieces each

3 tablespoons olive oil

1 small red onion, chopped

3 garlic cloves, finely chopped

1 small red pepper, cut into strips

1 small green pepper, cut into strips

675 g (1½ lb) tomatoes, skinned, seeded and roughly chopped

2 sprigs of thyme

1 small sprig of rosemary

15 g (½ oz) plain chocolate, finely chopped

100 g (4 oz) fresh or frozen shelled peas, thawed if frozen

Salt and freshly ground black pepper

Dry the duck legs and brown them briskly in the oil over a high heat in a wide, deep frying pan. Set aside. Reduce the heat and cook the onion, garlic and pepper strips gently in the oil until tender. Now add the tomatoes, thyme, rosemary, salt and pepper and about 150 ml (5 fl oz) water. Bring up to the boil. Return the duck legs to the pan and simmer for around 40 minutes.

Stir in the chocolate and the peas and cook for a final 5 minutes. Taste and adjust the seasoning. Serve with rice.

GRILLED DUCK BREASTS WITH PLUM SAUCE

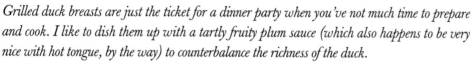

Grilled duck breasts are just the ticket for a dinner party when you've not much time to prepare and cook. I like to dish them up with a tartly fruity plum sauce (which also happens to be very nice with hot tongue, by the way) to counterbalance the richness of the duck.

These days, you can buy prepared duck breasts with no trouble, but if you are partial to duck, then it may make more sense to invest in a couple of whole birds. Why? Well, you can get two or three meals for 4 out of the brace and each one will taste totally different.

The great advantage of cooking breasts separately from the rest of the bird is that you can keep them rare, like a steak, as in this recipe and the one that follows. The legs are better cooked thoroughly, long and slow, in a small stew such as the Duck, Tomato and Pepper Stew on page 201. The carcase of the duck can be turned into stock (use the Chicken Stock recipe on page 168) which might then be used for a meal-in-a-bowl Duck Noodle Soup (page 198) and last but not least, the excess fat can be rendered down (page 198) and saved for sautéing potatoes.

If you don't want to grill the breasts, you can roast them in a hot oven instead, though you lose out on the hint of smokiness that grilling gives.

SERVES 4

4 duck breasts	Salt and freshly
Olive oil	ground black pepper

——— *For the plum sauce* ———

450 g (1 lb) plums, halved and pitted	1 bay leaf
1 cinnamon stick	1 tablespoon sherry vinegar
1 glass white wine	Sugar, to taste

Make the sauce first. Put the plums into a pan with the cinnamon, white wine and bay leaf. Place over a medium heat and bring gently up to the boil. Half cover and simmer quietly until the plums have all collapsed to a purée. Either pass through the fine blade of a mouli-légumes (vegetable mill) or rub through a sieve. While still warm, stir in the sherry vinegar, sugar to taste (3–4 tablespoons should be ample) and plenty of freshly ground black pepper. Set aside until needed.

Pre-heat the grill. When your guests are assembled, start grilling the duck. Place the breasts, skin-side to the heat, on a rack, fairly close to the grill – 7.5 cm (3 in) or so away.

Grill until well-browned and crisp. Turn the breasts over, brush quickly with oil and sprinkle with salt and pepper, then grill the cut side for 4 minutes. Let them rest in a warm place for 5 minutes while you re-heat the plum sauce.

To roast the breasts pre-heat the oven to 230°C/450°F/Gas Mark 8, brush the cut sides with oil and rub salt and pepper into the skin. Lay on a rack, skin side up for 10–15 minutes, until well-browned. Rest for 5 minutes before slicing.

If you are the patient sort, slice each duck breast and fan out on individual plates (stir any juices from the duck into the plum sauce), with a spoonful of sauce elegantly drizzled over. Or serve them up whole with the sauce on the side.

LACQUERED DUCK BREASTS

Double-brushing ensures that the glaze of soy sauce and honey cooks to a burnished, chestnut lacquer in the heat of the oven — a welcome contrast to the richness of the meat. Don't be tempted to use a classy high-price honey for this recipe. The intense heat will destroy its subtleties. A good, everyday honey will work just as well.

SERVES 2

1½ tablespoons clear honey
1 tablespoon soy sauce
¼ teaspoon Chinese 5-spice powder

2 boned duck breasts
Salt and freshly ground black pepper

Mix the honey and the soy sauce with the 5-spice powder and a generous grinding of pepper. Brush the mixture over the skin of the duck breasts. Leave for half an hour and then brush again with any remaining mixture. Place the breasts, skin-side up on a rack over a roasting tin.

Pre-heat the oven to 230°C/450°F/Gas Mark 8 and roast the duck for 10–15 minutes, if necessary covering with foil towards the end of the cooking time to prevent burning. Once they are cooked, leave the breasts to rest for 5 minutes in a warm place. Just before serving, slice each one and arrange on a warm serving plate.

CHINESE POACHED DUCK AND NOODLE SOUP

Chicken
& Poultry

This Chinese two-tier way of cooking duck — first roasting, then poaching — may seem rather long-winded, but the result is worth the extra modicum of work. Save any left-over poaching liquid to make a simple bowl of soup the next day.

SERVES 4

1.75–2.25 kg (4–5 lb) duck	4 tablespoons sugar
3 spring onions, sliced	2 star anise
1 cm (½ in) piece fresh root ginger, sliced	5 cm (2 in) cinnamon stick
600 ml (1 pint) light chicken stock, or water	4 cloves
4 tablespoons soy sauce	Salt and freshly ground black pepper
4 tablespoons rice wine or dry sherry	

Pre-heat the oven to 250°C/475°F/Gas Mark 9. Pierce the skin of the duck with a fork. Rub in a little salt and pepper and roast for 30 minutes until browned. Bring all the remaining ingredients to the boil in a pan or flame-proof casserole just large enough to take the duck. Add the duck, and enough boiling water to cover. Cover and simmer gently for half an hour. Check that the duck is cooked, then lift out and keep warm.

Strain the cooking liquid and measure 900 ml (1½ pints) into a wide frying pan. Boil until reduced by about half. Adjust the seasonings and serve with the duck.

NOODLE SOUP

Stock from cooking duck

1 layer Chinese egg thread noodles

Left-over scraps of cooked duck

Skim any fat from the remaining cooking liquid and boil down a little to concentrate the flavour, if necessary. Add the egg thread noodles and scraps of cooked duck. Simmer, stirring once or twice, until the noodles are done — a matter of minutes. Taste and adjust the seasonings.

ROAST GOOSE WITH PRUNE, APPLE AND APRICOT STUFFING

My aunt always used to cook a magnificent goose for our pre-Christmas family gathering if we weren't actually going to spend the big day together. She stuffed one end with fruit, the other with a forcemeat stuffing. This isn't exactly her recipe, but it is inspired by it. Some of her quince and apple compote, which she had made when the fruit of her quince tree were ripe in the autumn, was defrosted to accompany the bird. It's a lovely partnership if you can find some quinces, but otherwise a straightforward apple sauce, or even better the French Canadian Roast Apple Sauce on page 105, is excellent served with the bird.

SERVES 8

4–5.5 kg (9–12 lb) goose

——— For the fruit stuffing ———

100 g (4 oz) stoned prunes, roughly chopped

100 g (4 oz) dried apricots, roughly chopped

85 ml (3 fl oz) port

2 eating apples, peeled, cored and diced

1 small red onion, chopped

½ teaspoon ground cinnamon

¼ teaspoon ground nutmeg

Salt and freshly ground black pepper

——— For the forcemeat stuffing ———

1 small onion, chopped

1 celery stick, chopped

The goose liver, finely chopped

Finely grated zest and juice of 1 orange

225 g (8 oz) highest-quality pork sausagemeat

1 teaspoon fresh thyme leaves, or 1 level teaspoon dried thyme leaves

3 tablespoons chopped parsley

50 g (2 oz) soft breadcrumbs

1 egg, lightly beaten

Freshly grated nutmeg

Salt and freshly ground black pepper

——— For the quince and apple sauce ———

2 quinces, peeled, cored and diced

675 g (1½ lb) cooking apples, peeled, cored and cut into chunks

Juice of 1 orange

A generous slug of port

1 cinnamon stick

Sugar, to taste

First make the fruit stuffing. Soak the prunes and apricots for as long as possible in the port – overnight or even a couple of days if you remember. Mix with all the remaining fruit stuffing ingredients (don't worry that it seems sloppy – as the goose has a long, slow cooking time, it will all meld together loosely in the oven).

To make the forcemeat stuffing, mix together all the ingredients, adding just enough egg to bind.

Trim the excess fat from inside the goose. Put the forcemeat stuffing into the neck end of the goose, pressing it in firmly and then tucking the flap of skin neatly down around it. Secure firmly underneath with wooden cocktail sticks or a metal skewer. Put the fruit stuffing into the body cavity.

Pre-heat the oven to 190°C/375°F/Gas Mark 5.

Prick the skin of the goose all over with a fork. Season with salt and pepper. Lay some of the fat from the cavity over the thighs to keep them moist. Cover with foil and place on a rack in the oven with a tray underneath, so that you can empty out the fat regularly. Roast a 4 kg (9 lb) goose for 3 hours, a 4.5–5 kg (10–11 lb) goose for 3½ hours, and roast a 5.5 kg (12 lb) goose for 4 hours. Remove the foil 30–40 minutes before the end of the cooking time so that the skin can brown and crisp. To test, pierce the fattest part of the thigh with a skewer. If the juices run clear, then the bird is done.

Meanwhile, make the quince and apple sauce. Put the quinces into a pan with just enough water to cover. Simmer gently for about 30–40 minutes until barely tender. If necessary, boil hard to reduce the cooking liquid down to a scant few tablespoons. Add all the remaining sauce ingredients, except the sugar. Cover and cook until the apples have collapsed then add sugar to taste. Serve hot or cold.

Chicken
& Poultry

TURKEY ESCALOPES IN LEEK AND LEMON SAUCE

Turkey escalopes or turkey breast steaks take no time at all to cook (far quicker than, say, a whole chicken breast) and, as long as they are not overdone, are a most useful basis for a mid-week supper. They do need a sauce with a bit of oomph to it, though, since more often than not they are almost as light on taste as they are in colour. Here they are served with leeks and lemon, and scattered with a few chives just before serving to contrast with the paleness of the sauce.

SERVES 4

4 turkey escalopes	½ tablespoon Dijon mustard
25 g (1 oz) butter	Finely grated zest and juice of ½ large lemon
1 tablespoon sunflower oil	Freshly grated nutmeg
2 leeks, white part only, cut into matchsticks	Chopped chives
1½ tablespoons flour	Salt and freshly ground black pepper
300 ml (10 fl oz) milk	

Season the escalopes with salt and pepper. Melt the butter and oil in a wide frying pan. When foaming, add the escalopes and fry for about 3–4 minutes on each side, until lightly browned and just cooked through. If necessary, cook them in two batches. Remove from the pan and set aside.

Add the leeks to the pan and stir until they begin to wilt. Now sprinkle over the flour and stir for about 30 seconds. Gradually whisk in the milk, bringing the sauce to the boil and simmering for about 5 minutes, stirring occasionally, until thick and smooth.

Stir in the mustard, lemon zest, salt, pepper and nutmeg and return the escalopes to the pan, nestling them down into the sauce and overlapping slightly if necessary. Simmer for about 2 minutes, long enough to heat the turkey through thoroughly. Draw the pan off the heat and add enough of the lemon juice to sharpen the sauce without making it overwhelmingly acidic. Serve at once, scattered with chives.

ROASTED BONED AND STUFFED TURKEY THIGH

*A boned turkey thigh is big enough, when filled with a stuffing, to feed 4–6 people quite gener-
ously. Like a boned stuffed chicken, it is a boon for those of us who've never been too skilled with
the carving knife.*

*The stuffing I've used here is laden with dried wild mushrooms – porcini – and meaty flat-
cap mushrooms, though you might like to substitute the stuffing for the Galantine of Chicken with
Apricots and Pistachios on page 180. Buying muslin by the yard from fabric shops or department
stores works out very cheap. It is also sold in many kitchen shops, at a comparatively high price.
If you don't have any you can always substitute a clean J-cloth, but boil it first for 5 minutes and
rinse well.*

SERVES 4–6

1 turkey thigh, boned (see page 210)	25 g (1 oz) butter

—————— *For the stuffing* ——————

15 g (½ oz) dried porcini mushrooms	175 g (6 oz) pork sausagemeat
2 tablespoons oloroso sherry or Marsala	2 tablespoons breadcrumbs
½ onion, chopped	2 tablespoons chopped parsley
25 g (1 oz) butter	1 egg, lightly beaten
1 garlic clove, crushed	Salt and freshly ground black pepper
100 g (4 oz) flat-cap mushrooms, diced	

First make the stuffing. Soak the dried mushrooms in the sherry for half an hour.
Pick out the pieces of mushroom and chop finely. Let the sherry settle for 5 minutes or so, then carefully pour off, leaving the grit behind.

Fry the onion gently in the butter until tender. Now add the garlic and the fresh mushrooms and fry over a fairly high heat until the mushrooms are tender and any liquid
thrown off has evaporated. Add the dried mushrooms and the sherry and cook hard
until all the liquid has evaporated leaving just a moist mush. Cool slightly then mix with
the sausagemeat, breadcrumbs, parsley, salt, pepper and just enough egg to bind.

Pre-heat the oven to 200°C/400°F/Gas Mark 6.

Now for that turkey thigh. Melt the butter in a small pan and dunk a large square of
muslin right into it, so that it is thoroughly soaked. Lay it open on the worksurface and
place the thigh, opened out, flat on it, skin-side down. Spoon the stuffing down the centre

and draw the sides up and round. Roll up tightly in the buttered muslin and tie up both ends firmly with a piece of string.

Roast the turkey for 50–60 minutes. If you wish to serve it hot, unwrap the turkey thigh just before it goes onto the table. For a cold dish, leave the muslin *in situ* as it cools, and unwrap just before slicing.

Boning a turkey thigh

1. *With a sharp knife, cut along the length of the main thigh bone, right down to the bone.*

2. *Carefully scrape the meat away from the bone, then sever the joint and lift out the bone. Repeat with the drumstick so the thigh can be opened out flat.*

Feathered Game

Feathered
Game

I'm no hunter – I've never even managed to chip a clay pigeon, though to be fair I haven't had much practice – but I'm increasingly of the opinion that pheasant are wily birds. Throughout the shooting season I hardly ever catch a glimpse of one. From February onwards, however, when the season is closed, they are suddenly all over the place, strutting proudly across the roads and fields, burnished copper feathers gleaming in shafts of sun. 'Look at me,' they seem to be saying smugly, 'I gave those hunters the slip for months on end. Now I can revel in my freedom.' And indeed, they can, for some six glorious months, until autumn closes in again.

Of course, come autumn you only have to stroll down the aisles of a supermarket or past a specialist game dealer to realize that in fact my wily pheasant are in the minority. Pheasant and partridge are our most common game birds and they are amongst the many good things that the autumn months bring to our tables. Grouse, woodpigeon and wild ducks, such as mallard, widgeon and teal, through to rarer woodcock and snipe and a few more, back up to the commoner birds. Wee little quail are often classed as game birds, which is why you'll find them in this chapter, though these days they are always farmed.

Since there is more than enough scope to write a whole book about game (and if you develop a taste for game, there are several excellent books on the subject in print), in this chapter I'm concentrating on the most common of our game birds: pheasant, partridge, grouse, woodpigeon, mallard and quail.

In culinary terms, lumping all these birds together is rather misleading, since the range of flavours is enormous. At the milder end, pheasant and partridge are only a few shades more pronounced in flavour than a truly free-range chicken. Totally wild birds such as grouse and woodcock and snipe are dark-fleshed with a correspondingly intense taste. They've had to work their muscles a great deal harder, flying high and far to feed.

Cooking feathered game is no more taxing than cooking any form of poultry, providing you buy it fully prepared, which is how it is usually sold. As with a chicken, age is of major importance. Roasting is only for young birds in their first season (which doesn't mean that they aren't equally enjoyable cooked in other ways). By January they are already beginning to toughen up from all that dodging of the hunters' guns. You can still just about get away with roasting them, but they are veering towards the time when slower cooking methods are required. Second-season birds, those who escaped first time round, are inevitably too tough for roasting and must be slowly braised or casseroled to soften them up. The plus side is the deeper more complex flavour, which will go to make a sensational dish.

HANGING, PLUCKING AND DRAWING

Unless you live on or near a big game estate, where you are overwhelmed every year with the spoils of endless days' shooting, you will probably never have to deal with a freshly caught bird in all its plumage. I've a friend who occasionally turns up swinging a brace of pheasant as a present and though I have hung, plucked and eviscerated birds once or twice, I usually take the easy option, which is to pass the messy work on to a friendly local butcher. If this happens to you, it shouldn't be too difficult to locate a butcher who will do the business for you in return for a small consideration.

If you do fancy tackling the bird from scratch, then can I recommend that you seek the advice of someone who is familiar with the process, or at least go out and buy a good book on cooking game which will take you by the hand and guide you through. It's not that there's anything to be wary of, but plucking and eviscerating can be messy and proper hanging, which tenderizes the meat and develops the flavour, depends as much on weather as anything else and needs to be judged wisely.

BUYING FEATHERED GAME

You have two options here (excluding the poacher). One is to go to a major supermarket, where you can probably lay your hands on oven-ready pheasant, partridge, woodpigeon, mallard and quail. This will absolve you of any decision making – they will all be of good quality, young enough to roast and, relatively speaking, mildly flavoured.

Butchers who deal in game are easy to spot in the autumn as they usually set out a stunning display of their game birds, in feather, strung outside the shop for passers-by to marvel at.

A game dealer will be able to advise you properly. He will, for instance, be able to tell, roughly, the age of a bird – second-season birds are not sold so widely but when they are, they should be cheaper – and its sex. Hen birds are reckoned to be more tender, juicy and delicately flavoured than cocks, though they will be smaller.

The other advantage of buying from a proper dealer, rather than a supermarket, is that you can have some say in the length of time the bird is hung. Personally, I like game to have at least a hint of gaminess about it. What's the point of buying a pheasant that is so mild in flavour that it could just as well be chicken? On the other hand, seriously high

Feathered
Game

game that virtually walks off the plate on its own is too much even for me. Each to their own, as they say, and a game dealer will usually be able to supply you with what you want.

Don't expect immaculate perfection when buying game birds. The odd tear in the skin here and there, shot marks and slight damage are only to be expected. Mind you, you don't want a mangled lump with misshapen limbs that looks as if it has been run over by a car, either.

It's far easier to tell the age of a bird before it is plucked than after, but if you want to run your own checks on age on plucked birds, then look at the legs and the beak, if the head is still *in situ*. In young creatures the beak will be soft, but still pointed and the spur at the back of the male's leg will be malleable.

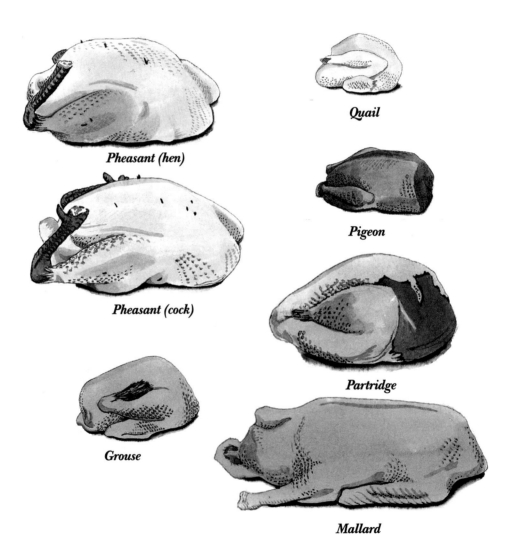

Pheasant (hen)

Pheasant (cock)

Grouse

Quail

Pigeon

Partridge

Mallard

I can't resist telling you about the Bursa test, though it is only really applicable to birds still in feather. It sounds far from tasteful, but may intrigue those of curious mind. Arm yourself with a tapered matchstick, then start searching the rear end of the bird for the bursa. This is a small dead-end hole situated somewhere between the vent and the tail (this area is usually removed when the bird is drawn, i.e. has its innards removed, which is why the test is not applicable to oven-ready game birds). Once you've located it, try to push in the matchstick. In a young bird you should be able to insert about 1 cm (½ in) all told. In older birds the bursa closes up, so if the matchstick won't go in, then you can be pretty sure you've been landed with a sexually mature pheasant. On the whole I prefer to stick with the dealer's recommendations.

As soon as you get your birds home, remove any plastic wrapping. If you are conscientious and thoughtful, you will gently prod and press the body all over to locate the lead shot, then ease it out. I have to admit that I rarely bother, preferring to warn diners that they may come across a little evidence that these birds met a speedy end after having led a blissful outdoors life. Either way, dry the flesh and store it in the fridge, covered loosely.

PHEASANT

(Season: 1st October–1st February)

Pheasant were introduced to this country, it is said, by the Romans along with dormice; once they'd done with invading, they thought, very sensibly, of their stomachs. Dormice didn't catch on long term, but pheasant proved a big hit, reappearing year after year, century after century on British tables. On many big estates they are bred in captivity, in order to be released into the wild. Most of their life is spent out in the open, though an element of domesticity is apparent as they run to the call of the gamekeeper, just like a flock of chickens. As a result they are plentiful and remarkably cheap to buy.

Pheasant are fairly mild in flavour (unless they've been hung to high heaven, but that won't be the case with shop-bought birds) and for anyone who is a little wary of game, they are probably the best starting point. A brace of pheasant, that is, a hen and a cock, will feed about 6 people. A hen on her own will do for 2–3, while a cock can stretch to feed 3–4 mouths. You can adapt practically any casseroled chicken recipe to pheasant most successfully.

Feathered
Game

PARTRIDGE

(Season: 1st September–1st February)

Partridges come in two models, the English or Grey, and the French or Red-legged. Generally, the Grey, indigenous partridge is considered better eating and is therefore the most sought after. Sadly, they are not as plentiful as they once were, though game eaters are not the ones to blame. Twentieth-century intensive farming methods have destroyed a good deal of the grey partridge's favoured habitat. Wilier red-legged partridges seem to cope with this far better. Though they may not be quite as estimably fleshed as their English cousins, they are certainly not to be rejected out of hand. In some ways, heretical though this may sound, they may be more useful to the cook, since they are not so over-shadowed by stronger, more vivid flavours.

In the end, the distinction between English and French may be largely academic if you are having to buy partridge from a supermarket or a small-scale game dealer. You take what you can get. Either way, the cooking methods are the same, dictated more by age than by variety.

Partridges are small birds, the hen weighing in at around 350–400 g (12–14 oz), the cock not much heftier at some 375–425 g (13–15 oz). I've always considered this a rather cussed, inbetween sort of size, since they are on the large side for a single portion yet on the small side for a two-person helping unless you bulk out the meal with plenty of other bits and bobs. The recipe, the other components of the meal, and the appetites of the diners, all need to be taken into consideration when calculating quantities.

QUAIL

(All year round)

Wild quail is now a protected species in this country, so all British quail that you come across will have been farmed. The Japanese quail, rather than our own native bird, is what we eat here, and it is available all year round. Despite its wee size, the quail is remarkably well-endowed. One alone makes a generous first course or a light main course for one person. They respond well to all manner of cooking, from grilling to roast-ing to casseroling, and being relatively lean, make good eating hot or cold.

GROUSE

(Season: 12th August–10th December)

Grouse are not as plentiful as they once were, which in part accounts for their comparatively high price. For many, they are *the* game bird par excellence, with a rounded, rich, gamey flavour that comes from feeding on heather-strewn highlands and moorlands. They are small birds and a singleton makes a perfect serving for one person. I like grouse roasted – in fact I don't think I've ever cooked them any other way, perhaps because I don't eat them often enough to become bored with the delicious flavour of juicy roasted young grouse.

WOODPIGEON

(All year round)

Woodpigeon are fairly common and reasonably priced and have no closed season, so you can enjoy them all year round. Their flesh is dark and moderately deep in flavour, though not overwhelmingly so. Assuming you have young birds, they should either be cooked very quickly or very slowly. In between and they tend to be tough. For roasting or grilling, they will need to be marinated and/or thoroughly barded or basted or both if they are not to dry out. Be patient when casseroling woodpigeon as even young birds take longer than one might expect. It makes sense, I think, to stew them a day in advance, so that you can give them ample time to tenderize without keeping a tableful of hungry people waiting.

MALLARD

(Season: 1 September–31 January, or 20 February below the high-tide mark)

Mallard is the most common of the wild duck and is the ideal bird for anyone who likes the taste of domesticated duck but not its fattiness. Mallard has more depth of flavour than farmyard duck, but it is not overpowering by any standards. Being a water bird it does have a thin layer of fat, but nothing approaching the chunky covering of domesticated breeds. A plump mallard will feed two to three people comfortably.

Feathered
Game

TECHNIQUES

BARDING

One of the much vaunted attributes of game birds is that they are lean and fat free, but this has its downside too. It means that the meat has a tendency to be dry, particularly when cooked by a dry method such as roasting. Barding is one answer (marinating before cooking and/or basting frequently during cooking are others). It means nothing more complicated than tying a thin sheet of pork fat (see page 91) or failing that some fatty streaky bacon or even better Italian pancetta or Eastern European speck over the breast and thighs with lengths of string, to protect them as they cook. If you use bacon, don't salt the bird before tying it in place.

Instead of barding, you can be extra generous with the butter (in which case you really must be rigorous with the basting) or you can tie butter papers or buttered greaseproof paper over the breast and legs instead of fat or bacon.

Whatever you do, remove the fat, bacon or paper 5–10 minutes before the end of the cooking time so that the birds can pick up a bit of colour.

ROASTING

Most game birds, especially the smaller ones, are best roasted at a high temperature, by which I mean about 230°C/450°F/Gas Mark 8, and consequently need good protection in the oven (see Barding above) and regular basting. At this temperature allow about 20–30 minutes for a mallard, 20 minutes for woodpigeon and 25–30 minutes for partridge. Grouse and pheasant do better in a cooler oven, say around 190°C/375°F/Gas Mark 5. Allow 45–60 minutes for a pheasant, 35 minutes for a grouse.

If you aren't going to make a full stuffing for game birds, it still pays to pop a little something extra into the central cavity. Halves or quarters of apple, orange (the sour spiciness of Seville oranges in January is extra good) or onion are perfect with or without a few herbs for their aroma. An extra knob of butter slipped inside always helps, but you might like to copy a trick learned from a French neighbour which is to pop a Petit Suisse, or a spoonful of full-fat fromage frais or cream cheese inside.

Traditional accompaniments to roast game birds include bread sauce, fried crumbs (see page 238), gravy, watercress and rowan or redcurrant jelly. Freshly fried home-made crisps are another classic, though true game crisps are latticed and rather a lot of bother when you are knee deep in the other trimmings and accompanying vegetables. You can cheat by crisping up high-quality bought crisps in a moderate oven.

TRUSSING

Trussing, whilst not absolutely necessary, keeps a bird neatly in shape while in the oven and helps to prevent some drying out of the legs and wings. Birds purchased oven-ready usually arrive ready-trussed, so make a note of how it's done, remove the string without cutting it, do what you need with the bird, then return it to its original state.

If your bird is untrussed then, with luck, you should be able to tuck the ends of the legs inside the opening to the central cavity. It may be easier to make slits in the skin and push the ends into those to hold them securely. Otherwise string, needle and thread, cocktail sticks and skewers can all be brought into play.

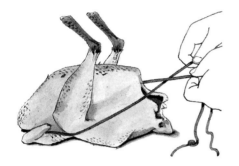

1. *Twist a length of string around the wing joints. Bring the ends forwards across the thighs and then cross the ends of string.*

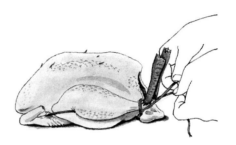

2. *Wrap the string around the thighbones to secure, cross the ends, then bring them down under the parson's nose and tie tightly.*

3. *Tuck the ends of the thighbones neatly into the stomach cavity*

219

Feathered Game

SPATCHCOCKING

To spatchcock a bird (and any bird can be spatchcocked, wild or domesticated, small or large), simply means to open it up flat. The French term *en crapaudine*, like a toad, gives you a graphic idea of what you are aiming for. A spatchcocked bird can be roasted or grilled whole.

The process is straightforward enough. Turn the bird breast-side down and, using a sharp knife or better still a pair of poultry shears or strong scissors, cut along the backbone from neck to tail. Snip out the backbone completely. Remove the wishbone. Turn the bird skin-side up and flatten out firmly with the heel of your hand to form a sort of butterfly shape.

To keep the bird flat as it cooks, thread skewer(s) through from one side to the other. The number and way will depend on the size of the bird.

1. *Set the bird breast-side down and cut along and through the backbone from one end to the other. Snip out the backbone, then cut out the wishbone.*

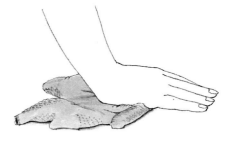

2. *Turn the bird over and press down firmly with the heel of your hand to flatten it.*

3. *For a large bird, thread skewers through diagonally from the wing tips to the legs.*

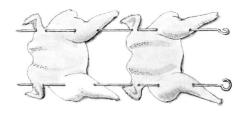

4. *Smaller birds can be skewered lengthways, 2 birds at a time.*

PHEASANT À LA NORMANDE

This is an old favourite from Normandy, where cream, apples, cider and Calvados flow freely. It is rich and delicious and worthy of a fine Sunday lunch party. If you don't have pheasant, guinea fowl is the next best thing, but a free-range chicken will do in its stead.

SERVES 6

75 g (3 oz) butter	150 ml (5 fl oz) medium cider
A brace of pheasant (see page 215)	150 ml (5 fl oz) crème fraîche
85 ml (3 fl oz) Calvados, apple brandy,	or double cream
or brandy if all else fails	A squeeze of lemon juice
5 eating apples, peeled, cored and	Salt and freshly
cut into 8 slices each	ground black pepper

Melt 50 g (2 oz) of the butter in a flameproof casserole large enough to take the two pheasant whole. Brown the birds briefly but thoroughly in the butter, then reduce the heat. Pour in the Calvados and set alight at arm's length with a match. When the flames have died down, nestle both birds breast-side down in the casserole. Add 2 apples' worth of slices and season with salt and pepper. Pour in the cider, then cover and leave to cook slowly for about 45 minutes, turning the birds upright after half an hour.

While the birds cook, fry the remaining slices of apple briskly in the rest of the butter until browned. Set aside until needed.

When the pheasant are cooked through, transfer them to a serving dish, tuck the fried apple slices around them and keep warm. Set the casserole over the hob and add the cream. Bring up to the boil, stirring and let it reduce to a good consistency. Rub the sauce through a sieve, pushing through some of the disintegrating pulp from the apples, then taste and adjust the seasoning, adding a dash or two of lemon juice to heighten the flavours. Pour a little of the sauce around the pheasants and serve the rest separately.

PHEASANT WITH MUSHROOMS
IN A CREAM SAUCE

I've eaten variations on this theme several times, always at the homes of people who are dealing with copious hauls of game from local shoots. It is an ideal way to use up left-over cooked pheasant, but that's not something I have much of in my larder. In fact it is good enough to justify roasting a brace of birds from scratch. They can be cooked and the meat stripped off the bones a day in advance. For this recipe, I prefer to cook the pheasant at a high temperature, since the flesh will get a second dose of heat in the sauce. I like it served with baked potatoes, but rice would go with it nicely as long as it was saved from overwhelming pallor by generous dots of chopped parsley.

SERVES 6

2 pheasants	1 branch of thyme
2 thin sheets of pork fat or 2 butter papers	2 sprigs of parsley
25 g (1 oz) butter	300 ml (10 fl oz) double cream
1 tablespoon oil	A squeeze of lemon juice
3 shallots, sliced	A little chopped parsley
8 flat-cap mushrooms, thickly sliced	Salt and freshly ground black pepper
1 glass of dry white wine	

Pre-heat the oven to 230°C/450°F/Gas Mark 8. Season the pheasants inside and out with salt and pepper. Tie the pork fat or butter papers over the breasts and roast for 30–45 minutes, laying on one side for the first 10 minutes then on the other side for the second 10 minutes, and turning breast upwards for the final part of the cooking time. Let the pheasants cool, then strip off all the meat and cut or tear into bite-sized pieces.

Warm the butter and oil in a wide, deep frying pan and sauté the shallots until tender, without browning. Raise the heat and add the sliced mushrooms. Fry until the mushrooms are tender and most of the liquid they release has evaporated. Pour in the wine, add the thyme, parsley and cooked pheasant. Bring up to the boil and let it bubble until almost all the liquid has evaporated. Now add the cream and salt and pepper. Bring up to the boil and let it simmer for 4–5 minutes to reduce the sauce and blend the flavours, stirring occasionally. Remove the herbs, then taste and adjust the seasoning, adding a squirt or two of lemon juice to lift the flavours. Serve with a sprinkling of chopped parsley.

ROAST PHEASANT WITH OATMEAL AND BLACK PUDDING STUFFING

I love this stuffing with its slightly knobbly texture (make sure it is oatmeal, not rolled or porridge oats, that you use), but even if you prefer to use some other mixture or leave the birds unstuffed, you'll still find the roasting method a good one. All lean, feathered game has a tendency to dryness, so it is important to be generous with the fat, to baste frequently and give adequate protection from the heat of the oven. Don't be tempted to skimp.

SERVES 4 – 6

2 pheasants	½ bunch watercress
40 g (1½ oz) butter	Salt and freshly ground black pepper

——— *For the stuffing* ———

2 leeks, white part only, chopped	150 g (5 oz) medium oatmeal
40 g (1½ oz) butter	2 tablespoons chopped parsley
100 g (4 oz) black pudding, skinned and diced or crumbled	

——— *For the gravy* ———

450 ml (15 fl oz) pheasant or chicken stock	A dash of lemon juice
70 ml (2½ fl oz) port	

Make the stuffing first. Sweat the leeks in the butter over a gentle heat in a covered pan for 5–10 minutes until tender. Stir in the black pudding, oatmeal, parsley and salt and pepper. Cook for a few minutes, stirring, until the oatmeal has absorbed all the leek juices. Taste and adjust the seasoning. Cool slightly and stuff into the cavity of the pheasants. Seal up the openings with wooden cocktail sticks.

Heat the oven to 190°C/375°F/Gas Mark 5. Smear the birds with the butter, season with salt and pepper and set in a roasting tin, on their sides with one leg stuck up in the air. Roast for 15 minutes. Turn the birds onto the other side and roast for a further 15 minutes. Set them right way up (i.e. breast upwards) and roast for a final 20 minutes or until cooked. Each time you turn the birds, baste with the pan juices.

Transfer the pheasants to a heated serving dish and keep warm. Pour any excess fat from the roasting tin, then set on the hob. Add the stock and port and bring up to the boil, scraping in all the brown goo on the bottom of the pan. Boil until reduced by half. Add a squirt of lemon juice, then taste and adjust the seasoning. Serve with the pheasants. Tuck little tufts of watercress around the birds just before dishing up.

Pheasant with Grapes and Walnuts

This pheasant casserole is pure autumn at its golden, mellow best. It really belongs to a French October, when grapes and fresh walnuts are being harvested, but what the hell? It's good for a daydream or two back in Britain on a chilly late autumn day.

SERVES 4

450 g (1 lb) seedless white grapes

40 g (1½ oz) walnut pieces

75 g (3 oz) shallots, sliced

15 g (½ oz) butter

1 tablespoon sunflower oil

1 large pheasant

1 bouquet garni (see page 33)

1 tablespoon flour

150 ml (5 fl oz) dry white wine

150 ml (5 fl oz) pheasant or chicken stock

Salt and freshly ground black pepper

Cut 225 g (8 oz) of the grapes in half. Skin the remaining grapes (this can be done while the pheasant is cooking) then cut these in half too. Spread the walnuts out on a baking sheet and toast in the oven (around 200°C/400°F/Gas Mark 6) for 4–7 minutes, shaking occasionally, until browned. Tip into a wire sieve and shake to dislodge the papery skins then set aside.

Cook the shallots gently in the butter and oil in a flame-proof casserole which is just large enough to take the pheasant; do not let them brown. Scoop out and reserve. Raise the heat and brown the pheasant briskly all over. Take out of the pan and return the shallots to it, together with the halved, unskinned grapes and the bouquet garni. Put the pheasant back, breast downwards, and sprinkle over the flour. Pour in the wine and stock then season with salt and pepper. Cover and simmer gently for 40 minutes (or longer if it's a tough old thing) until the pheasant is cooked. Transfer to a serving dish and keep warm while you finish the sauce.

Sieve the sauce, pressing the grapes to extract the last drops of flavour. Boil hard to reduce by about one third, then add the skinned grapes and walnuts. Bring up to the boil and simmer for 1 minute then taste and adjust the seasoning. Spoon some of the grapes and walnuts around the pheasant and serve the sauce separately.

BRAISED PHEASANT WITH RED CABBAGE AND SAUSAGES

Long-braised red cabbage has become an established favourite (its origins are probably Germanic), and makes a good repository for pieces of pheasant and meaty sausages to cook in. A happy exchange of flavours takes place and you end up with a hearty, filling meal.

SERVES 6

1 red cabbage, shredded	1½ tablespoons sherry vinegar
1 large onion, sliced	or red wine vinegar
2 cooking apples, peeled, cored	85 ml (3 fl oz) water
and roughly diced	450 g (1 lb) good pork chipolatas
50 g (2 oz) raisins	or other sausages
50 g (2 oz) light muscovado sugar	1 tablespoon sunflower oil
6 allspice berries, lightly bruised	1 large pheasant, cut into 8 pieces (see
2 blades of mace	page 165)
Juice of 1 orange	Salt and freshly ground black pepper
300 ml (10 fl oz) red wine	

Pre-heat the oven to 150°C/300°F/Gas Mark 2. Layer the cabbage, onion, apples and raisins in a casserole, sprinkling with the sugar and a little salt and pepper, and tucking in the spices as you go. Mix the orange juice, wine, vinegar and water and pour over. Cover tightly and cook for 2 hours, stirring occasionally. There should be enough liquid to keep it moist, but if it threatens to dry out at any point add a little water or another slurp of wine.

Meanwhile, prick the sausages all over and brown in the oil over a high heat, then set aside. Brown the pheasant pieces over a high heat in two batches so as not to overcrowd the pan. Reserve along with the fat.

Once the cabbage has been cooking for 2 hours, bury the sausages and pheasant pieces down in the mass of purple. Pour any cooking fat over the top (though if you prefer it can be left out), cover again and return the casserole to the oven. Cook for a further 1–1½ hours, until the pheasant is done. Taste and adjust the seasoning.

Either serve straight from the cooking pot or, for a more elegant presentation, excavate the pheasant and sausages, arrange round the edge of a serving dish and mound up the cabbage in the centre.

Partridge with Cabbage

This is a marriage that occurs in French, Italian, Spanish and Portuguese cooking, and no doubt elsewhere too. It is a homely, warming combination, a peasant dish to fill the stomach on a cold day. It's suitable for older partridge, if needs be, and is an excellent way to stretch two birds generously around four people.

SERVES 4

1 white or green cabbage	2 bay leaves
3 tablespoons olive oil	4 juniper berries, crushed
2 plump partridges	Stock
100 g (4 oz) lardons (see page 102)	225 g (8 oz) Italian pure pork sausage,
2 large carrots, sliced	or chipolatas
1 large onion, sliced	Salt and freshly ground black pepper
2 garlic cloves, chopped	

Pre-heat the oven to 170°C/325°F/Gas Mark 3. Quarter the cabbage and cut out the tough stem. Shred the leaves finely and pile into a bowl. Pour over enough boiling water to cover, leave for 1 minute, then drain thoroughly. Make a bed of cabbage in the bottom of a casserole.

Heat half the olive oil in a frying pan and brown the partridges briskly all over. Place in the casserole. Fry the lardons in the same fat then add the carrots and onion and fry until golden brown. Scoop into the casserole. Add the garlic, bay leaves, juniper berries, salt and pepper, and then cram in the remaining cabbage. Season again. Add enough hot stock to come about half-way up the cabbage. Cover tightly and cook in the oven for 2 hours.

Meanwhile, if using large sausages, twist the links to form smaller ones. Prick with a fork, then fry briskly in the remaining oil to brown. When the partridges have been cooking for about an hour, tuck the fried sausages down into the cabbage, cover again and return to the oven to complete the cooking.

ROAST PARTRIDGE WITH ROAST PEARS

Partridge goes well with pears and not just on the first day of Christmas. This is a lovely way of dressing up plain roast partridge — the scented sweetness of the hot pear highlights the savouriness of the meat. Since the flesh is lean to the extreme, it is important, especially late in the season, to keep it moist and well basted throughout the cooking period if it is not to dry out and toughen up.

If you are neat-fingered, try to core the pears from the bottom upward, leaving the stalks pertly in place.

SERVES 2

40 g (1½ oz) butter	2 teaspoons redcurrant jelly
2 small partridges	A grating of nutmeg
1 tablespoon oil	300 ml (10 fl oz) perry or cider
4 shallots, halved	2 juniper berries, coarsely crushed
2 pears, cored but not peeled	Salt and freshly ground black pepper
1 tablespoon currants	

Pre-heat the oven to 200°C/400°F/Gas Mark 6. Rub 15 g (½ oz) of the butter over the breast of each partridge. Season with salt and pepper, then place in a roasting tin. Heat the oil over a fierce heat and fry the shallot halves until they are thoroughly browned all over and beginning to soften. Set aside. Score a thin line around the girth of each pear, through the skin only. Mix the currants with the jelly, the remaining butter and a sprinkling of nutmeg and pepper, then stuff into the pears.

Stand the pears in a dish and pour the perry or cider around them. Tuck in the pieces of shallot and the juniper berries too. Cover with a dome of foil and roast in the oven for half an hour. Remove the foil and raise the oven heat to 240°C/475°F/Gas Mark 9.

Pop the partridges into the oven too and roast for 25–30 minutes, basting frequently with their own juices and a spoonful or two from the pears. Check the pears occasionally to make sure they do not overcook. Serve the partridges surrounded with the pears and shallots. Strain the juices from both dishes and mix to serve as a thin gravy, seasoning with salt and pepper.

PERDICES ESTOFADAS CON CHOCOLATE

This is an altogether more robust sort of a stew from Spain. You can use young partridge, but it is admirably suited to older birds. It is a pretty straightforward recipe, the one twist being the final enrichment of the sauce with a square or two of dark chocolate. This adds an almost unfathomable richness and depth. Though in Spain the fried potatoes are considered part and parcel of the dish, I'm not sure that I wouldn't prefer to eat it with a tangled heap of buttered and parsleyed noodles.

SERVES 2-4

2 good-sized partridges, cut in half	300 ml (10 fl oz) dry white wine
About 2 tablespoons olive oil	1 tablespoon sherry vinegar
1 large onion, chopped	20 g (¾ oz) bitter or plain chocolate, grated
8–12 garlic cloves, peeled but whole	Salt and freshly ground black pepper
2 cloves	Fried potato slices to serve, optional
1 bay leaf	

Brown the partridges in 2 tablespoons of oil in a frying pan over a high heat. Transfer to a casserole. Fry the onion in the same oil, adding a little more if needed, then transfer to the casserole. Add all the remaining ingredients except the chocolate and potatoes. Bring up to a gentle simmer, cover tightly and continue simmering for about 45–60 minutes (or longer if necessary), until the partridges are tender. Transfer to a warm serving dish, surround with fried potato slices, if using, and keep warm while you finish the sauce.

Stir the chocolate into the remaining liquid in the pan and simmer for another 2–3 minutes. Rub the contents of the pan through a sieve, pushing through as much of the onion and garlic as you can to thicken and flavour the sauce. Stir, then taste and adjust the seasoning. Pour the sauce over the partridges and potatoes and serve.

Feathered
Game

PARTRIDGE KORMA

The mild, scented creaminess of a korma is perfect for partridge, enhancing without overwhelming. It is best to use young birds for this one, but if you have to take older specimens, stew them gently for longer, increasing the amount of water added to the pan a little so that it doesn't dry out. Be patient when adding the yoghurt to the pan, and don't try to rush it by throwing it in all at once. Do remember to point out to those eating the korma that the whole spices are not meant to be chewed and swallowed.

SERVES 4-6 AS A LIGHT MAIN COURSE

85 ml (3 fl oz) sunflower or vegetable oil

3 partridges, cut into quarters

1 large onion, very finely chopped

2 garlic cloves, crushed

2.5 cm (1 in) piece fresh root ginger, grated

1 cinnamon stick

8 green cardamom pods, bruised

4 cloves

½ dried red chilli

250 ml (8 fl oz) Greek yoghurt

150 ml (5 fl oz) double cream

Salt

Fresh coriander leaves, to serve

Heat 2 tablespoons of the oil in a wide heavy casserole over a high heat and brown the partridge pieces briskly, then set aside. Add the remaining oil to the pan and reduce the heat slightly. Add the onion and fry until golden, stirring frequently. Now add the garlic and ginger and continue stirring until the onion begins to brown. Next put in the cinnamon, cardamom and cloves and continue frying for 3 minutes, stirring all the time. Add the chilli and fry for a few seconds, then stir in a generous heaped tablespoon of the yoghurt. Stir for a minute or so until the moisture has evaporated, then add another tablespoon of yoghurt and stir again for a minute or so. Repeat until all the yoghurt has been incorporated.

Now put in the partridge pieces, salt and a generous 150 ml (5 fl oz) boiling water. Turn the heat down, cover and simmer very gently for half an hour or until the partridge is tender. By now, the sauce should have thickened (don't worry if it looks a bit curdled), with the oil separating out from it. Stir in the cream, let it simmer for another couple of minutes, then taste and adjust the seasonings. Sprinkle with coriander and serve with saffron- or turmeric-scented rice.

SAUTÉED QUAIL WITH LEMON, GARLIC AND GINGER

This is not a dish to be served at a horribly formal best-behaviour kind of a meal. Tackling quail with knife and fork alone is a frustrating experience at the best of times, but particularly in this case. You can get a couple of mouthfuls of the breast meat quite neatly, but that's about it. No, to really enjoy quail, you've got to use fingers and be prepared to get them sticky. That's fine by me — there's nothing I like better than being able to get really stuck in and forget etiquette altogether. As long as there are plenty of napkins to go round, and with luck a couple of finger bowls, I'm more than happy to abandon cutlery.

So, save this recipe for a meal to be shared with good friends or family, when you really want to give them a treat. It is terrifically simple, and wonderfully delicious into the bargain. The thin slices of garlic and ginger cook to a crisp, imparting their flavour to the oil and the tender quail, and then there's the sharpness of the lemon to offset the rest.

One quail each is just enough to make a light main course or a generous starter.

SERVES 4

4 quails	1 cm (½ in) piece fresh root ginger,
Juice of ½ lemon	cut into thin slivers
4 tablespoons olive oil	1 tablespoon finely chopped parsley
3 garlic cloves, sliced	Salt and freshly ground black pepper

Using a sturdy pair of scissors, proper poultry shears or a sharp knife, cut the quails in half. Rub their skin with salt and pepper, then marinate in the lemon juice for half an hour. Drain, reserving the lemon juice, and pat dry.

If you have one large frying pan that will take all the quails in one layer, then whizzo — use that. Otherwise, settle for two frying pans, or cook the quails in two batches.

Heat the oil until hot. Add the garlic and ginger and fry, stirring, for about a minute. Push the flavourings to one side and add the quails, skin-side down. Cook over a medium-hot flame until well browned. Turn down the heat slightly, then turn over the quails and give them another 5 minutes or so until just cooked through. Take the quails, ginger and garlic out of the pan and keep hot. If you're cooking this in two batches, add the second lot to the pan now and cook as the first.

Pour the lemon juice into the pan and let it sizzle for 1 minute, then pour over the quail, sprinkle with parsley and serve, providing plenty of napkins for those sticky fingers.

Roast Quail with Peperonata on Polenta

This is a more substantial quail recipe, the small birds extended with a pepper stew and a mound of golden polenta. The peperonata can be made in advance, but the polenta and quail must be cooked just before serving. For this dish, and in general, I like my polenta quite runny, so I tend to use a fair amount of water in proportion to cornmeal. The proportions given on most packets tend to produce a stiffer mush, however, and since different brands vary radically (from 'instant', to 'fast cooking' to 'slow') it's very hard to be precise about this. In general, the best advice is to go with the packet ratio, increasing the water quantity by about one quarter if you like your polenta on the soft side.

SERVES 4

4 garlic cloves	2 tablespoons olive oil
4 quails	Salt and freshly ground black pepper

For the polenta

Around 225 g (8 oz) polenta	3 tablespoons freshly grated Parmesan
50 g (2 oz) butter	

For the peperonata

1 onion, sliced	450 g (1 lb) good tomatoes, skinned
3 tablespoons olive oil	and roughly chopped
4 red peppers, sliced	1 tablespoon tomato purée
1 garlic clove, crushed	1 teaspoon sugar (unless your tomatoes
	are exceptionally good)

The peperonata will definitely be better made a day in advance if you can. Sauté the onion in the olive oil until lightly browned. Add the peppers and garlic and cook for a further couple of minutes. Cover the pan and let them cook down gently in their own juices for 10 minutes. Now add the remaining ingredients, bring up to the boil, then simmer gently for half an hour, uncovered, stirring occasionally. Taste and adjust the seasoning and re-heat when necessary. Any left-overs will be just as good cold.

Pre-heat the oven to 230°C/450°F/Gas Mark 8. Put a clove of garlic inside each quail. Brush generously with the olive oil and season with salt and pepper. Roast for about 20 minutes.

When it comes to the polenta, check the packet instructions and the ratio of water to polenta (see the introduction to this recipe). I use a slightly unorthodox method of

preparing the cornmeal, but find that it produces fewer lumps. Here it is: put the polenta into a heavy-based pan and gradually stir in the water. Set over a moderate heat and bring up to the boil, stirring. Let it heave and bubble until cooked (again, timing depends on the type of polenta, so refer to the packet) stirring frequently, particularly towards the end of the cooking time. When done, draw off the heat, stir in the butter and Parmesan and place great dollops of it on each plate. Top with warm peperonata and then perch a quail on the top of each heap. Serve a.s.a.p.

QUAGLIE AL DIAVOLO

As with the recipe for sautéed quail, this is a fingers job, par excellence. *The quails, opened out flat, are marinated with paprika and cayenne (al diavolo means devilled, from both the colour and the heat), then grilled. You can use the same recipe for partridge, though you'll have to allow a little more cooking time.*

Either way, these devilish quails are extra nice served with mashed potato and celeriac or parsnip in winter, or with hot rice mixed with a couple of spoonfuls of Greek yoghurt and chopped parsley in summer.

4 quails, spatchcocked	Salt
(see page 220)	

——— *For the marinade* ———

4 tablespoons olive oil	1 teaspoon cayenne pepper
Juice of 1 lemon	1 teaspoon paprika

SERVES 4

Spear the quails on wooden skewers to keep them flat and place in a shallow dish. Mix all the marinade ingredients and pour over the birds. Leave for at least an hour, and a lot longer if possible

Pre-heat the grill thoroughly, then grill the quail, skin-side towards the heat, for about 7–8 minutes. Turn over and grill the bony side for a further 5 minutes, by which time they should be done to a turn. Brush them a couple of times with the marinade as they cook. Season with salt. Eat with the fingers and let the juices run down your chin.

GRILLED WOODPIGEON
ON TOASTED CIABATTA

Finger-lickin' good, suitably messy and not for hoity-toity occasions. The toasted bread catches the juices, but you'll still need to use your fingers for the grilled woodpigeon. Tackle the birds first, wipe your chin with nice napkins, then sink your teeth into the bread and tomato. If you can't get woodpigeon, substitute quails.

SERVES 4

4 woodpigeon, or quails, spatchcocked (see page 220)   2 tomatoes, sliced

1 ciabatta loaf, split in half lengthwise   A pinch of sugar

Olive oil   A small bunch of watercress

Salt and freshly ground black pepper

——— *For the marinade* ———

Juice of 1 lemon   ¼ teaspoon cayenne pepper

4 tablespoons olive oil   A pinch of cinnamon

½ teaspoon dried oregano

Spear the woodpigeon flat on wooden skewers. Mix all the marinade ingredients and pour over the woodpigeon, rubbing it in well. Leave for 1 hour or more. Make sure that at least the last half hour is at room temperature.

Grill the pigeons, breast side to the heat first, for 8 minutes, then turn over and give the other side a further 7–9 minutes. Quickly toast the split sides of the ciabatta and cut each piece in half. Drizzle over a little olive oil to moisten, lay the tomato slices on top and season with a pinch of sugar, salt and pepper, then lay a spatchcocked pigeon on each piece of bread. Tuck a few sprigs of watercress around them and serve immediately.

PIGEON AUX PRUNEAUX

This is a dark, rich game casserole, with a hint of sweetness given by the prunes. Adjust the cooking time to suit your birds; they remain tender when cooked very briefly as in the grilled woodpigeon recipe, but any longer and they toughen up before they soften once more. Some woodpigeon take longer to reach this stage than others.

Topping the list of ingredients here are two pig's trotters. If the thought of eating trotters makes you uneasy, don't worry. Their main purpose is to give the sauce a velvety unctuousness that is quite impossible to reproduce otherwise, so don't leave them out. I like the texture of the trotters themselves, but if you're not so sure about them, remove from the casserole before serving.

SERVES 4

2 pig's trotters	1 cinnamon stick
25 g (1 oz) butter	1 bay leaf
1 tablespoon oil	2 sprigs of thyme
4 woodpigeon	1½ tablespoons flour
12 small pickling onions or shallots, peeled	16 prunes
1 carrot, diced	2 sprigs of parsley
1 celery stick, diced	300 ml (10 fl oz) red wine
100 g (4 oz) streaky bacon, cut into strips	Salt and freshly ground black pepper

Singe or shave any hairs off the pig's trotters. Place them in a pan and cover with water. Bring up to the boil, cover and simmer for 1 hour, skimming any scum from the cooking liquid. Reserve the liquid and trotters.

Melt the butter and oil in a flameproof casserole. Quickly brown the pigeons then remove and reserve. Add the onions, carrot, celery and bacon to the pan with the cinnamon, bay leaf and thyme. Stir to coat with fat, then lower the heat, cover and sweat gently for 10 minutes.

Sprinkle with flour and stir. Return the pigeons to the pan, together with the pig's trotters, prunes, parsley, wine and 600 ml (1 pint) of the trotters' cooking liquid. Season lightly with salt and pepper. Bring up to the boil, cover and simmer gently, turning the pigeons over occasionally, for 45–60 minutes, or longer if necessary, until the birds are tender.

ROAST GROUSE WITH ALL THE TRIMMINGS

This is more or less the classic British way to serve roast grouse. In fact the same accompaniments – gravy, fried crumbs, bread sauce, watercress and redcurrant or rowan jelly – are just as likely to turn up with practically any roast game bird. As a final extra you might like to add some warm potato crisps, home-made, if you have the time, but use bought ones and heat through in the oven if not.

Instead of popping the liver inside the bird, you could fry it briefly in butter, then mash and spread it on pieces of fried bread. Pop the birds onto the bread as soon as they are cooked, while you finish off the gravy and any vegetables that accompany this spread.

If you really can't lay your hands on thin sheets of pork back fat (see page 91), then you could use strips of streaky bacon instead, though the stronger flavour is far more noticeable and intrusive, even with a gamey bird like grouse.

SERVES 4

4 grouse	A handful of watercress
50 g (2 oz) butter	Salt and freshly ground black pepper
4 thin sheets of pork back fat	Redcurrant or rowan jelly, to serve

———— *For the gravy* ————

600 ml (1 pint) game stock	1 bouquet garni (see page 33)
1 carrot	1 small glass port

———— *For the game crumbs* ————

50 g (2 oz) fresh or slightly stale white breadcrumbs	25 g (1 oz) butter

———— *For the bread sauce* ————

300 ml (10 fl oz) full-cream milk	A little grated nutmeg
1 small onion	25 g (1 oz) butter
2 cloves	Cayenne pepper
50 g (2 oz) fresh white breadcrumbs	

The bread sauce can be made the day before and re-heated when needed. You can make it in a pan directly over the heat, but for best results, use a double boiler (a purpose-made one or a bowl set over a pan of simmering water). Put the milk into the bowl or pan with the onion, stuck with the 2 cloves. Bring very slowly up to scalding point, draw off the heat, cover and leave to infuse for half an hour. Discard the onion and add the breadcrumbs, beating well so that they absorb all the milk. Season with nutmeg and salt and stir in the butter. Re-heat when needed and serve with a light dusting of cayenne pepper.

It's worth preparing the stock for the gravy well in advance too. Put the game stock into a pan with any giblets (except the liver) from the grouse, the carrot, and the bouquet garni. Bring up to the boil and boil until reduced by half. Strain.

Pre-heat the oven to 190°C/375°F/Gas Mark 5. Prepare the birds by putting about 15 g (½ oz) butter into the cavity of each one, along with its liver. Season with salt and pepper. Tie a jacket of pork fat over the breast and upper legs with string. Roast for 35–45 minutes, removing their jacket of fat for the last 10 minutes so that they can brown.

Meanwhile, fry the crumbs in the butter over a moderate heat, stirring constantly so that they colour evenly. Tip into a bowl lined with kitchen paper (or a doily, if you like), as soon as they are a good hazelnut brown. The paper absorbs some of their fat, making them less greasy – discard the kitchen paper before serving, but if the edges of the doily don't look too grease-spattered and you like the frills, leave it in place.

Once the grouse are done, transfer to a warm serving dish and keep warm. Spoon as much fat as you can from any juices in the roasting tin, and place over the hob. Add the reduced stock and bring up to the boil, stirring. Stir in the port and simmer for a few minutes to reduce and drive off the alcohol. Season and strain into a gravy boat. Tuck tufts of watercress around the grouse and serve up forthwith, presenting crumbs, gravy, redcurrant or rowan jelly and the bread sauce alongside.

ROAST GROUSE WITH BLACKBERRY SAUCE

The seasons for blackberries and grouse get going at vaguely the same time, give or take a few weeks and depending on the weather. This is very handy as they go together rather well. The fruitiness of the blackberries is strong enough to match the full flavour of the grouse. If you have time to go out gathering, use wild blackberries. Cultivated ones never quite match up when it comes to taste, though they do have the advantage of being far less pippy. Crème de mûre, blackberry liqueur, is sold in some supermarkets and off licences, but the more common crème de cassis, blackcurrant liqueur, makes a good stand-in.

SERVES 2

2 grouse	Salt and freshly
25 g (1 oz) butter	ground black pepper

—————— For the sauce ——————

300 ml (10 fl oz) game or chicken stock	½ tablespoon sugar
3 tablespoons crème de mûre	100 g (4 oz) blackberries
or crème de cassis	15 g (½ oz) cold butter, diced

Pre-heat the oven to 190°C/375°F/Gas Mark 5. Smear the breasts of the grouse liberally with the butter then lay a strip of non-stick baking parchment or greaseproof paper over the top and secure with string. Place in a roasting tin and roast for 35–45 minutes.

Once they are done, place on a serving dish and keep warm. Skim as much fat as possible from the juices in the roasting tin, then place over the hob. Add the stock, the crème de mûre or the crème de cassis and the sugar. Bring up to the boil, stirring and scraping in all the brown residues on the bottom of the pan. Boil until reduced by two-thirds.

Add the blackberries, salt and pepper and simmer for 30 seconds or so, then add the diced butter a few pieces at a time, shaking the pan so that they melt into and thicken the juices. Spoon the blackberries and a little of the sauce around the grouse and serve the remaining sauce separately.

ROAST MALLARD WITH CRANBERRY AND ORANGE GRAVY

In this recipe I've used both fresh cranberries and cranberry juice (which is now available from many supermarkets) to make a gravy to partner roast mallard. It's a delicious combination of tart fruitiness with the gamey flavour of wild duck.

SERVES 2-3

1 mallard	75 g (3 oz) cranberries
A generous 15 g (½ oz) butter	Juice of 1 orange
300 ml (10 fl oz) game or chicken stock	15 g (½ oz) sugar
1 tablespoon flour	Salt and freshly ground black pepper
150 ml (5 fl oz) cranberry juice	

Pre-heat the oven to 230°C/450°F/Gas Mark 8. Season the mallard well, then smear the breast with the butter. Sit in a roasting tin and pour half the stock around it. Roast in the oven for 25–35 minutes, depending on how rare you like it. Baste frequently with its own juices, adding a little more stock if the pan threatens to burn dry. When the duck is done, transfer to a warm serving dish and keep warm in the oven.

Pour the roasting juices into a jug, leaving just enough to moisten the base of the tin. Let the juices settle for a couple of minutes and skim off any fat. Place the tin over a low heat and sprinkle with the flour. Stir until lightly browned, scraping in all the roasting residues. Add all the remaining ingredients to the pan, including the cooking juices. Bring up to the boil, stirring constantly, and simmer for a few minutes until thickened. Taste and adjust the seasoning.

Roast Mallard with Orange Crumb Crust

Orange doesn't only go with domesticated duck – it transfers well to the leaner flesh of wild duck as well. In this recipe it flavours a crust of crumbs encasing a mallard. The crumbs are heavily laden with butter, which keeps the bird from drying out in the oven.

SERVES 2–3

1 mallard	1 tablespoon finely chopped parsley
1 small eating apple, quartered and cored	Finely grated zest of ½ orange
40 g (1½ oz) butter	1 tablespoon orange juice
50 g (2 oz) fresh white breadcrumbs	Salt and freshly ground black pepper

Pre-heat the oven to 230°C/450°F/Gas Mark 8. Skin the mallard and place the apple quarters in the cavity. Melt the butter and cool until tepid. Mix the breadcrumbs with the parsley, orange zest, salt and plenty of pepper. Add the butter and the orange juice and mix evenly so that all the crumbs are well soaked in butter.

Press the crumb mixture firmly over the mallard, making sure that the breast in particular is well coated. Set the bird in a roasting tin and roast for 25–35 minutes, depending on how well cooked you like your duck. Rest for 5 minutes in the oven with the heat turned off and door slightly ajar, before serving.

WILD DUCK WITH LENTILS

It doesn't have to be duck — other game birds would do just fine — but the combination of the dark, savoury duck meat with the melting lentils is an out-and-out winner. This is my idea of the perfect winter lunchtime dish. My version of this time-honoured partnership is adapted from Good Game *by Victoria Jardine-Paterson and Colin McKelvie, published by Swan Hill Press.*

Though I haven't tried it, it occurs to me that it might be almost as good with domesticated duck. One large one should be ample. Prick the skin and roast for 25–30 minutes.

SERVES 4 - 6

2 mallard	1 carrot, quartered
¼ lemon	1 bouquet garni (see page 33)
2 garlic cloves, crushed	100 g (4 oz) lardons (see page 102)
3 tablespoons olive oil	12 pearl onions, skinned
120 ml (4 fl oz) dry white wine	A sprig of parsley
225 g (8 oz) brown or green lentils	50 ml (2 fl oz) duck, game or
1 garlic clove, peeled but whole	rich chicken stock
1 onion, halved	Salt and freshly ground black pepper

Pre-heat the oven to 230°C/450°F/Gas Mark 8. Rub the inside and outside of the two mallard with the lemon quarter, crushed garlic, salt and pepper. Let them stand for half an hour if you have the time, then brush generously with some of the oil. Place in a heat-proof dish, pour the wine around them and roast in the oven for 20 minutes.

Meanwhile, put the lentils into a pan with the whole clove of garlic, the halved onion, quartered carrot and bouquet garni. Add enough water to cover thoroughly and bring gently up to the boil. Simmer quietly for 15–30 minutes (this will vary according to the type of lentils), until almost cooked, skimming off any scum. Drain.

Fry the lardons briskly in the remaining oil until browned. Scoop out and transfer to a casserole. Keep the heat high and fry the pearl onions fiercely in the same fat until browned all over and softening.

Put the ducks into the casserole with their pan juices, then spoon the fried pearl onions around them. Add the sprig of parsley. Spoon in the lentils (with all their bits of carrot and onion) and pour in the stock. Bring up to the boil, reduce the heat, cover and simmer for a further 30–40 minutes. Taste and adjust the seasoning. To serve, ladle the lentils out onto a serving dish and pop the ducks on top, either in their full glory, or quartered if that seems more appropriate (it may well be easier to hack them into portions in the privacy of the kitchen than to attempt carving them at the table).

Furred
Game

Furred Game

For centuries deer hunting has been the preserve of king and aristocracy and with that went the pleasure of feasting on the meat of the catch, the venison. Wild boar, long extinct in this country, hunted out of sight, was also fair game for the powerful. The poor had to make do with the smaller, less regal animals that scampered and streaked through the countryside, and usually that meant rabbit and hare.

These days matters are quite different. Venison is shedding its exclusivity, wild boar is making a reappearance, while hare, the only one of the foursome that is not farmed at all, is increasing in price. Only wild rabbit stays relatively cheap, as the price of domesticated rabbit inches up. The poor old poacher has been quite done out of his job.

The thought of cooking furred game gives many people the heebie-jeebies, but it shouldn't. Venison has a few more variables than beef, but fundamentally the approach is much the same (and most venison is no stronger in flavour, either). Wild boar requires barely any more application than cooking a decent piece of free-range pork, which in itself is far simpler than cooking over-lean mass-produced pork. Domesticated rabbit can be compared to chicken, wild rabbit just needs patient slow casseroling. The only furred game that requires a touch of fortitude is hare, a bloody meat if ever I saw one, and with a strong smell that belies its superb flavour. Still, if you can't face handling it, most butchers will do all the preparation, leaving only a few moments of discomfort for the uneasy cook as it goes into the pan.

You can be reasonably certain that the venison and domesticated rabbit sold in supermarkets will be tender and in good condition, though I would warn against frozen imported rabbit which I've always found unbelievably tasteless. However, as with feathered game, your greatest ally when it comes to choosing any of these animals is a good game dealer. He or she will be able to advise on the merits of farmed versus wild, this breed or that, hanging and depth of flavour, and give you an idea of age where appropriate. Use his knowledge and expertise as much as you can and never be wary of showing your ignorance. I've learned more from good butchers (and still do) than I ever have from books!

HANGING

Practically all meat needs hanging, but for wild game it is essential, with one exception and that is the very first grouse of the season. The race to get the earliest grouse onto the plate on the 'glorious twelfth', the very day the season opens, prevents hanging, though I think that many keen grouse eaters would prefer to wait a day or two for properly hung grouse.

When meat is first slaughtered it is tough and lacking in flavour. The function of hanging is to break down and soften muscle fibre and while doing so, to develop flavour in much the same way as you would expect the taste of cheese or wine to improve with ageing.

Hanging is not the same as rotting, though it is related and both processes are brought about by the meat's own enzymes, released and free to work changes on the flesh. To hang meat properly and safely demands a good deal of skill. Conditions are crucial. Temperature and humidity levels need to be carefully controlled to prevent the growth of unwanted bacteria (i.e. rotting). Length of hanging time will vary according to the type of meat and to the taste of the consumer. An awful lot of mass-produced meat is hung for only the minimum of time, which accounts to some degree for its muted flavour.

To hang game, you don't need to have a purpose-built thermostatically controlled room. Many people hang their own game birds in an outhouse, hung high and well away from possible marauders. A good flow of air is essential. Under these circumstances, hanging time will depend as much on weather as on the type of bird.

Furred Game

VENISON

(Season: varies according to breed and sex. Farmed venison is available all year round.)

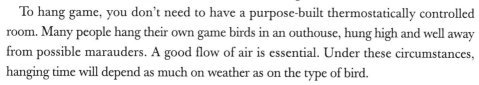

For years I've been convinced that wild venison was inevitably gamier than farmed. Certainly, most of the wild meat that I've eaten has had the kind of depth of flavour that I love, making most of the farmed venison seem insipid in comparison. As it turns out, this discrepancy in flavour is not the inevitable outcome of lifestyle, but has more to do with husbandry, age and handling after slaughter. Wild venison can be as mild as a daisy, while farmed can be intensely gamey. It just so happens that most of the time the reverse is true. Gaminess is not to everyone's taste it must be said, but I happen to like it in moderation. Tell your supplier what you want and he should be able to oblige.

Wild venison also has a reputation for being tough. This has more to do with age than anything else. A springy young beast will always be more tender than an old codger. Well-judged hanging diminishes toughness, but can't do away with it altogether. Meat from older animals (farmed or wild) is best casseroled or pot-roasted slowly to break down the fibres.

Flavour, as well as tenderness or toughness, is dependent, too, on species. Red deer has the most forceful flavour but is probably the chewiest. Roe deer (which in France is given the specific name *chevreuil* on menus) is the most tender and has an excellent flavour, not too strong, but nowhere near insipid – a combination which makes it the hot favourite. Fallow deer fall somewhere between the two.

Having said all that, farmed venison is still a less daunting meat to approach for those who are not old hands at cooking game. The variables are less variable, the product is

Furred Game

closer to being uniform but not, I'm glad to say, always exactly the same. The taste is usually no more pronounced than that of beef. As with any animal, tenderness depends on the cut, but since you can be pretty sure that it is young meat, you can be certain that the choice cuts will not strain the jaws of family or guests.

All venison is lean, which is currently being plugged as a major selling point. The rub is that you will probably have to add fat in one way or another to keep it moist, particularly if roasting. So it's not necessarily quite as virtuous as you might have thought.

CUTS AND COOKING

Roasting

The haunch (leg) is the classic cut, and a magnificent sight it can be too. Loin and saddle (double loin on the bone) are the other two prime roasting joints. I've also found boned rolled shoulder makes a good roasting joint and is much cheaper than the rest!

Frying

Saddle steaks (medallions) and leg steaks are perfect for quick pan-frying, as are venison chops, and should always be cooked pink. Cook the pinkness out and they will be tough and dry.

Grilling

Since venison is such a lean meat, great care must be taken when grilling. Baste frequently and don't overcook. Steaks and chops, as long as they are not cut too thin, can be grilled.

Stewing and casseroling

Leg makes marvellous stews and needs relatively little cooking time. Shoulder, neck and breast are cheaper, with just as much flavour, though they require a little more time in the pot.

ROASTING VENISON

The best advice I have come across on roasting venison is in Julia Drysdale's *Classic Game Cookery*, which actually lives up to its name. I quote: 'Venison goes on cooking itself long after it comes out of the oven. If it is a good enough haunch to be roasted then it should not be overcooked. I usually panic when I see the first slice, thinking it is far too bloody, but by the time I start to eat it, it appears rather grey.'

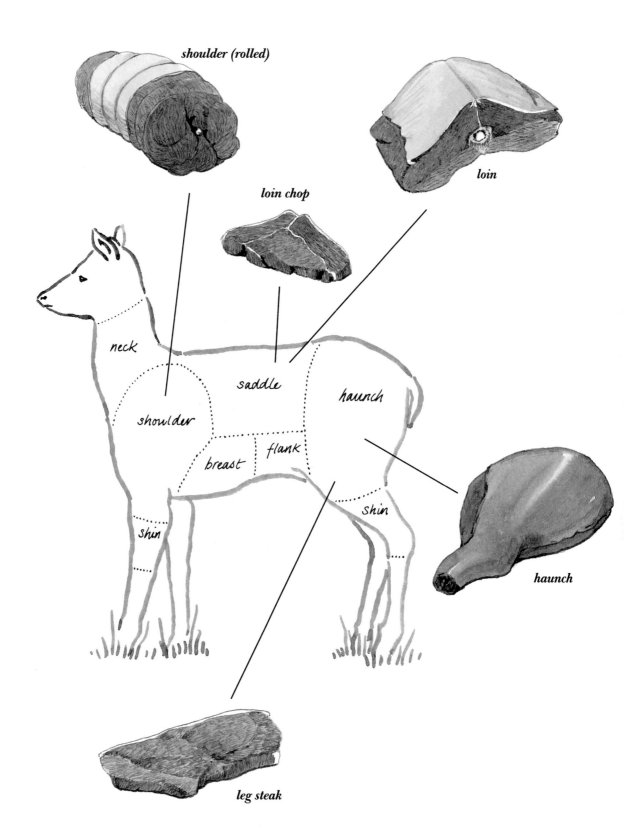

shoulder (rolled)

loin chop

loin

neck

saddle

haunch

shoulder

flank

breast

shin

shin

haunch

leg steak

Furred
Game

Since venison is a lean meat, it benefits greatly from larding. In other words, threading thin strips of pork fat (see page 91) through the meat with a larding needle. If you don't have a larding needle, then make slits in the meat with a thin-bladed knife and push the fat in with the handle of a teaspoon. The joint will also need a generous smearing of butter or olive oil. General opinion seems to be that marinating is superfluous with a really good young haunch of roe venison. Besides, to make a noticeable difference to the texture you would have to marinate it for almost a week. A shorter dunking in a marinade may add extra flavours and help to keep the exterior from drying out.

Back to Julia Drysdale, who suggests roasting the prepared joint in a moderately hot oven (190°C/375°F/Gas Mark 5). 'Baste frequently – preferably every 10 minutes. It should take about 15 minutes per 450 g (1 lb) if it is large and 20 minutes per 450 g (1 lb) if it is smaller (under 1.6 kg or 4 lb). This should make it slightly pink.'

Carving a haunch of venison

Hold the meat securely with a carving fork and slice it horizontally, parallel to the bone.

WILD BOAR

True wild boar was driven into extinction in this country some 300 years ago, though it still roams and rootles in parts of France, Italy, Germany, and other European countries. When you get the real McCoy, as you may occasionally on the continent, it is a fully flavoured, dark, rich meat.

In this country 'wild' boar is farmed, though not in any great quantity. Some of it will be pure-bred from continental stocks, but a good deal is cross-bred with domesticated breeds of pig. If you want to be sure that you are purchasing pure-bred meat, then ask if it comes from stock that has been registered with the British Wild Boar Association, who will accept nothing less.

Pure- or cross-bred, the animals will have been raised in huge enclosures with ample space to rootle and snuffle at a certain degree of liberty. They get a fair amount of exercise, but nothing to match the scope of the continental wild boar. I've yet to try British wild boar that has the kind of gamey flavour of real wild boar, though to be honest I can't claim any depth of knowledge in this matter as my experience has been limited. The boar that I have cooked and eaten has tasted very good, but really not much more than a marginally emphasized replica of first-rate free-range traditional-breed pork.

This gives the lead when it comes to the cooking of the meat. Many of the wonderful European ways of cooking wild boar are designed to fit a very gamey flesh. Some of them are just too overwhelming for our own version. On the whole, I would advise treating it like the best pork, making allowances, particularly if roasting, for the fact that it may be leaner.

Furred Game

RABBIT

Let me be honest and up-front about this. I'm not too keen on wild rabbit. I don't like the flavour much and it is tough. Washing, or marinating in vinegar, will dampen the flavour. Lazy casseroling will tenderize it. Even so, I'd rather have domesticated rabbit any day.

Domesticated rabbit bears more resemblance to chicken, though the flavour is detectably different. It is tender enough to roast – the saddle or back, on its own, is a real treat – or even to grill if it has been well marinated and is frequently basted. It is excellent in casseroles and stews, where it combines just as well with creamy white sauces as with darker tomato or wine-based sauces. It is, as they say, a most versatile meat.

HARE

Hare has a gamey flavour and an even gamier smell, but don't let that put you off. It is a delicious meat when properly cooked. Steaming dark jugged hare served with mashed potato, or thick, rich Italian hare sauce over pasta – the very thought makes my mouth water. Hare makes some of the most superb warming winter dishes, scenting the house as they cook with the most appetizing, savoury smell.

Hare is no longer as cheap as it once was, but I still reckon it is a bargain. One plump animal will feed six people comfortably. However, it is horribly messy and bloody to prepare. I'm not very squeamish, but I still try to get it over and done with as quickly as possible. As a result, I usually ask the butcher to prepare and joint it for me fully, though technically speaking it is no different from chopping up a rabbit.

If you don't use the liver to thicken the sauce (mashed up and stirred in towards the

end), save it to make liver pâté, in the same way as you make chicken liver pâté, adding a little more butter and smearing very thinly on toast to allow for its powerful flavour.

JOINTING A RABBIT OR HARE

Find the v-shaped pelvis at the base of the spine. Cut through the meat that lies between the pelvis and the leg, right to the spine. Locate the leg joint, bend the leg back to loosen it then slice through on each side releasing the two meaty hind legs. For casseroling, you may want to divide each hind leg into two parts.

Locate the leg joint between the front legs and body, bend the legs back to loosen and then sever.

With a sharp knife cut off the bony bit at the rear end of the saddle (the fleshy back) and cut off the ribcage from the other end. Trim away the belly flaps – save all of these bits for the stockpot. You can either leave the saddle whole for roasting or chop it firmly in half or thirds (across the body) for casseroling. Poultry shears make an easier job of this as you will have to cut through the backbone.

1. *Cut through the meat that lies between the pelvis and the leg on each side, then cut off the hind legs.*

2. *Bend back the front legs to loosen them, then cut them off.*

3. *Cut off the bony bit at the rear end of the saddle and cut off the ribcage from the other end.*

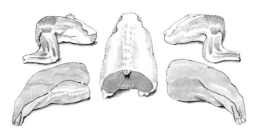

4. *You will now have 5 pieces: the saddle, hindquarters and forequarters.*

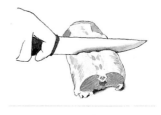

5. *Either leave the saddle whole for roasting or divide it into 2 or 3 portions for casseroling.*

CASSEROLE OF RABBIT WITH WHITE WINE AND MUSHROOMS

The French are very keen on rabbit. In the small village that I know well in France, many people raise their own rabbits for the table. I often used to see our neighbour out cutting swathes of grass from the verges to take home to feed her small livestock. In this recipe with distinctly French overtones, the jointed rabbit is bathed in a creamy sauce flavoured with mushrooms. I use shiitake mushrooms if I can get them, but ordinary button mushrooms will do fine.

SERVES 4

1 rabbit, cut into 10 pieces	600 ml (1 pint) chicken stock
225 g (8 oz) mushrooms, button or,	1 bay leaf
better still, shiitake	2 tablespoons chopped parsley
16 pearl onions	40 g (1½ oz) beurre manié (half butter, half
Seasoned flour, for dusting	flour mashed thoroughly together)
2 tablespoons oil	150 ml (5 fl oz) crème fraîche or double cream
25 g (1 oz) butter	A squeeze of lemon juice
120 ml (4 fl oz) dry white wine	Salt and freshly ground black pepper

Either get the butcher to joint the rabbit for you or joint as on page 252, cutting all 4 legs into 2 pieces and the saddle in half. Quarter the button mushrooms or slice the shiitakes thickly. Top and tail the pearl onions, cover with boiling water and leave for 30 seconds, then drain and skin.

Toss the rabbit in seasoned flour. Heat half the oil with half the butter in a wide frying pan and brown the rabbit in two batches. Transfer to a flame-proof casserole. Add a little more butter and oil to the pan and sauté the mushrooms over a high heat until browned. Scoop out into the casserole. Add the remaining oil and butter to the frying pan and brown the pearl onions. Into the casserole with those, too.

Pour the wine into the frying pan and bring up to the boil, scraping in the residues from frying. Boil until reduced by half. Pour over the rabbit then add the stock, bay leaf, half the parsley, salt and pepper. Bring up to the boil, half cover and simmer for 45 minutes or until the rabbit is tender. Scoop out the rabbit, mushrooms and onions and keep warm.

Pour the juices into a wide frying pan and boil hard until reduced by half. Reduce the heat to a bare simmer and add the beurre manié in small knobs, stirring it in. Cook for a further 3–4 minutes without boiling. Stir in the cream and a touch of lemon juice. Taste and adjust the seasoning. Pour over the rabbit and scatter with the remaining parsley.

SADDLE OF RABBIT WITH SUN-DRIED TOMATOES EN CROÛTE

You can bone out the saddles to give neat tiny little fillets, but in fact it is much easier to handle them whole – just warn your fellow diner that there is a bone hidden in the centre of the pastry parcel. Save the legs to make a pie like the one on page 256 and treat yourselves to this most delicious way of presenting the choicest part of a rabbit.

SERVES 2

A little sunflower oil	225 g (8 oz) puff pastry
2 saddles of rabbit	6 pieces of sun-dried tomato, cut into strips
35 g (a generous 1 oz) butter	2 sage leaves
2 shallots, sliced	1 egg yolk
1 garlic clove, finely chopped	Salt and freshly ground black pepper

Pre-heat the oven to 220°C/425°F/Gas Mark 7. Heat a little sunflower oil in a frying pan over a high heat and brown the meat all over as quickly as possible, then set aside.

Reduce the heat under the pan and let it cool for a few minutes. Add half the butter and sauté the shallots until tender. Add the garlic, cook for a minute or two longer and then draw off the heat.

Put a baking tray in the oven to warm. Roll the pastry out thinly into a rectangle, then divide into two. Make a bed of fried shallots in the centre of each piece of pastry, dot with the remaining butter and scatter with the sun-dried tomatoes. Snuggle the rabbit saddles on top, season with salt and pepper and finally lay the sage leaves on the saddles. Bring the pastry up over the meat, moistening the edges with a little water, and seal neatly. Turn over so that the joins are underneath. Place on a lightly dampened baking tray (not the one in the oven) and, if you have time, let the parcels rest for half an hour or more in the fridge. Bring back to room temperature before cooking and brush with the egg yolk.

Pop into the oven, setting the tray with the parcels of rabbit on the hot baking tray for an instant blast of heat. Bake for 15 minutes until puffed and golden brown. Serve hot or warm.

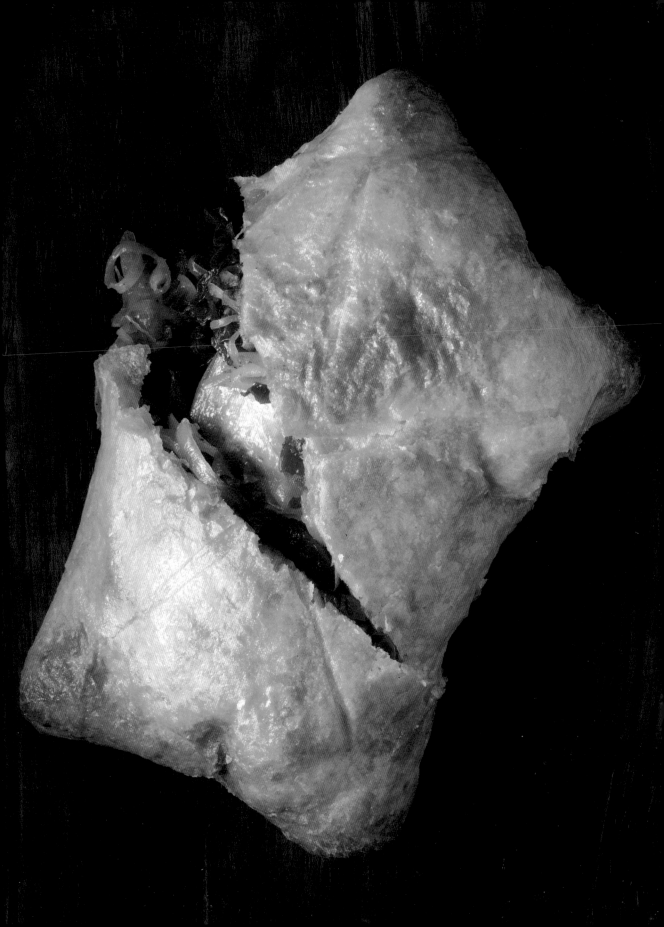

Furred
Game

RABBIT AND CELERIAC PIE

The light meat of rabbit goes very well with celeriac, that ungainly knobbly root vegetable. Together they make a sensational filling for a pie. Either use the meat from a whole rabbit or the leg meat from two rabbits (the exact quantity is neither here nor there in something like this), saving the saddles to roast on their own or use in the recipe on page 254.

SERVES 6

1 rabbit, jointed, or the hind and back legs of 2 rabbits

Seasoned flour, for dusting

2 tablespoons sunflower oil

25 g (1 oz) butter

100 g (4 oz) streaky bacon, cut into strips

1 onion, chopped

1 celery stick, diced

1 large carrot, diced

1 small celeriac, peeled, diced and turned in lemon juice

1 bouquet garni (see page 33)

85 ml (3 fl oz) Noilly Prat

450 ml (15 fl oz) strong chicken or rabbit stock

Freshly grated nutmeg

150 ml (5 fl oz) double cream

A dash of lemon juice

225 g (8 oz) shortcrust pastry

1 egg yolk, beaten with 1 tablespoon water

Salt and freshly ground black pepper

Strip all the meat from the bones and cut into 2.5 cm (1 in) cubes, more or less. Dust with flour and brown briskly in half the oil and butter in a frying pan, then transfer to a saucepan.

Add the remaining oil and butter to the frying pan and fry the bacon in the fat. Scoop out and add to the rabbit. Now pop in the onion, celery, carrot and celeriac, together with the bouquet garni. Turn to coat, then cover and sweat over a low heat for 15 minutes, stirring once or twice. Pour in the Noilly Prat, raise the heat and boil until it has almost evaporated. Sprinkle over a tablespoon of flour, stir well and gradually stir in the stock. Bring up to the boil and pour over the rabbit. Season with salt, pepper and a little nutmeg. Simmer gently for 30 minutes until the rabbit is almost done and the liquid much reduced. Stir in the cream, and again let it bubble down until the sauce is fairly thick and unctuous. Taste and adjust the seasonings, adding a dash of lemon juice. (You could serve it just as it is now, never mind the pastry!)

Pre-heat the oven to 200°C/400°F/Gas Mark 6.

Spoon the rabbit and celeriac stew into a pie dish. I use a 30 cm (12 in) oval dish, but whatever the shape, the filling should come up to within 1 cm (½ in) of the rim. Roll out the pastry to form a lid for the pie, then cut off a long narrow ribbon of pastry all round the edge. Using the egg yolk and water wash, moisten the edges of the dish and lay the ribbon of pastry round the edges. Brush with more egg and water wash, then lay the lid over the top. Trim and crimp the edges neatly, pressing down gently to seal. Make a hole in the centre to allow the steam to escape, give the top of the pastry a brush with the egg wash and bake for 20–30 minutes until nicely browned. Serve steaming hot.

LAPIN À LA MOUTARDE

Lapin à la Moutarde is one of France's most popular ways to cook rabbit and there are many versions of the recipe. The one I use is based on a recipe I cut out of a French children's magazine (I still have a scrapbook filled with their recipes, which were always first rate) when I was about 10 years old. It works so well that I've never seen any reason to try other methods! The heat of the oven kills the heat of the mustard, so if you want a slight tingle, stir in a little more at the end.

SERVES 4

3 tablespoons Dijon mustard	1 onion, sliced
2 tablespoons sunflower oil	120 ml (4 fl oz) water
1 rabbit, jointed or 4 rabbit joints, weighing	50 ml (2 fl oz) dry white wine
about 1 kg (2 lb) in total	150 ml (5 fl oz) double cream
1 large carrot, sliced	Salt and freshly ground black pepper

Pre-heat the oven to 200°C/400°F/Gas Mark 6. Mix the mustard with the oil, salt and pepper and smear all over the rabbit joints. Make a bed of the carrot and onion in a roasting tin that's just large enough to take the rabbit joints in a snug single layer. Pour in the water, then lay the rabbit pieces on top.

Roast for 25–30 minutes, basting frequently with the pan juices, until the joints are cooked through. Test by piercing the thickest part of a thigh with a skewer. If the juices run clear, then they are ready. If they are still pinkish, pop them back into the oven for another 5–10 minutes, then test again.

Lift the rabbit joints onto a warm serving dish and keep hot. Pick out the vegetables and discard. Set the roasting tin on the hob and pour in the wine. Bring up to the boil, stirring, and boil hard until reduced by about two-thirds. Now add the cream, stir well and bring back to the boil. Let it bubble for a few more minutes, then taste and adjust the seasonings. Pour over the rabbit and serve.

MY MOTHER-IN-LAW'S
HARE CASSEROLE

When my mother-in-law came to stay one Christmas, she arrived bearing a tupperware container full of hare marinating in red wine. She proceeded to make the most superb hare stew. This is not her exact recipe but it replicates roughly what I saw as I watched her work. My only input was the left-over gravy from the turkey, which was thrown in to aid and abet the sauce!

SERVES 6

1 hare, jointed	1 sprig of thyme
1 onion, sliced	1 bay leaf
2 carrots, cut into pieces about 5 cm (2 in)	6 juniper berries, crushed
long, and quartered lengthwise	450 ml (15 fl oz) good game stock or
2 tablespoons olive oil	left-over thin gravy
25 g (1 oz) butter	1–2 tablespoons tomato ketchup
Flour, for dusting	1 tablespoon redcurrant jelly
1 sprig of rosemary	Salt and freshly ground black pepper

——— *For the marinade* ———

2 glasses of red wine	2 bay leaves
1 carrot, sliced	1 sprig of thyme
1 onion, sliced	4 juniper berries, lightly crushed

Mix the marinade ingredients and pour over the hare. Leave to marinate for at least 12 hours and up to 2 days, turning occasionally. Take the hare out of the marinade and dry thoroughly. Strain the marinade and reserve.

Fry the onion and carrots in half the oil and butter until browned and tender. Transfer to a casserole. If necessary, add a little more oil and butter to the pan. Dust the hare in flour and fry briskly until browned, in batches if necessary. Add them to the casserole and tuck in the herbs and juniper berries with them. Sprinkle over a tablespoon of flour.

Pre-heat the oven to 150°C/300°F/Gas Mark 2. Pour the excess fat out of the pan and add the marinade. Bring up to the boil, scraping in all the frying residues, then pour over the hare. Bring the stock to the boil in the frying pan and add that too. Finally, season and stir in the ketchup. Cover and transfer to the oven and cook gently for 3–4 hours, until the meat is so tender it is practically falling off the bone. Stir in the redcurrant jelly, then taste and adjust the seasoning. Serve with mashed potato and braised red cabbage.

CZECH HARE AND PLUM STEW

This is an adaptation of a Czech recipe for hare stew with a plum sauce. When testing it, I made two versions, one with cream, the other without, and couldn't decide which I liked best, so I give them both. The first is fruitier, the second richer.

SERVES 4–6

1 medium onion, grated	3 allspice berries, crushed
3 rashers green streaky bacon, diced	1 bay leaf
50 g (2 oz) butter	2 wide strips lemon zest
1 hare, cut into 12 pieces, i.e. each leg halved	2 tablespoons redcurrant jelly
and the saddle cut into 4	1 tablespoon tomato purée
5 black peppercorns, crushed	Salt and freshly ground black pepper

——— *For version 1* ———

450 g (1 lb) purple plums, pitted and quartered

——— *For version 2* ———

275 g (10 oz) purple plums, pitted	150 ml (5 fl oz) crème fraîche
and quartered	or double cream

Both versions

Cook the onion and bacon gently in the butter in a flame-proof casserole without browning. Add the hare, spices, bay leaf and lemon zest, salt and 300 ml (10 fl oz) of water. Cover and simmer very gently until the hare is tender – about 1½ hours – turning the pieces occasionally.

Meanwhile, place the plums in a pan with just enough water to prevent them from burning. Simmer gently until the fruit is soft, then pass through a sieve. Add this purée to the hare, together with the redcurrant jelly and tomato purée.

Version 1

Stir well, then simmer for a final 15 minutes. Lift the meat out of the pot and keep hot. Strain the sauce, taste and adjust the seasonings, then pour over the hare and serve.

Version 2

Stir well, then stir in the cream. It may curdle at first, but don't be alarmed. Raise the heat slightly, let it bubble and cook down. Stir occasionally and after 10–15 minutes you will have a rich, unctuous sauce. Lift the meat out of the pot and keep hot. Strain the sauce, taste and adjust the seasonings, then pour over the hare and serve.

ESTREMOZ DRY HARE SOUP

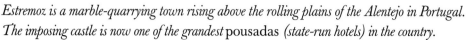

Estremoz is a marble-quarrying town rising above the rolling plains of the Alentejo in Portugal. The imposing castle is now one of the grandest pousadas *(state-run hotels) in the country.*

We ate in the baronial dining room. The game season had begun a few days earlier, and this 'dry soup' was the star turn of the meal. It's more of a stew than a soup – just enough liquid is added to the finished dish to moisten the underneath of the bread topping while the upper part bakes to a crisp. Save the remaining stock to serve as a soup or to add to another dish. I buy salted pork fat from an Italian delicatessen, which also sells Spanish chorizo, *not quite the same as Portuguese* chouriço, *but a fair substitute. Instead of hare, you could make the 'soup' with a brace of mallard.*

SERVES 6 AS A MAIN COURSE

1 hare or 2 mallards, cut into pieces	6 large Savoy cabbage leaves
1 onion, quartered	150 g (5 oz) *chouriço*, or *chorizo*, skinned
150 ml (5 fl oz) dry white wine	and thickly sliced
2 sprigs of parsley	8 sprigs of mint
100 g (4 oz) smoked or salted pork fat	4 large thick slices of stale bread, halved
(see above), sliced	Salt and freshly
2 large carrots	ground black pepper

Put the hare or mallards into a large pan with the onion, wine, parsley, pork fat, salt and pepper. Cover generously with water and bring up to the boil. Skim off any scum and simmer for 45 minutes.

Cut the carrots into 4 cm (1½ in) lengths and quarter lengthwise. Shred the cabbage leaves thickly, discarding the thicker part of the stem. Add the carrots and *chouriço* to the pan with half the mint and simmer for 15 minutes before adding the cabbage. Continue cooking for a further 15 minutes. Remove from the heat and leave to cool. Strain and reserve the cooking liquid. Pick out the hare or mallard and strip the meat from the bones. Discard the bones and the bedraggled bits of parsley and mint.

Pre-heat the oven to 220°C/425°F/Gas Mark 7.

Arrange the vegetables and pork fat in a wide casserole and lay the meat and remaining mint on top. Add enough of the cooking liquid to barely cover the meat and vegetables. Cover with foil and bake for 20 minutes. Lay the bread on top and press down lightly. Return to the oven for 20–30 minutes until the bread is browned. Serve immediately.

ITALIAN PASTA WITH HARE SAUCE

It's worth taking the time to make this sauce properly – it benefits from being cooked a day in advance, if that's any help – since it is so wonderfully rich and earthy. It comes from Tuscany where it is ladled over wide noodles called pappardelle. Here, tagliatelle may have to stand in.

SERVES 6

1 hare, jointed	3 sprigs of thyme
2 tablespoons olive oil	1 level tablespoon flour
75 g (3 oz) pancetta (or unsmoked streaky	50 ml (2 fl oz) Marsala
bacon), cut into narrow strips	120 ml (4 fl oz) red wine
1 onion, chopped	450 ml (15 fl oz) good game or veal stock
1 celery stick, finely diced	A squeeze of lemon juice
1 carrot, finely diced	Freshly grated nutmeg
1 garlic clove	Salt and freshly ground black pepper

—— To serve ——

450 g (1 lb) pappardelle or tagliatelle	A knob of butter
A little chopped parsley	Freshly grated Parmesan

Strip the meat off the bones of the hare and cut it into small strips, around 2.5 cm (1 in) long – a messy business. You can cook the whole pieces in the stew and strip the meat off later, but all in all it takes much longer that way.

Heat the olive oil in wide frying pan or saucepan and fry the pancetta until browned. Set aside. Now add the onion, celery and carrot and fry until browned – this may take some time, but keep the heat high and stir every couple of minutes. Next, add the garlic, the hare meat and the thyme. Stir for 2–3 minutes, then sprinkle over the flour. Stir again and moisten with the Marsala and wine. Mix well and bring up to the boil. Now add the stock and season with salt and pepper. Bring up to the boil again, then reduce the heat to low, cover and let it cook gently for 2 hours until the meat is so tender that it is collapsing. Stir and check every now and then, adding a little extra liquid if necessary.

By the time it is done, the sauce should be rich and dark and thick and creamy. If needs be, help it along a bit by mashing down some of the bits of meat and veg with a fork. Add a squeeze of lemon juice and a scraping of nutmeg to lift the flavours then taste and adjust the seasoning.

Drop the pasta into a pan of boiling salted water and cook until *al dente*. Drain quickly and then pile into individual serving dishes. Spoon the hot hare sauce over it, sprinkle with a little parsley, dot with butter and serve with freshly grated Parmesan.

Elizabeth David's
Cephalonian Hare

As Elizabeth David wrote, this is '…a dish from the Ionian islands, but of Italian origin…This may sound an outlandish dish, but try it. The lemon flavour, the garlic, and the olive oil have an excellent effect upon the cloying and dry qualities of hare.'

She was absolutely right. It is undoubtedly delicious with its intense (but not overwhelming) lemony taste and it makes a most welcome change from the more usual, less piquant types of hare stew that we are used to. I should warn you, however, that it doesn't look terribly enticing, but the smell from the pan should get you over that drawback. A sprinkling of chopped parsley will improve presentation.

SERVES 6

Juice of 6 lemons	12 cloves of garlic, peeled but whole
1 hare, jointed	2 teaspoons dried oregano
Good olive oil, for frying	1 glass red wine
1 onion, sliced	Salt and freshly ground black pepper

Pour the lemon juice over the hare, season with salt and pepper and leave for at least 12 hours, to marinate. Take out of the marinade and pat dry.

Cover the bottom of a capacious, heavy-based pan with 5 mm (¼ in) of olive oil. Set over a moderate heat and when hot, add the onion. Let it brown slightly, then add the hare pieces and brown them on both sides. Now add the garlic, oregano and red wine. Season well. Cover and simmer gently for 2½–3 hours.

VENISON, CHESTNUT AND FRUIT STEW

This is a big, rich, warming winter stew, tempered with spices, sweetened with apricots and prunes, and gilded with mealy chestnuts. A sumptuous feast.

Don't be tempted to substitute tinned chestnuts for fresh. They are far too soggy and will collapse and disappear into the stew. Fresh ones may be a bore to peel, but they are worth every minute of tedium.

SERVES 6

100 g (4 oz) dried apricots	1 onion, sliced
100 g (4 oz) pitted prunes	2 tablespoons sunflower or vegetable oil
50 ml (2 fl oz) brandy	1 cinnamon stick
225 g (8 oz) fresh chestnuts	2 strips dried orange peel
1.25 kg (2½ lb) venison	900 ml (1½ pints) water
½ tablespoon coriander seeds	Salt and freshly
1 tablespoon flour	ground black pepper

Put the dried fruit to soak in the brandy. It won't cover them, but that doesn't matter. Leave for ½–1 hour, turning occasionally, so that they suck up the alcohol.

Score a cross in the curved side of each chestnut then place in a pan, cover with water and bring up to the boil. Simmer for 1 minute and turn off the heat. No more than one or two at a time, take the chestnuts from the water and strip off the tough outer skin and the brown papery inner skin. As the chestnuts cool, this becomes harder work, so if necessary, bring the water back to the boil. Set the peeled chestnuts to one side.

Pre-heat the oven to 150°C/300°F/Gas Mark 2.

Cut the venison into 5 cm (2 in) square pieces, about 2.5 cm (1 in) thick. Dry-fry the coriander seeds in a heavy-based frying pan over a high heat, until they start to pop. Tip into a bowl and when cool, crush with a pestle or the end of a rolling pin. Mix with the flour.

Cook the onion in the frying pan, in the oil, until lightly browned and then scoop into a flame-proof casserole. Raise the heat and brown the venison pieces in three batches. Transfer to the casserole and sprinkle the flour and spice mixture evenly over the meat. Add the cinnamon stick, the dried fruits, the orange peel and salt.

Tip the excess fat out of the frying pan and pour in the water. Bring up to the boil, scraping in the meaty residues from frying. Pour over the contents of the casserole, cover and immediately transfer to the oven. Cook for 2 hours, then stir in the chestnuts. After another hour or so, the meat should be very tender and the sauce should have reduced and thickened up nicely. If necessary, however, uncover the casserole and cook for another 20 minutes or so to cook off some of the liquid. Taste, adjust the seasoning and serve with mashed potatoes or buttered noodles.

VENISON AND MUSHROOM TOAD IN THE HOLE

Venison sausages make a tremendous toad-in-the-hole and it tastes even better when a few mushrooms are thrown in as well.

SERVES 4

8 venison sausages	2 eggs, lightly beaten
Dripping or sunflower oil, for frying	175 ml (6 fl oz) milk
6 flat-cap mushrooms	175 ml (6 fl oz) water
175 g (6 oz) flour	Freshly ground black pepper
¼ teaspoon salt	

Pre-heat the oven to 200°C/400°F/Gas Mark 6. Put the sausages into a 20 x 30 cm (8 x 12 in) roasting tin with a good knob of dripping or 1–2 tablespoons of oil and pop into the oven for 20–30 minutes, turning once or twice, until they are just cooked through. As soon as they are in the oven, wipe the mushrooms clean, quarter them and then add to the pan with the sausages.

While they are sizzling in the oven, make the batter. Sift the flour with the salt and make a well in the centre. Add the eggs and about half the milk. Gradually whisk into the flour, adding the rest of the milk and the water as you go, to make a smooth batter. Stir in a generous grinding of pepper.

When the sausages are just cooked, remove them from the tin, along with the mushrooms, and set aside. Raise the oven temperature to 220°C/425°F/Gas Mark 7 and pop the tin back in for 5 minutes. When hot, quickly remove the tin from the oven, give the batter a quick stir and pour it into the tin. Spoon the sausages and mushrooms into the batter and return it immediately to the oven. After 15 minutes, reduce the heat back down to 200°C/400°F/Gas Mark 6 again and cook for a further 20 minutes or so until the batter is puffed, crisp and brown.

PAN-FRIED VENISON WITH PORT AND ORANGE SAUCE

A quick but elegant way to deal with plain venison chops. Dried sour cherries are now available from several of the smarter supermarkets and delis and have a marvellous flavour. If you can't get any, you could substitute large raisins or even a handful of little currants. It won't be quite the same, but it will still taste fine.

I've used this recipe both for venison chops and for prime venison saddle steaks. Quantities will vary according to cut and variety of deer, so you'll have to use your head when it comes to buying. The butcher should be able to advise you if you are ordering in advance.

SERVES 4

50 g (2 oz) dried sour cherries	1 shallot, very finely chopped
Juice of 1 orange	150 ml (5 fl oz) port
8 small venison chops, or 8 small saddle steaks	150 ml (5 fl oz) venison, beef or chicken stock
(see above)	2 tablespoons redcurrant jelly
25 g (1 oz) butter	½ teaspoon Dijon mustard
1 tablespoon oil	Salt and freshly ground black pepper

Soak the dried cherries in the orange juice for half an hour. Dry the chops or steaks. Heat the butter and oil in a pan over a moderate heat. Fry the chops in the fat for about 5–8 minutes on each side until cooked almost to your liking, then set aside.

Add the shallot to the pan and cook gently, until tender. Drain the excess fat from the pan, then deglaze with the port, bringing it up to the boil and scraping in the residues from the pan. Let it bubble until reduced almost to nothing, then add the stock, orange juice and cherries. Boil until reduced by half. Now stir in the redcurrant jelly and mustard. Stir until the redcurrant jelly has dissolved into the sauce. Taste and adjust the seasoning, then spoon a little over and around the chops and serve the rest of the sauce alongside.

SWEDISH BRAISED VENISON

Shoulder of venison is astoundingly cheap. Demand is almost entirely for haunch or saddle, so suppliers are happy if they can sell other parts even at a relatively low price. This is a good recipe for cooking shoulder, which can be dry if roasted naked in the oven. It is slightly adapted from a recipe in Julia Drysdale's Classic Game Cookery.

SERVES 6 - 8

2.75 kg (6 lb) shoulder of venison	300 ml (10 fl oz) crème fraîche or double
50 g (2 oz) pork back fat, or streaky bacon, cut	cream mixed with soured cream
into thin strips	1 tablespoon redcurrant jelly
40 g (1½ oz) butter	1 tablespoon arrowroot
300 ml (10 fl oz) beef or venison stock	Salt and freshly ground black pepper

Pre-heat the oven to 220°C/425°F/Gas Mark 7. Make small slits all over the venison and push in strips of fat. Season with salt and pepper and place in a greased roasting tin. Dot with the butter and roast for 15 minutes. Reduce the heat to 170°C/325°F/Gas Mark 3. Mix the stock with the cream and pour over the meat. Cover and cook for a further 2 hours, basting frequently, until the meat is tender.

Transfer the venison to a serving dish and return it to the oven with the heat turned off and the door slightly ajar. Leave to relax for 15 minutes or so while you finish the sauce.

Skim the fat from the cooking juices as best you can and strain the juices back into the roasting tin. Place on the hob, over a gentle flame and stir in the redcurrant jelly. Mix the arrowroot to a paste with a little of the juices, then stir back into the tin. Simmer for a minute or so, stirring constantly, until smooth and thickened. Taste, adjust the seasoning and serve with the meat.

MAURITIAN CURRY DE CERF

Mauritian curries and stews are born out of a blending of many styles of cooking. French, Indian, Chinese and African flavours all come together, often in one large pot. This curry, cooked in a wok, has a distinctly exotic flavour. They use a special type of small tomato, called a pomme d'amour, that is more acidic than a salad tomato but with an intense flavour. Here, a slightly underripe tomato is the best substitute. If necessary, you can always soften the acidity towards the end of the cooking time with a little sugar.

SERVES 6

2–3 tablespoons sunflower oil

1.5 kg (3 lb) tender venison steak, cut into 4 cm (1½ in) cubes

2 onions, finely chopped

2 garlic cloves, crushed

1 cm (½ in) piece fresh root ginger, finely chopped

1½ tablespoons mild curry powder

5 curry leaves (if you can get them)

2 sprigs thyme

2 tablespoons chopped parsley

350 g (12 oz) tomatoes, skinned, seeded and roughly chopped

2 tablespoons chopped coriander leaves

Salt and freshly ground black pepper

Heat the oil in a wok over a high heat and brown the venison in 2–3 batches. Scoop out and set aside. Sauté the onions in the same oil until golden brown. Now add the garlic and ginger and sprinkle over the curry powder. Stir and fry for about 3 minutes. Next add the curry leaves, if using, the thyme, parsley, tomatoes, salt and pepper. Stir for a couple of minutes more. Pour in about 150 ml (5 fl oz) water and bring up to the boil. Return the meat to the pan and simmer for 10–15 minutes until the sauce has thickened and the meat is just cooked through. Taste and adjust the seasoning and serve sprinkled with coriander.

VENISON, APPLE AND CRANBERRY PARCELS

The astringent fruitiness of cranberries makes them ideal partners for all kinds of game. In this recipe they are cooked to a mush with apples to go into the filling for some pastry-wrapped parcels of venison.

The parcels can be put together up to 8 hours in advance (take them out of the fridge half an hour before baking) and zipped into the oven shortly before supper.

SERVES 4

2 eating apples, peeled, cored and chopped	4 venison steaks, cut 2 cm (¾ in) thick
100 g (4 oz) cranberries	1–2 tablespoons oil
50 g (2 oz) caster sugar	1 egg yolk
1 clove	450 g (1 lb) puff pastry
½ teaspoon ground cinnamon	Salt and freshly ground black pepper

Put the apples, cranberries, sugar and spices in a pan with 3 tablespoons of water. Cover and bring slowly to the boil, stirring once or twice. Uncover and cook hard until very thick – some 8–10 minutes should do it. Leave to cool and thicken. Fish out and discard the clove if you can find it.

Meanwhile, brown the venison steaks quickly over a high heat in as little oil as you can get away with. Let them cool too.

Pre-heat the oven to 220°C/425°F/Gas Mark 7.

Beat the egg yolk lightly with a tablespoon of cold water. Divide the pastry into four and roll each piece out into a circle large enough to wrap one of the steaks in. Lay a steak in the centre of each circle, season with salt and pepper and spread a quarter of the cranberry and apple sauce over the steak. Brush the edges of the pastry with egg wash and bring up over the steak, pinching the edges together to form a neat pasty-like parcel. Transfer to a baking tray and brush with egg wash. Bake in the oven for 15 minutes then reduce the heat to 190°C/375°F/Gas Mark 5 and give them a final 15 minutes.

WILD BOAR WITH SWEET AND SOUR SAUCE

(Cinghiale in Agrodolce)

❦

I remember being very impressed by the sight of wild boar hams hanging from the rafters of small, dark shops in the town of Norcia in Italy's Sibillini mountains. They were covered in dark wiry hair, left on to show that they were more than mere domesticated pig. Truly wild boar still roam here and there in Italy and this recipe is really designed for their meat, rather than the semi-farmed wild boar we get here. Nonetheless, it doesn't seem out of place. The candied peel, pine kernels and raisins all mix well with our wild boar, and would, I think, not be too much for a joint of first-rate free-range pork. I've come across several versions of this recipe, but Elizabeth David's remains one of the best. Be prepared, it yields up only a small amount of sauce, but the flavour is powerful.

SERVES 4 – 6

Haunch or fillet of wild boar, weighing around 1–1.5 kg (2–3 lb)	2 tablespoons caster sugar
	3 tablespoons red wine vinegar
100 g (4 oz) fatty ham or pork fat, cut into strips	50 g (2 oz) candied peel, cut into strips
25 g (1 oz) butter	25 g (1 oz) pine kernels
1 tablespoon olive oil	50 g (2 oz) raisins

——— *Cooked marinade* ———

1 carrot, sliced	1 sprig of rosemary
1 celery stick, sliced	4 allspice berries or juniper berries, crushed
1 onion, sliced	1 cinnamon stick
50 ml (2 fl oz) olive oil	8 black peppercorns
1 bay leaf	3 garlic cloves, sliced
2 sprigs of thyme	450 ml (15 fl oz) red wine

Make the marinade first, allowing it plenty of time to cool. Fry the carrot, celery and onion in the olive oil over a snappy heat until lightly browned. Add all the remaining marinade ingredients, bring up to the boil and simmer for 20 minutes. Leave to cool. Slide the wild boar into a hole-free plastic bag, pour in the marinade, knot the bag and place in a dish. Leave to marinate for at least one day or better still 2–3 days, turning every now and then.

Pre-heat the oven to 180°C/350°F/Gas Mark 4.

Dry the meat and lard with the ham or pork fat. Reserve the marinade. Stand the meat in a roasting tin and smear with butter, then spoon over the olive oil. Roast in the oven

allowing 33 minutes per 500 g (30 minutes per lb), basting occasionally with a couple of spoonfuls of the marinade. Rest for 20 minutes in a warm place (e.g. the oven with the heat off and the door ajar) before carving.

Strain the remaining marinade and boil down until reduced by half. Put the sugar into a small, heavy pan with 2 tablespoons of water and stir over a low heat until the sugar has completely dissolved. Stop stirring and cook until caramelized to a rich brown. Draw off the heat and add the vinegar at arm's length (it's bound to spit). Stir and then mix in the reduced marinade, candied peel, pine kernels and raisins. Just before serving, mix in the juices from the roasting tin and serve with the wild boar.

Oven-Roast Wild Boar Steaks with Potatoes and Garlic

This is a particularly good, simple way of cooking steaks of wild boar, though I think that it could well be used for free-range pork if you can't find any wild boar.

SERVES 6

6 wild boar steaks	1 large sprig of rosemary, snapped in two
85 ml (3 fl oz) olive oil plus a little for frying	3 garlic cloves, crushed
900 g (2 lb) potatoes, peeled and cut roughly into 2.5 cm (1 in) chunks	150 ml (5 fl oz) dry white wine
1 teaspoon thyme leaves	Salt and freshly ground black pepper

Pre-heat the oven to 180°C/350°F/Gas Mark 4. Brown the steaks in a little olive oil over a high heat. Lay them, overlapping, in a roomy oven-proof dish and fill the gaps around them with potatoes. Sprinkle over the thyme leaves, tuck the sprigs of rosemary between the steaks and smear the garlic around the meat and potatoes. Season generously with salt and pepper and drizzle over the white wine. Now trickle 85 ml (3 fl oz) olive oil over the potatoes and cover the dish with foil.

Bake for 1–1½ hours until the meat and potatoes are both tender. Raise the heat to 230°C/450°F/Gas Mark 8, uncover the dish and return to the oven for a final 10–15 minutes to brown. Serve immediately.

Offal

Offal

When a friend, who is a chef, and his family came to stay with us in France, I reckoned that here was the ideal opportunity to indulge in some of the more unusual bits and bobs of offal that one can buy much more readily across the Channel. Even if the rest of the clan refused, he and I could tuck in. Gleefully, I headed off to town, down to the butcher who specializes in offal. I returned clutching a bag of *rognons blancs* and *amourettes*, in other words, testicles and spinal cord. He was appalled. Everyone was appalled. In the end I threw them out, vastly disappointed.

Offal does not merely divide the human race into two, those who do and those who don't eat it; it is far more divisive than that. There are many degrees of offal-lust and offal-loathing. My love of offal of all types puts me at the extreme limit. There's little I will not try and while I can understand that some people find the whole lot repulsive, I fail to see why for others this bit of internal paraphernalia is to be relished but that other part, not so very far distant, is repulsive.

Still, that is the way matters are, and there is absolutely no point in trying to convince a confirmed offal-loather of whatever degree that they should try the object of their dislike. At best, one might persuade people to try something new to them, before prejudice sets in.

Though I can think of no particular type of offal that repulses me because of what it is, or its erstwhile function, that does not mean I will eat any old piece of tosh that is set in front of me. The offal of some animals tastes so much nicer than that of others, and the way it is cooked can make all the difference.

STORAGE

Offal has a very short shelf-life. Use it if you can on the day you buy it, or the very next day, failing that. Take it out of its plastic bag as soon as you get it home and put it into a shallow dish. Store it in the fridge, loosely covered with clingfilm or silver foil so that it can breathe.

Your nose is the best guide to its state of freshness. If it is at all pongy, then chuck it straight in the bin. When you are actually at the counter buying the stuff, use your common sense. If any bit of offal looks tired and miserable, with dry patches, then it shouldn't be on sale at all. Transfer your custom elsewhere.

LIVER

Calf's liver is the unassailable king of the clan, with its marvellous sweet delicate flavour, melting tenderness and correspondingly high price tag. It is possible to buy British-raised calf's liver, which you know will have come from an animal raised in relatively comfortable conditions (it's all too easy to forget that calf's liver is veal liver), but the demand is high and restaurateurs grab all they can.

A leap takes you down to lamb's liver, pleasant and very palatable but no match for the king. Then comes pig's liver and trailing last and least in culinary interest is ox liver. Chicken, poultry and game-bird livers have their own hierarchy, but they can all be used more or less interchangeably, allowing for the fact that the liver of game birds will be more powerfully flavoured.

I must admit that my enthusiasm for liver stops short of ox liver, which I find just too dominant and overwhelming in flavour to enjoy, however many steps I take to tame it. Pig's liver is another matter, and though I can't profess enormous enthusiasm, I do think it has some merits. A couple of hours soaking in milk (longer if possible) draws out much of the rankness of pig's liver, leaving it mild enough to fry quickly in strips (tossed in seasoned flour first). Otherwise, I find it only really comes into its own in French-style pâtés, and good old English faggots.

PREPARING LAMB'S AND CALF'S LIVER

Lamb's and calf's livers need little in the way of preparation other than trimming and with any luck they will come neatly trimmed and ready for the pan. Always check before you cook though and cut any stray gristle or tubes clean away. Ask the butcher to slice calf's or lamb's liver for you – he or she is likely to make a better, more even job of it than you will at home. A scant 1 cm (½ in) thick is about right for frying, while for grilling it's better to go for a marginally thicker slice.

Whether you fry or grill, make the heat powerful and keep the time to a minimum. The idea is to end up with a nicely browned outside and an interior that is still pink, though not raw. Lamb's liver can be substituted for calf's in most recipes and though the results are unlikely to scale great gastronomic heights, you will still end up with a fine supper dish.

PREPARING CHICKEN AND POULTRY LIVERS

By and large, most chicken livers these days turn up well-cleaned and trimmed, but it still pays to check over them carefully, removing any traces of yellow-green bile that might ruin them with its bitter taste.

Poultry livers freeze well, so I tend to save individual livers from duck or game-birds (having checked for bile) in the freezer until I have enough to make a decent batch of pâté (see page 289).

Offal

HEARTS

Lamb's, calf's and pig's hearts are not the food of romance, I'll grant you that. In fact, my butcher says they are not the food of anything much at all these days, apart from cats and dogs. Younger human generations tend to pass them by – real hearts are distinctly lacking in gastronomic allure. They are cheap but you won't win many brownie points for dishing up an economic plateful of braised hearts.

The standard way of cooking heart of any type is to braise it into submissive tenderness, but in fact lamb's and calf's hearts taste far nicer, remaining beautifully tender, when cooked briefly with a high heat, which on the whole means grilled or fried.

PREPARING LAMB'S OR CALF'S HEARTS

First trim off the layer of fat around each heart. Use a sharp knife or small pair of kitchen scissors and take off as much fat as you can without cutting them to shreds. Then remove any tubes and arteries and other unpleasant-looking bits and bobs. Rinse thoroughly, inside and out, under the cold tap and drop into a bowl of lightly salted water until needed.

PREPARING PIG'S HEARTS

Pig's hearts are less fatty than lamb's, but trim off what fat there is all the same, then remove tubing and gristle. Rinse them really thoroughly under the cold tap to get rid of blood clots and other nasties, then soak in lightly salted cold water for at least 20 minutes.

PREPARING OX HEARTS

Don't. Cheap they may be, but it takes an inordinate amount of braising time and a myriad of ingredients to make them at all palatable. Once you've paid for all that, you might just as well have gone for something marginally more expensive.

SWEETBREADS

First of all, let me put paid to one myth. The term sweetbread is not a euphemism for testicles. There are plenty of those, but sweetbreads, lovely little things that they are, are quite distinct. In anatomical terms, sweetbreads are the thymus glands, well removed

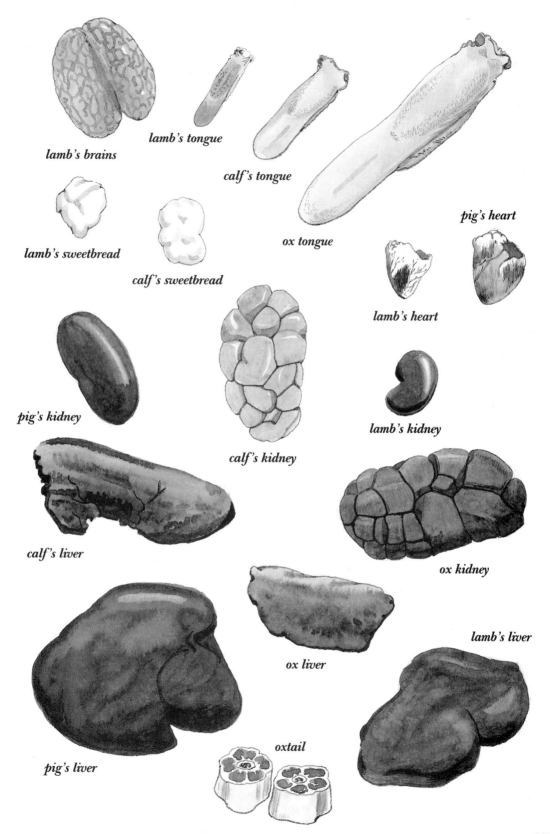

lamb's brains

lamb's tongue

calf's tongue

ox tongue

pig's heart

lamb's sweetbread

calf's sweetbread

lamb's heart

pig's kidney

calf's kidney

lamb's kidney

calf's liver

ox kidney

pig's liver

ox liver

lamb's liver

oxtail

Offal

from the reproductive organs. They have a delicate flavour and a smooth, milky texture, which I've always found immensely appealing. Lamb's sweetbreads are what you are most likely to come across. Calf's sweetbreads, the most highly rated of all, are no longer sold in Britain. The sweetbreads of other animals are rarely seen.

Buying sweetbreads in this country can be a frustrating business. Few butchers carry them as a regular day-to-day line, unless, that is, you live in an area with a large Greek or Turkish community, in which case you may strike lucky. Most butchers, however, are happy to buy them in for you if you give a day's notice. A few will also keep frozen sweetbreads, which aren't at all bad.

The preparation of sweetbreads takes a little time, but most of it can be done up to a day in advance. Soak the sweetbreads in cold water for 2 hours – this dissolves any blood and gunk. Drain and put them into a pan with enough cold water to cover. Bring to the boil and simmer for 5 minutes. Drain and trim the sweetbreads, removing the skin, fat and ducts. Sandwich the sweetbreads between two plates, set a weight on top (a couple of tins of something or other will do) then leave in the fridge for at least an hour to firm up.

BRAINS

It is no longer possible to buy beef or veal brains in this country, but at least lamb's brains are still available. Like sweetbreads, you will probably have to order them in advance, unless you live near a good Greek or Turkish butcher who seem to have them in far more regularly.

Brains have a melting, creamy texture that I adore, though I can in this particular case understand why some people, even those who will happily eat other forms of offal, cannot stomach the thought of eating them. They are prepared in much the same way as sweetbreads, first by soaking in cold water for several hours to dissolve away traces of blood, then by blanching briefly in salted water. Serve them hot, straight away, or re-heat whole in the frying pan. I love them with caper butter (see page 294), but any sauce with an edge of sharpness will do them justice.

KIDNEYS

Let me deal with ox kidneys immediately. Cook them for your pets, by all means, but be wary when it comes to cooking them for humans. It's not that they are inedible, just hardly worth the bother, since the powerful flavour needs to be muted by a long soak in milk or water, or by prolonged cooking. They are on the hefty side, weighing in at around 450 g (1 lb) each. The only place I use them is in a steak and kidney pie or pudding (see page 297), where the lengthy cooking time and partnership with other ingredients will beat them into submission. The one positive thing about ox kidneys is the jacket of fat that surrounds them. This is real suet, which is absolutely the thing to use for the best suet crust, sweet or savoury. Trim it off, nick out any messy bits and chop very finely, or whizz briefly in the processor.

Pig's kidneys are fine for everyday cooking. Sliced or cubed they need only brief frying or grilling. Calf's or veal kidneys are a great delicacy, as is the liver, but British calf's kidneys are a rare and sought-after commodity. If you are lucky enough to be able to lay your hands on some, slice and cook them lightly and serve with a cream sauce – the recipe for Rognons à la Moutarde on page 302 would fit the bill perfectly.

That leaves cute little lamb's kidneys, which are the ones I cook most often. They need little preparation, cook quickly and have a suitably light flavour and good texture. You will need 2–3 per person, depending on how they are cooked. Usually they are sold ready-trimmed and naked, but from time to time you may be lucky enough to come across lamb's kidneys still enclosed in their natural casing of fat. Whenever I see them, I snap up a couple to bake for my supper. Protected and basted by the layer of fat, they are tender and moist, needing nothing more than salt and pepper to season them.

PREPARING KIDNEYS

If necessary, cut and/or pull away any fat, then peel off the thin membrane that surrounds the kidney. With larger kidneys, such as ox, calf's and pig's, slit open and cut out the tough core with tubes and gristle from the centre, then cube or slice. There's no need to fiddle around with the core of lamb's kidneys. Depending on the recipe, leave them whole, or slit open from the outer edge towards the core so that they can be opened out flat.

TESTICLES

I once spotted a tray of perfect, glossy white globes, neatly nestled together in Liverpool's covered market. They were boldly labelled 'goolies'. No messing about there, though the French euphemism is far more genteel. Across the Channel they are known as *rognons blancs*, white kidneys. Sweetbreads, by the way, are something completely different and have their own entry (see page 276).

In fact, testicles are nothing like kidneys at all. If you can bring yourself to cook them, you will find that they have a firm but soft, bland texture that is perfectly pleasant but needs a lift in the form of some sharpish addition, if only a squeeze of lemon juice. If the testicles have not already been skinned, slit the outer skin, which comes away easily, and slice off the knobbly bit at either end. Slice what remains thickly, fry quickly and they are done…and I bet no one would ever guess what they were eating if they weren't told.

TONGUE

Ox tongue is a great favourite of mine, but it has to be cooked at home. The stuff that comes sliced paper-thin in vacuum packs is totally tasteless in comparison. It's worth stamping down any squeamishness you may have and trying real tongue for a change. Buy a tongue that has been cured, i.e. brined or pickled, which enhances the flavour and improves the colour. Avoid tongues with exaggeratedly pointed tips. Ask the butcher whether it will need soaking to remove excess salt. Most of the time, the ones I've bought can go straight into the pan.

To cook, put the tongue into a large saucepan with a few flavourings such as a bouquet garni (see page 33) and maybe a quartered carrot and onion, plus a stick of celery and water to cover. Bring to the boil and simmer gently for 3–4 hours until the meat can be pierced easily with a skewer. Remove from the pan, let it cool slightly, then strip off the now-vile-looking tough outer skin, which will come away with the smallest of yanks. If necessary, trim off any bits of bone and gristle at the thicker end (though a good butcher should have already dealt with these).

The tongue can be eaten hot when it is first cooked or left to cool then re-heated thoroughly later by simmering in a fresh pan of water for 30–40 minutes. Of course, it will be lovely cold, too, sliced not too thinly and served with fruity chutneys or Cumberland sauce. Save some for sandwiches.

Little wee lamb's tongues weigh in at around 100 g (4 oz) each and come, like ox tongues, fresh or cured. Basically they are treated in much the same way as ox tongue, reducing all the timings to match their size.

MARROWBONE

Marrowbone jelly, the waxy white core (which when cooked turns into a rich, unctuous goo) that sits in the centre of the leg and shin bones of beef or calves, was highly appreciated by the Victorians, but these days it is often overlooked. All to the good, for those of us who like the stuff, as the bones remain very cheap to buy. When ordering, ask your butcher to saw the bones into 5–7.5 cm (2–3 in) lengths. If you don't you'll be lumbered with whole bones and no way of getting at the marrow, which is immensely frustrating.

You can roast or poach the marrowbones to serve as a starter (see page 308), but the marrow itself can be used to enrich sauces and risottos. If you want to use only the marrow, ask the butcher if he can extract it for you by cracking open the cut marrowbone. If he won't, then be very specific about getting the bones in short lengths and poach them for a minute or two to soften them just enough to scoop it out.

OXTAIL

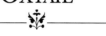

Oxtail stew is one of the great joys of winter, thick and rib-sticking, with a rich velvety texture that comes neatly packaged inside this most unprepossessing part of the animal. Oxtails don't look too attractive in their raw state, but get the butcher to chop them up into individual joints and then cook them slowly for a good 3–4 hours or until the meat falls from the bones at a gentle touch (if it is clingy, then it needs more cooking). Everyone who tucks in will be delighted with the result.

TROTTERS

Pig's trotters are considered quite a treat in France, where the *charcutier* (pork butcher and *traiteur*) will sell them fully cooked and breaded, needing no more than to be grilled and dished up. They are gelatinous, well-flavoured and filling (but bony) and, if that's the kind of thing you like, delicious.

Over here, pig's and calf's trotters are more likely to be used to enrich stews. They add some of the glutinous quality that you get with oxtail, and can be eaten along with the rest of the meat or discarded, as you like. Calf's trotters in particular are highly gelatinous and will thicken sauces to such an extent that they set firmly in the fridge.

Offal

BLACK PUDDING

Black pudding is a traditional favourite in the north of England, not to mention Scotland and Ireland. I remember being amazed by the queues at the famous black pudding stall on my trips to Bury Market when I was a student in Manchester. Customers would walk away, holding their steaming puddings in a sheet of paper, garnished with a trail of mustard, big grins on their faces.

Black pudding is made of ox blood, with chunks of fat, onion, grains, herbs and spices. I like to serve it fried in slices with apple (see page 310), but you can also grill it, if you are a touch more calorie conscious. I met one producer who swore blind that the best thing to serve with black pudding was marmalade! Throughout the Iberian peninsula, black puddings are added to stews of various pork meats, vegetables and beans and excellent they are too. If you do add black pudding to a stew, leave it firmly in its skin. If you peel it, the pudding will dissolve away to nothing.

HAGGIS

I do love a good haggis. This is perhaps Scotland's most important contribution to gastronomy, born, as so many fine dishes are, out of poverty and the meanness of the gentry. In the past, the rich landlords snatched away all the good meat, leaving the poor with the sheep innards and little else. From these they created haggis – boiled pluck, or in other words, the liver, heart and lights, very finely minced with oatmeal, fat, salt and lots of pepper, then stuffed into the stomach or intestine. The whole lot is boiled up again to cook the grain and meld the flavours.

What you buy is already fully cooked and just needs to be re-heated. Wrap it in foil (then if it bursts, it won't collapse completely) and re-heat it in a pan of barely simmering water. Timing will depend on the size of your haggis and is usually given on the packaging or label. Haggis is always served with bashed neeps and tatties (mashed swede, also known as turnip in Scotland, and mashed potato, both with lots of butter). My cousin adds a delicious Sassenach's touch with a thick, home-made tomato sauce, spiked with a shot or two of whisky.

Sautéed Calf's Liver with Balsamic Vinegar and Sage

The Italians love lightly sautéed calf's liver with sage, and so do I and so does my husband, who has made something of a speciality of cooking liver this way. It takes only minutes to rustle up and is the kind of supper dish we really appreciate when we've both had a hard day. A real treat.

Be sure to add the vinegar after the pan is off the heat. Over-heating balsamic vinegar destroys much of its aroma, leaving it flat and dull. Though you can cook lamb's liver this way, it's really a recipe to save for the marvellous, tender sweetness of more expensive calf's liver.

SERVES 2

2 slices calf's liver cut 1 cm (½ in) thick and weighing 225–350 g (8–12 oz) in total

3 tablespoons olive oil

50 g (2 oz) shallots, thinly sliced

3 large or 6 small sage leaves

1 tablespoon balsamic vinegar

Salt and freshly ground black pepper

Season the calf's liver with salt and pepper. Heat the olive oil in a wide frying pan over a medium heat. Add the shallots and fry gently until golden and tender. Raise the heat and add the calf's liver to the pan. Cook for about 1 minute on the first side, by which time it should be nicely browned (if not, crank the heat up a bit more), then turn over, add the sage to the pan and cook the other side for 1–3 minutes depending on how well done you like your liver and bearing in mind that to overcook calf's liver is well nigh a mortal sin and a terrible waste of money.

Transfer the calf's liver to a warmed serving dish. Remove the pan from the heat, pour the vinegar into it and stir. Pour over the liver and serve. Very nice with mashed potato, flavoured with olive oil and Parmesan.

Offal

FEGATO ALLA VENEZIANA

Liver and onions! Not the British version, but the Italian one, where the onions are cooked down slowly to a melting sweetness to form a bed for quickly fried, tender calf's liver. A blissful combination. If it makes life easier, the onions can be cooked up to a day in advance, then re-heated while you fry the liver.

SERVES 2 GENEROUSLY

350 g (12 oz) calf's liver, or lamb's liver	1½ tablespoons chopped parsley
2 tablespoons olive oil	½ tablespoon balsamic or sherry vinegar, or
25 g (1 oz) butter	red wine vinegar
2 onions, thinly sliced	Salt and freshly ground black pepper

Cut the liver into pieces about 2.5 cm (1 in) square. Set aside for the moment. Heat half the olive oil and half the butter in a wide saucepan. Add the onions and 1 tablespoon of parsley, stir, then cover and cook slowly for 30 minutes, stirring once or twice. Remove the lid, raise the heat and continue cooking until golden – another 10 minutes or so. Season with salt and pepper and scoop out onto a serving dish. Keep warm, if necessary.

When the onions are nearly done, heat the remaining oil and butter in a separate pan. Sauté the calf's liver over a high heat for 1–2 minutes. Draw off the heat, drizzle over the vinegar and season with salt and pepper. Stir, then spoon onto the onions. Scatter with the remaining parsley and serve.

ISCAS A LISBOA

This way of cooking liver is immensely popular in Lisbon – it's usually just known as Iscas, or liver, plain and simple. It can be made with lamb's or pig's liver, though I have to say that it tastes best of all with calf's liver. If you do use pig's liver, soak it in milk for half an hour before marinating to draw out some of its coarser flavour.

Some recipes for Iscas a Lisboa include potatoes to eke out the meat, but if they're not cooked with the liver, boiled potatoes are considered the essential accompaniment.

SERVES 4–6

175 ml (6 fl oz) dry white wine

2 tablespoons white wine vinegar

1 bay leaf, snapped in two

3 garlic cloves, crushed

900 g (2 lb) calf's, lamb's or pig's liver (see above), thinly sliced (less than 1 cm/½ in)

3 tablespoons olive oil

100 g (4 oz) smoked back bacon, diced

Salt and freshly ground black pepper

Mix the wine, wine vinegar, bay leaf, garlic and salt and pepper to make a marinade. Pour over the liver, cover and leave in the fridge to marinate for at least 2 hours, preferably overnight. Bring back to room temperature before cooking:

Take the liver out of the marinade and pat dry. Strain the marinade and reserve. Heat the oil in a pan and fry the bacon over a moderately high heat until just crisp. Reduce the heat a little and add the liver. Cook briefly for about 1½ minutes on each side if it is pig's liver, 1 minute on each side for lamb's or calf's liver. Transfer the liver and bacon to a heated serving dish and keep warm.

Pour the marinade into the pan, raise the heat and bring to the boil, scraping in the residues from the meat. Cook hard over a high heat until reduced by about half. Taste and adjust the seasoning. Pour over the liver and bacon and serve.

ALBANIAN LIVER

❦

Despite the name, this is actually a Turkish recipe, usually served as part of a mixed meze *or hors d'oeuvre. The briefly fried liver is piled up with sweet fried onions, lashings of thick yoghurt and lots of fresh mint leaves. I usually serve it as a first course on its own and it has been known to convert non-liver eaters to rampant enthusiasm, clearing the last slivers before anyone else can lay their hands on them. If you want to turn it into a light main course for a summery lunch, then accompany it with a tomato and olive salad, perhaps a green salad too and lots of hunks of sturdy peasant-type bread.*

All the Turkish cookbooks I own give a very simple recipe for Albanian Liver – the strips are tossed in flour seasoned generously with paprika, fried, and served at room temperature. This version is based on one described to me by my friend Martin Lam at Ransome's Dock restaurant in Battersea.

SERVES 4 AS A FIRST COURSE

450 g (1 lb) lamb's liver, trimmed

2 tablespoons flour

1 tablespoon paprika, plus extra to garnish

85 ml (3 fl oz) olive oil

1 large onion, thinly sliced

150 ml (5 fl oz) Greek yoghurt

12 mint leaves, roughly torn up

Salt and freshly ground black pepper

Cut the liver into long strips, about 2 cm (¾ in) wide. Mix the flour with the paprika, salt and pepper. Coat the strips of liver in the seasoned flour. Heat 4 tablespoons of the olive oil in a wide frying pan over a brisk heat. Fry the strips of liver, in two batches if necessary, for about 2–3 minutes, until browned, but still pink in the centre. Drain briefly on kitchen paper. Fry the sliced onion in the same oil, adding more if needed, gently at first then raising the heat, once they are tender, to brown them. Drain on kitchen paper.

Place the warm liver in a shallow dish, top with a generous dollop of yoghurt, then scatter over the fried onion and the mint leaves. Drizzle a tablespoon or so of fresh olive oil over the top, dust with a little paprika and serve.

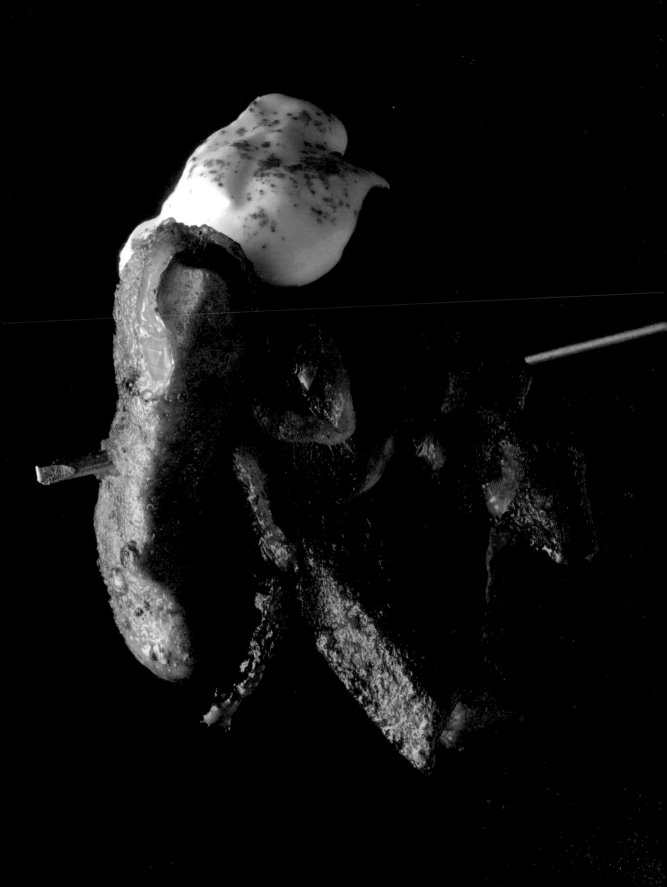

Offal

CHOPPED LIVER

---❧---

Chopped liver is the Jewish answer to butter-laden chicken liver pâté, and it is every bit as good, with a special sweetness from the fried onions. For this recipe the livers should be cooked a little longer than usual, so that they are no longer pink at the centre. Having said that, there's nothing to be gained from cooking them for so long that they are as tough and dry as rubber. Don't be tempted to whizz them up in a processor which will produce a smooth texture that is quite wrong. A small degree of knobbliness is a boon.

Serve the chopped liver as a first course with toast or use it as a sandwich filling.

SERVES 6

---

450 g (1 lb) chicken livers

1 large onion, chopped

3 tablespoons sunflower oil, or rendered chicken fat (see page 205)

3 hard-boiled eggs, chopped

Chopped parsley and/or an extra chopped hard-boiled egg

Salt and freshly ground black pepper

Pick over the chicken livers and remove any greenish-yellow bits. Quarter larger livers. Fry the onion gently in the oil or fat in a frying pan large enough to take the livers as well. When the onions are translucent, add the livers and plenty of salt and pepper. Cook gently, stirring frequently, until the livers are well-cooked.

When the livers are done, tip them into a bowl and add the eggs. Mash well together using a potato masher, if you have one, or a large fork, until the mixture is grainy. Spoon into a dish and, just before serving, garnish with a little chopped parsley, or extra chopped boiled egg.

CHICKEN LIVER PÂTÉ

I've been making chicken liver pâté for donkey's years, and it never fails to please. It's quick and easy, and makes a lovely first course served with little French cornichons or pickled caper berries (from smart delis) and toast, though usually we just dig into it for lunch, smearing it on bread or crackers with unwonted abandon.

It is also a most adaptable pâté. I usually flavour it with nothing more than a shot of sweet sherry, or Madeira or port, or whatever sweetish fortified wine I can find a few slurps of, but some people prefer a shot of brandy in it or like to add some crushed green peppercorns, a hint of garlic or a smattering of thyme leaves. Of course, you could leave the alcohol out altogether, but it wouldn't be half so nice.

When I'm lucky enough to have a few livers from game birds or a rabbit, I use them instead of, or as well as, chicken livers. These gamey livers are highly flavoured, so I add a little more butter to soften the edge, and smear it on toast with a modicum of restraint.

SERVES 4

225 g (8 oz) chicken livers

100 g (4 oz) butter

1 tablespoon sweet sherry, Madeira, port or brandy

Salt and freshly ground black pepper

Pick over the chicken livers, removing any greenish yellow bits. Cut any larger livers in half. Melt 40 g (1½ oz) of the butter and fry the livers over a moderate heat until browned on the outside but still pink inside. Tip the contents of the pan either into a food processor or into a pestle and mortar (depending on whether you want a smooth- or rough-textured pâté), scraping out all the butter and brown frying residues. Add the alcohol and remaining butter, salt and pepper and pound together until roughly amalgamated or blend until smooth.

Taste and adjust the seasoning, transfer the mixture to a bowl, smooth down and leave to set in the fridge.

Offal

CROSTINI DI FEGATINI DI POLLO

Toasted bread (preferably grilled over a barbecue for a hint of smokiness) topped with a hash of chicken livers is one of the most appetizing of all Italian crostini, served as a preamble to a meal, with drinks, or as a rustic first course.

It is essential to use absolutely the best-quality bread, cut fairly thickly, so that it can soak up the juice. Sometimes, instead of grilling, I brush the bread generously with olive oil and bake it in a moderate oven until golden brown and crisp through and through. If you like garlic, then you can highlight it by rubbing the toasted or baked bread with a cut clove of garlic, before piling on the livers.

SERVES 4

4 large or 8 small slices good bread, cut thickly	Olive oil
	A little chopped parsley

——— For the sauce ———

225 g (8 oz) chicken livers	5 anchovy fillets, chopped
3 tablespoons olive oil	1 tablespoon capers, rinsed and chopped
1 onion, chopped finely	85 ml (3 fl oz) Marsala or dry white wine
2 garlic cloves, crushed	Salt and freshly ground
2 sage leaves	black pepper

Pick over the chicken livers, removing any greenish-yellow bits. Cut any large livers in half or quarters then fry in 2 tablespoons of the olive oil until they are just firm. Scoop out and chop finely.

Add the remaining oil to the pan and fry the onion and garlic gently until tender but without browning. Return the chicken livers to the pan with all the remaining sauce ingredients (adding only a little salt as the anchovies will provide some) and simmer for about 4 minutes, mashing the livers down to a coarse purée.

Grill the bread, moisten with a trickle of olive oil and spread with the hot chicken liver sauce. Scatter over a little chopped parsley and serve immediately.

CHICKEN LIVER, BACON AND PLUM KEBABS

Threading up these skewers of chicken liver and bacon-wrapped plum is a bit messy, but worth it in the end. The bacon is multifunctional – it serves to keep the plums from collapsing in the heat and adds a pleasing saltiness to contrast with the sweetness of the fruit and livers.

SERVES 4

350 g (12 oz) chicken livers	275 g (10 oz) thinly sliced
450 g (1 lb) red or purple plums	green streaky bacon

————— *For the basting mixture* —————

2 garlic cloves, crushed	½ teaspoon freshly ground black pepper
½ teaspoon ground coriander	50 ml (2 fl oz) dry sherry
½ teaspoon paprika	50 ml (2 fl oz) olive oil

Pick over the chicken livers and remove any greenish-yellow traces. Cut larger livers in half or quarters. Quarter the plums and discard the stones. Snip the rinds off the bacon and stretch the rashers out thin by dragging the back of a knife along them. Snip each rasher in half, and wrap each half around a piece of plum.

Thread the chicken livers and wrapped plums alternately onto 4 skewers. Mix all the basting mixture ingredients, brush over the kebabs, then grill, turning and basting frequently, until the livers and bacon are just cooked. Serve immediately.

MOROCCAN LIVER AND HEART BROCHETTES

A few years ago we stayed with colleagues of my husband's in Casablanca. A fascinating town, though not the romantic location you would like it to be. Our hosts were keen to cook Moroccan food for us and we feasted on mountains of couscous and spiced fish. Abdu cooked us these kebabs, grilling them over hot charcoal in an earthenware brazier on the tiny balcony of their flat.

This is a good recipe for lamb's liver, though naturally calf's will taste even better. Briefly exposed to heat, the pieces of heart remain amazingly tender. When measuring out the chopped parsley and spices don't worry about being too precise. Err on the side of generosity rather than genteel restraint.

SERVES 4–6

450 g (1 lb) calf's or lamb's liver	1 tablespoon paprika
2–3 lamb's hearts	½ teaspoon freshly ground black pepper
3 tablespoons chopped parsley	2 tablespoons olive oil
3 garlic cloves, crushed	Salt
2 teaspoons ground cumin	

Trim the liver and heart, removing the tough sinews and any obvious tubes, but leaving a good portion of the fat on the heart. Cut into cubes about 2.5–4 cm (1–1½ in) across. Put into a bowl and mix with all the remaining ingredients except the salt, turning well with your hands so that all the meat is evenly coated. Cover and leave to marinate for at least 4 hours.

Thread skewers with either liver or heart, keeping the two meats separate as far as possible, as the liver cooks a little more quickly.

Grill over charcoal, or under a hot grill, turning until the meats are just done. With the liver it's just a matter of a few minutes, so that the outside is browned but the inside still slightly pink. The heart will take a few minutes longer, 5–8 minutes maximum, depending on the heat of the grill. Season with salt and serve immediately.

HEARTS BRAISED WITH RED WINE AND ROSEMARY

This is a rich stew of hearts and carrots in red wine. Use either pig's or lamb's hearts – lamb's hearts have a slightly more refined flavour but there's not a massive difference as there is, say, between calf's and pig's liver.

SERVES 4 – 6

4 pig's hearts or 5 lamb's hearts	2 sprigs of parsley
About 2 tablespoons olive oil	450 ml (15 fl oz) red wine
2 onions, thinly sliced	300 ml (10 fl oz) hot water or light stock
3 garlic cloves, chopped	2 tablespoons red wine vinegar
450 g (1 lb) carrots, thickly sliced	Finely grated zest of 1 lemon
2 sprigs of rosemary	1 tablespoon finely chopped parsley
1 bay leaf	Salt and freshly ground black pepper

Pre-heat the oven to 180°C/350°F/Gas Mark 4. Trim the hearts but leave whole. Heat 2 tablespoons of oil in a frying pan and brown the hearts. Place in a casserole. Fry the onions in the same oil, adding a little more if needed, until lightly browned. Add the garlic and cook gently for another couple of minutes. Spoon into the casserole and tuck in the carrots. Tie the rosemary, bay leaf and parsley sprigs in a bundle with string to make a bouquet garni and add to the casserole.

Pour the wine into the frying pan and bring up to the boil, scraping in the brown gloop from the bottom of the pan. Pour over the hearts and add the vinegar and hot water or stock. Season well. Cover, transfer to the oven and cook for 2–2½ hours, or until the hearts are tender. Mix together the lemon zest and chopped parsley.

To serve, lift out and slice the hearts. Arrange in a dish with the carrots and onions and pour over the sauce. Sprinkle with the lemon and parsley.

Offal

SWEETBREADS WITH CAPER BUTTER

Caper butter is nothing more than melted butter, sharpened with a little lemon juice and dotted with capers. It is often spooned over fried skate, but finds a welcome home over tender sweetbreads.

SERVES 4

450 g (1 lb) prepared and cooked lamb's sweetbreads (see page 276)

75 g (3 oz) unsalted butter

1½–2 tablespoons lemon juice

2 tablespoons capers, roughly chopped

Salt and freshly ground black pepper

A little finely chopped parsley, to serve

Slice the larger pieces of sweetbread in half lengthwise. Heat about 25 g (1 oz) of the butter in a frying pan until it foams. Fry the sweetbread pieces for a few minutes on each side until lightly patched with brown. Scoop out onto a warmed serving dish and keep warm. Pour away the butter, and then return the pan to the heat. Add the remaining butter to the pan and heat until it darkens to a fine hazelnut brown. Keep a careful eye on it as you don't want it to burn. Pour over the sweetbreads. Quickly return the pan to the heat one final time, add the lemon juice and the capers, stir around for a second or two, then pour over the sweetbreads. Season with salt and pepper, sprinkle with a little parsley, then dish them straight up.

SWEETBREADS
WITH GOOSEBERRY SAUCE

Tart, green gooseberries make a pretty summer sauce for breaded sweetbreads. Both sweetbreads and sauce can be prepared in advance. All you need do at the last minute is fry the sweetbreads and gently re-heat the sauce.

SERVES 4

450 g (1 lb) prepared and cooked lamb's sweetbreads (see page 276)

Breadcrumbs, for coating

1 egg, beaten

Oil, for frying

Salt and freshly ground black pepper

——— For the sauce ———

225 g (8 oz) gooseberries

A knob of butter

1 tablespoon sugar

1 tablespoon chopped chives

First, make the gooseberry sauce. Don't bother to top and tail the gooseberries, just put them straight into the pan with the butter, sugar and 3 tablespoons of water. Cover and cook over a gentle heat for a few minutes until the juices begin to run. Uncover and cook until all the gooseberries have collapsed. Push through a sieve and season to taste with a little salt and plenty of pepper. Set aside until needed.

Slice the larger pieces of sweetbread in half lengthwise. Dip first in the beaten egg and then coat in breadcrumbs. Fry gently in oil until nicely browned. Season with a little salt. Meanwhile, re-heat the sauce, stir in the chives and serve with the sweetbreads.

SWEETBREADS À LA CASTILLANE

This is a dish from my childhood and one that I adored. My mother made it for us as a special treat every now and then (the alcohol burns off so we didn't end up drunk). The sweetish sauce, made with bananas, apples and cream, sounds a bit odd, but it is totally irresistible. Remember when poaching the sweetbreads to save 300 ml (10 fl oz) of their cooking liquor for the glaze.

SERVES 6

675–900 g (1½–2 lb) prepared and cooked lamb's sweetbreads (see page 276)

4 medium eating apples, roughly chopped, core and all

75 g (3 oz) butter

4 small, very ripe bananas

A little sugar, optional

A squeeze of lemon juice

A liqueur glass of brandy

120 ml (4 fl oz) double cream

Salt and freshly ground black pepper

Slice the sweetbreads into pieces about 1 cm (½ in) thick. Stew the apples in 25 g (1 oz) of the butter in a covered pan until very tender. Pass through a sieve and throw away the remains of the peel and core. Mash the bananas thoroughly and mix with the apple purée. Sweeten if necessary, and add a little lemon juice – very good apples and scented bananas will need hardly any additions. Keep the purée warm.

Brown the sweetbreads in the rest of the butter; turn the heat up high and pour in about 150–300 ml (5–10 fl oz) of their cooking liquor, little by little, so that it reduces to a rich glaze on the sweetbreads. Arrange the sweetbreads on the fruit purée. Quickly add the brandy to the pan and bring to the boil, scraping in all the pan juices. Stir in the cream and cook gently for a few minutes. Season with salt, pepper and a squeeze of lemon juice and pour over the sweetbreads. Serve immediately with plain boiled rice.

STEAK AND KIDNEY PUDDING

There is nothing in the world to beat our own steak and kidney pud – at least when it is made properly. The very thought of that pale, steaming, fragrant crust enclosing the velvety darkness of melting pieces of steak and kidney swathed in rich gravy makes my mouth water.

I have tried short-circuiting the method, popping the filling ingredients straight into the crust and then steaming it for ever and a day (which is, I'm sure, the way that it was originally made), but the end result is always disappointingly thin and I could probably charge entry to the kitchen as a public sauna.

No, to make the ultimate, unctuous, devastating steak and kidney pudding, you must cook the filling before it goes into the pudding itself. In fact, this has several advantages besides mere deliciousness. The filling can be made a day in advance and the fat skimmed off when cold, and then the pudding will need no more than an hour and a half's steaming, leaving the crust lighter and less soggy. Incidentally, I think rump makes a marginally better pud, but there's not a lot in it. If you want to make a truly serious steak and kidney pud, then buy fresh suet from the butcher and chop it finely yourself.

SERVES 6

———— *For the filling* ————

50 g (2 oz) butter	600 ml (1 pint) beef or chicken stock,
2–3 tablespoons sunflower oil	or 300 ml (10 fl oz) beef or chicken stock
1 large onion, chopped	and 300 ml (10 fl oz) Guinness or stout
900 g (2 lb) rump or chuck steak, trimmed	275 g (10 oz) flat-cap mushrooms,
and cut into 2.5 cm (1 in) cubes	halved and sliced
225–350 g (8–12 oz) ox or veal kidney,	1 bouquet garni (see page 33)
trimmed and sliced	Salt and freshly ground black pepper
1½ tablespoons plain flour	

———— *For the suet crust* ————

350 g (12 oz) self-raising flour	½ teaspoon salt
1 teaspoon baking powder	175 g (6 oz) prepared suet

Heat 25 g (1 oz) of the butter and 1 tablespoon of oil in a wide frying pan over a medium heat. Add the onion and fry until golden then set aside. Add half of the remaining butter and oil to the pan and turn the heat up high. Brown the meat in two batches (three if the pan is on the small side), then scoop out and reserve. Add the remaining butter and oil, if necessary, and quickly brown the kidney. Set aside. Pour any excess fat from the pan and sprinkle over the flour. Gradually pour in the stock, stirring constantly, then the Guinness if using, scraping in all the browned bits from the meat. Bring to the boil, still stirring.

If the frying pan is big enough, return the meat, kidneys and onions to it, adding the mushrooms, bouquet garni, salt and pepper. Otherwise transfer them all to a flame-proof casserole. Either way, cover and simmer gently on the hob for 2–3 hours, stirring occasionally, or transfer to the oven, set to 150°C/300°F/Gas Mark 2 and cook for 2–3 hours until the meat is tender and the sauce reduced to a pleasing thickness. Taste and adjust the seasoning. Cool and skim off any congealed fat.

To make the crust, sift the flour with the baking powder and salt. Mix in the suet and just enough cold water to make a firm dough. Roll out on a well floured board to make a large circle. Cut out a quarter and set aside for the lid. Drop the rest into a generously buttered 1.75 litre (3 pint) pudding basin, so that the centre sits on the base of the basin and the outer edges of the pastry overhang the rim of the bowl. Using your fingers, gently press the dough into the corners of the basin and round to line it completely, pinching the cut edges together.

Fill the crust with the steak and kidney stew, stopping about 2.5 cm (1 in) below the rim of the basin. Roll out the remaining pastry to form a lid for the pudding. Lay over the pudding and dampen the edges of the overhang. Flip them over on to the lid, and press together to seal neatly.

Take a large sheet of silver foil or greaseproof paper and make a double pleat down the centre. Lay over the pudding basin and tie in place securely with string. Leave the ends trailing and loop them over and under the string on the outside of the basin, then knot to form a string 'handle' to lift the pudding in and out of the pan with.

Stand the pudding, on a small trivet if you have one or an upturned saucer, in a large saucepan, and pour enough boiling water around it to come about two-thirds of the way up the basin. Bring to the boil, then reduce to a simmer. Cover tightly (make a dome of silver foil if the lid won't fit) and leave it to simmer for 1½ hours. Check the water level regularly and top up with more boiling water as needed.

Serve the pudding straight from the basin: lift it out of the pan and remove the string and foil or paper. Wrap a clean white napkin or tea-towel around the basin and present the pudding proudly.

Offal

Kidney and Mushroom Parcels

In this recipe, the kidneys are baked, but protected from the drying heat of the oven with a moist stuffing and a wrapping of puff pastry. The golden brown parcels of kidney look neat and pretty on the plate and can be made in advance (though not too long in advance or the pastry will be sodden), so that they are ready to pop into the oven when needed.

SERVES 2 AS A MAIN COURSE OR 4 AS A STARTER

½ onion, finely chopped

1 garlic clove, finely chopped

1 tablespoon olive oil or 15 g (½ oz) butter

100 g (4 oz) mushrooms, finely chopped

1 tablespoon finely chopped parsley

A dash of lemon juice

4 lamb's kidneys

225 g (8 oz) puff pastry

1 egg, beaten

Salt and freshly ground black pepper

Fry the onion and garlic gently in the olive oil or butter without browning until tender. Add the mushrooms, parsley, lemon juice, salt and pepper. Continue cooking, stirring constantly, until virtually all the liquid has evaporated and the mixture is thick, dark and moist. Taste and adjust the seasonings, then leave to cool.

Pre-heat the oven to 230°C/450°F/Gas Mark 8.

Split the kidneys in half. Sandwich the halves back together with a thick layer of the mushroom mixture in between. Season with salt and pepper.

Roll out the pastry very thinly and divide into four. Wrap each kidney in a quarter of the puff pastry and lay on a baking sheet, neatly tucking the joins underneath. Rest in the fridge for 15 minutes. Brush with beaten egg, then bake in the oven for 10 minutes until puffed and golden. Turn the heat down to 190°C/375°F/Gas Mark 5 and cook for a further 15 minutes. Serve immediately.

KIDNEYS TURBIGO MA FAÇON

The proper recipe for Kidneys Turbigo demands a demi-glace sauce, which is the kind of thing that may well be readily to hand in the kitchens of a French restaurant but takes far too long to make to be of any great use to a domestic cook. This then is Kidneys Turbigo made my way, with nothing more recherché *than a tomato and white wine sauce. It is a hearty dish of kidneys, mushrooms and chipolata sausages. Lovely with sautéed potatoes or rice.*

SERVES 4-6

15 g (½ oz) butter	1 teaspoon sugar
1 tablespoon sunflower oil	1 small glass of dry white wine
6 lamb's kidneys, split in half	1 sprig of thyme
8 chipolatas	1 small sprig of rosemary
225 g (8 oz) button mushrooms	1 bay leaf
1 garlic clove, crushed	Salt and freshly ground black pepper
1 x 400 g (14 oz) tin chopped tomatoes	Finely chopped parsley, to serve

Melt the butter with the oil in a frying pan over a medium heat. Fry the kidneys fairly swiftly until just cooked (don't overdo them, though, as they are going to have to sit around for a while). Scoop out of the pan and set aside. Now fry the chipolatas and set them aside with the kidneys. Next, fry the mushrooms over a keen heat until tender and scoop out.

Add the garlic to the pan and swish around for a few seconds. Tip in the tomatoes with their juice, then add the sugar, wine and herbs (except for the parsley) tied together with a piece of string. Season with salt and pepper and bring to the boil. Simmer for about 15 minutes until the sauce is well reduced with not a trace of wateriness. Taste and adjust the seasoning. Return the kidneys, chipolatas and mushrooms to the pan and let them simmer for a couple of minutes to heat through. Sprinkle with parsley and serve immediately.

ROGNONS À LA MOUTARDE

These are Rolls Royce kidneys, napped in cream and speckled with grains of mustard, a veritable feast for anyone who is partial to the inner organs. Serve with plain buttered noodles and maybe some mangetout or spinach on the side and you can be tucking in in less than half an hour.

Though kidneys with a mustard sauce is a particularly fine combination, this method is widely adaptable to other meats (sliced chicken breast, perhaps). You will have to adjust the frying times to suit, of course, but the final additions of wine, cream and mustard are standard.

SERVES 4

12 lamb's kidneys	4 tablespoons crème fraîche or double cream
1 shallot, finely chopped	2 tablespoons coarse-grained or Dijon mustard
25 g (1 oz) butter	A little chopped chervil or parsley
1 tablespoon sunflower oil	Salt and freshly ground black pepper
150 ml (5 fl oz) white wine	

Cut the kidneys in half. Sauté the shallot gently in the butter and oil in a wide frying pan until tender. Raise the heat and add the kidneys. Fry briskly for about 3 minutes. Pour off the excess fat, then tip in the white wine. Bring to the boil and simmer, stirring once or twice, until the wine has almost boiled away. Now stir in the cream, the mustard and a little salt and pepper. Leave to bubble steadily for a minute or so to reduce the cream slightly, then taste and adjust the seasoning. Stir in the chervil or parsley and serve immediately.

ROGNONS BLANCS AU VIN BLANC

Rognons blancs, white kidneys, is the polite French term for testicles. They really are very good and very tender, cooked quickly with parsley, garlic and a dose of white wine. Honestly!

If the butcher hasn't already skinned the testicles for you, just slit open the loose outer skin, which will come away neatly, needing only to be severed along the line that anchors it to the main part. Trim off the ends as well, rather as if you were dealing with a lemon.

SERVES 2 BRAVE BODS

4 lamb's testicles, skinned	1 generous tablespoon chopped parsley
25 g (1 oz) butter	A squeeze of lemon juice
50 ml (2 fl oz) white wine	Salt and freshly ground black pepper
1 large garlic clove, crushed	

Slice the testicles about 1 cm (½ in) thick. Melt the butter in a frying pan over a medium heat. When it is foaming, pop in the testicle slices. Fry until patched with brown on both sides. Pour the wine around the slices and let it simmer down for a few minutes until almost totally evaporated, turning the slices once or twice. Lift them out onto a serving plate and keep warm. Quickly stir the garlic into the buttery juices, cook for a few seconds, then stir in the parsley, a generous squeeze of lemon juice, salt and pepper. Pour over the testicles and dish up promptly.

TONGUE WITH RAISIN AND ALMOND SAUCE

Tongue is easy to cook, though it does require a few hours' steady simmering. This can be done up to 24 hours in advance (once skinned, let it cool, then keep covered with foil in the fridge), so that all you need do on the day is re-heat it and make the sauce. If you haven't got a full complement of eight to feed, don't dismiss the idea out of hand. Left-over tongue is good cold, especially in sandwiches with a fruity chutney, or made into a gratin like the one on page 305.

This sauce is a Germanic one, sweet and sharp, just the thing to bring out the full flavour of the tongue. It does no harm to make it an hour or two in advance and re-heat it.

SERVES 8

1 whole cured ox tongue	1 onion, quartered
1 celery stick, quartered	1 bouquet garni (see page 33)
1 carrot, quartered	6 peppercorns

——— *For the sauce* ———

25 g (1 oz) butter	75 g (3 oz) raisins, soaked and drained
2 level tablespoons flour	50 g (2 oz) currants, soaked and drained
300 ml (10 fl oz) red wine	Zest of ½ lemon, shredded
300 ml (10 fl oz) light chicken or ham stock	1 cinammon stick
5 tablespoons red wine vinegar	50 g (2 oz) slivered almonds
50 g (2 oz) caster sugar	Salt and freshly ground black pepper

Put the tongue into a large pan and tuck the vegetables around it with the bouquet garni and peppercorns. Add enough water to cover, bring to the boil and simmer for 3–4 hours. Test with a skewer to see if it is tender. Take the tongue out of the pan, trim off the skin (which will look rather revolting by now) and any odd bits of bone and gristle at the thicker end. If not serving immediately, cool and wrap loosely in foil.

To re-heat the tongue, pop into a pan of boiling water and leave to simmer for another 30 minutes or so. Drain, slice and serve hot with the sauce.

To make the sauce, melt the butter and stir in the flour. Cook over a gentle heat, stirring, until the roux is light brown with a nutty smell. Gradually mix in the wine and then the stock and vinegar. Add the sugar and stir to dissolve. Add all the remaining ingredients, bring to the boil and simmer for 20 minutes until reduced to a good consistency. Taste and adjust the seasoning. Re-heat when needed and serve with the tongue.

TONGUE GRATIN

This is a good way of using up left-over tongue, but I reckon it's worth cooking a whole tongue just so that you can make a gratin and have the rest cold with chutney; two radically different ways of serving tongue, so no one should complain about repetition. To cook the tongue, use the method given in the recipe on page 304.

SERVES 4

450–675 g (1–1½ lb) cooked, sliced tongue

———— *For the sauce* ————

½ onion, finely chopped	150 ml (5 fl oz) Madeira, Marsala or port
25 g (1 oz) butter	1 bay leaf
25 g (1 oz) flour	2 sprigs of parsley
300 ml (10 fl oz) stock from cooking	1 tablespoon Dijon mustard
the tongue, if it isn't too salty,	Salt and freshly ground
or chicken or veal stock	black pepper

———— *To finish* ————

Fine breadcrumbs	A little extra butter

Pre-heat the oven to 200°C/400°F/Gas Mark 6. First make the sauce. Sweat the onion gently in the butter in a covered saucepan for 10 minutes until tender. Sprinkle over the flour and stir, uncovered, until the roux darkens to a hazelnut brown. Gradually stir in the stock, a little at a time as if making a white sauce, then follow with the Madeira, Marsala or port. Add the herbs. Simmer for 20 minutes, stirring occasionally, until the sauce is good and thick. Fish out and discard the bay leaf and parsley. Stir in the mustard, and season with plenty of pepper, and salt if it needs it.

Spoon a little of the sauce into a 30 cm (12 in) gratin dish, then cover with a layer of tongue. Repeat until the tongue is all used up and spoon over the remaining sauce. Spread a generous layer of breadcrumbs over the top and dot with butter. Bake for 25–30 minutes until the crumbs are nicely browned. Serve immediately.

RISOTTO MILANESE

This is perhaps the greatest of all risottos. It can be served as a first or main course on its own, though it is also the classic accompaniment to Osso Buco *(see page 147). The bone marrow is an optional extra but it does add a marvellous, though virtually unidentifiable, richness. When ordering it from your butcher, explain that you want to extract the marrow from the bones and ask him to saw them into short lengths, 5 cm (2 in) or so, to make this easier. Two bones should give you enough marrow.*

The quantity of saffron depends entirely on your taste and pocket. A full ⅛ teaspoon gives a glorious daffodil-yellow colour, half that reduces it to primrose and a mild hint of saffron. A very generous pinch of saffron threads is about equivalent to ¹⁄₁₆ teaspoon. Dry-fry it briefly to crisp the threads then pound them to a powder.

SERVES 4 – 6

1.2 litres (2 pints) chicken stock	2 shallots, finely chopped or 1½ tablespoons
¹⁄₁₆–⅛ teaspoon powdered saffron or 1–2	finely chopped onion
generous pinches of saffron threads	350 g (12 oz) arborio or other risotto rice
(see above)	120 ml (4 fl oz) dry white wine
75 g (3 oz) butter	50g (2 oz) freshly grated Parmesan
50 g (2 oz) beef marrow,	Salt and freshly ground
roughly chopped	black pepper

Bring the stock to the boil, turn down the heat and keep it at a low simmer. Pour 2 tablespoons of hot stock over the saffron and leave it to steep.

Melt two-thirds of the butter in a heavy pan. Add the beef marrow and shallots or onion and fry gently until tender, without browning. Add the rice and stir for 1 minute until translucent. Pour in the wine and simmer over a medium-low heat until almost all the liquid has been absorbed, stirring constantly.

Add a generous ladleful of the hot stock and simmer until almost all the liquid has been absorbed, stirring constantly. Repeat, adding 1 ladleful of stock at a time, until the rice is tender but still *al dente*, i.e. firm but not chalky and hard. Add the saffron and its soaking liquid after the risotto has been simmering for about 20 minutes. You may find that you don't need all of the stock, but if you don't have quite enough, finish with hot water; the finished risotto should be creamy and wet, but not swimming in liquid. Stir in the remaining butter (or more!), the Parmesan, pepper and salt to taste. Serve immediately, with extra Parmesan for those who want it.

ROAST MARROWBONE WITH PARSLEY, SHALLOT AND CAPER SALAD

Queen Victoria, it is said, was most partial to roast marrowbone jelly smeared on toast, and well she might be. These days it is a forgotten pleasure, quite unknown to many. I can see that it might not be everyone's cup of tea, but marrowbones are so cheap that you might as well try it. St John's Restaurant in London's Clerkenwell is the only place I know where they put marrowbone on the menu. Chef Fergus Henderson accompanies them with this most sensational parsley, shallot and caper salad, which cuts the richness of the marrowbone jelly.

SERVES 4

4 marrowbones, sawed into 5–7.5 cm (2–3 in) lengths	8 slices thin toast, made with light rye bread if possible
4 tablespoons flour	

For the salad

A bunch of flat-leaf parsley	2–3 teaspoons lemon juice
4 small shallots, halved and thinly sliced	3 tablespoons olive oil
2 tablespoons capers	Salt and freshly ground black pepper

Pre-heat the oven to 150°C/300°F/Gas Mark 2. There are three methods for cooking the marrowbone. The traditional way is to seal the ends with a flour and water paste. Mix the flour with just enough water to make an extremely thick paste. Smear it over the cut ends of the bones right up to the edges. Stand upright in a roasting tin and roast for 1½–2 hours. Chip off the paste before serving.

Sometimes the marrow leaks out with only the paste and so I prefer to wrap each bone tightly in silver foil, then roast as for the paste-sealed bones.

The third alternative is to paste the ends as before and then also wrap each bone in foil. Poach in water for 2 hours.

For the salad, cut the parsley leaves from the stalks and mix with the shallots and capers. At the very last minute, dress with lemon juice, olive oil, salt and pepper. Taste and adjust the balance of lemon to oil and the seasoning.

Serve 3 lengths of marrowbone per person (the classic way to present them is wrapped in white napkins), alongside a mound of salad, with a couple of pieces of toast. If you can't get proper long marrow spoons to scoop the insides out with, then lobster picks (!) or even skewers and small teaspoons will do the job. Smear the rich marrow onto the bread, season with salt and top with a little of the salad. Delicious!

OXTAIL STEW

Oxtail makes a brilliant, sticky stew but all too often it is forgotten and ignored. A shame, as it is far more economical than cubes of expensive beef. Don't think of the heavy weight of the bones as wasteful, either. They are what yield up that special velvety texture which is the hallmark of an oxtail stew.

The seasonings for this oxtail stew are similar to those used in a French daube, an aromatic collection of orange zest, spices, herbs and a generous slurp of red wine. The stew positively benefits from being cooked in advance and re-heated thoroughly 24 hours later. Lift congealed fat off the surface first.

SERVES 4 – 6

2 oxtails weighing about 1.5 kg (3 lb) in total, jointed	5 cm (2 in) cinnamon stick
Seasoned flour, for dusting	3 cloves
3 tablespoons olive oil	½ bottle red wine
2 onions, sliced	2 sprigs thyme
3 garlic cloves, sliced	2 bay leaves
450 g (1 lb) carrots, peeled and thickly sliced	1 sprig rosemary
4 wide strips orange zest, dried or fresh	Salt and freshly ground black pepper

Coat the oxtail in seasoned flour and brown in the oil in a flame-proof casserole over a high heat. Lift out the oxtail and set aside. Reduce the heat and add the onions and garlic, and extra oil if needed. Fry gently, without browning, until the onions are tender.

Return the oxtail to the pan with all the remaining ingredients and enough water to cover. Bring to the boil, skim the scum from the surface, then cover and simmer for 3 hours. Uncover and continue simmering for a further 1–2 hours, stirring occasionally, until the meat falls easily from the bone and the sauce has thickened. Alternatively, the stew can be cooked in the oven, set to 150°C/300°F/Gas Mark 2. Adjust the heat so that it simmers happily.

Skim the fat from the surface, then taste and adjust the seasoning. Serve with potatoes or noodles.

BLACK PUDDING WITH APPLE AND MASHED POTATOES

This is not so much a recipe as an idea. The French often serve black pudding with fried apple slices, mashed potato and, of course, lots of French mustard, which is milder than our own. You could grill the black pudding if you wish or replace the mash with, perhaps, hot lentils or fashionable polenta (see page 233). The caramelized apple slices, though, are a stroke of genius and I wouldn't change them for the world.

SERVES 4

25 g (1 oz) butter

1 tablespoon sunflower or vegetable oil

12 slices black pudding

2 eating apples, cored and cut into eighths

A little chopped parsley

——— *For the potatoes* ———

900 g (2 lb) potatoes

50–75 g (2–3 oz) butter

A little full cream milk

Salt

Make the mashed potatoes in the usual way; boil the potatoes in their skins (or better still, bake them if you have the time). Peel and mash in the pan while still warm. Beat in the butter and salt. Place the pan over a medium heat and start to add milk, trickling it down the side of the pan and beating it in energetically with a big spoon. Keep going until the potatoes are light and fluffy and about as thick as you like them. I prefer my mash fairly soft and verging on sloppy, but you may well prefer something a little sturdier. Taste and adjust the seasoning. Re-heat when needed and spoon into a serving dish.

Shortly before sitting down to eat, heat half the butter and half the oil in a frying pan over a high heat until the foaming subsides. Fry the black pudding slices on both sides. Transfer to a dish lined with kitchen paper. Add the remaining butter and oil to the pan and fry the apple slices briskly, until browned. Drain briefly on kitchen paper, then arrange the apple and black pudding over the mashed potatoes. Sprinkle with a little chopped parsley and serve.

Alternative names for

Meat cuts

BEEF

Forerib

Back rib, best rib, bottom rib, chine, crop, eye of rib, fine chine, fore chine, foresye roast, prime rib, rib, rib roast, rib steak, rolled roast, second rib, short rib, sirloin, standing rib, wing rib

Chuck

Back rib, backs eye, blade and chine, braising steak, chain, chine, chuck and blade, chuck roll, crop, draught, low chine, middle rib, neck end, pony, rib, rib eye, rib eye steak, rib roast, rib rolled, rolled rib, short rib, shoulder, shoulder piece, spord, standing rib, top rib, top shoulder

Blade

Blade and chine, blade and feather, blade bone, blade roll, blade round, blade steak, blade top, chine, chuck and blade, false fillet, feather, feather and blade, Glasgow fillet, middle rib, mock fillet, salmon cut, shoulder, shoulder fillet, spale bone, top chuck, top crop, top of blade, top of chuck, top rib

Thick Rib

Back rib, blade, boxeater, bread and butter cut, chuck rib, clod, crop, elbow steak, Jacob's ladder, ladder staves, leg of mutton cut, leg tops, market hand, marking cut, middle rib, middle runner, palace rib, pale

bone, plate, plate runner, rib, rib draught, runner, savoy, short rib, shoulder, shoulder steak, steak meat, thick flat rib, thick end, thick rand, thick runner, top chuck, top rib

Thin Rib

Brisket, flat rib, Jacob's ladder, ladder staves, leg of mutton cut, middle rib, mince, plate, rand, rib, rib end, score, short rib, side rib, thin end staves, thin flat rib, thin rand, thin runner, thin top rib, top rib

Brisket

Can be divided into point end and plate:

Point end

Best end, bosum, bosum end, breast side, coast, crop end, heartspoon, horseshoe, middle brisket

Plate

Breast side, coast, flank, forequarter flank, heartspoon, navel, nine holes, nine skins, rand, rolled loin, seam end, single rib, spoon end, sweet rib, target

Neck

Chuck steak, lyre, shoulder, sticking, sticking piece

Clod

Bosum, fore vein, gorrister, gullet, hough, knee bone, marrow bone runner, neck, pot roast, round bone, runner, shoulder, shoulder lyre, skink, sloat, soft skin, spode, sporn, sticking, thick brisket, vein

Shin

Hough, knee, leg, nap, nap bone, skink

Leg

Hough, nap, shin, skink

Topside

Best end, buttock, corner case, corner cut, corner piece, hind lift, hinderbone, in lift, insteak, middle cut, minute steak, round, round steak, rump, rump steak, top lift, top rump

Silverside

Can be divided into silverside and aitch bone:

Silverside

Bottom, bottom rump, hind lift, insteak, in stick, out lift, pope's eye, round, round steak, rump, salmon cut, shellbone, tail draft, topside, underlift

Aitch bone

Cocked hat, corner piece, corner rump, face steak, lip end, middle cut rump, point rump, round, rump, rump cut, rump end, rump joint, shellbone, short rump, tag end, tail end, tail end rump, tip of rump

Thick Flank

Ball of rump, bed, bedpiece, bed steak, brail, braising steak, buttock, buttock steak, carving, chandler cut, chandler steak, crown steak, face of round, first cutting, flank side, fleshy end, frying steak, kernel right, loin's end, mouse, pin round, pope's eye, prime end steak, raw beef ham, round, round steak,

rump, rump steak, second steak, soft side, split piece, stewing steak, tea beef, top rump, topside, white steak

Rump

Aitch bone, chump, heuk bone, hip bone, pin bone, point, point steak, pope's eye, steakbone, steakpiece

Sirloin

Can be divided into sirloin and wing rib:

Sirloin

Best end loin, best end sirloin, entrecote, fillet end, loin, porterhouse steak, rib, sirloin steak, T bone steak

Wing rib

Foresye, rib end, rib roast, ribs loin, roast steak, sirloin, wing end

Fillet

Undercut

Thin Flank

Boiling rib, brisket, hindquarter flank, plate, pot roast, soft flank, tail of flank

Rump

Goose skirt, rump skirt, skirt, skirting, skirt steak, thick skirt, thin skirt

LAMB

Shank

Foot end, front end, gigot, half end knuckle, half leg, half leg knuckle, half leg shank, hough, knuckle, knuckle end, knuckle end leg, knuckle leg, leg, middle cut gigot, middle fillet, shank end gigot, shank end half leg, shank end leg, shank of leg

Fillet End of Leg
Best end, centre cut gigot, chump, chump chops, fillet centre gigot, fillet end, fillet end half leg, fillet leg, gigot, gigot chops, half fillet end leg, half leg, half leg fillet, leg chops, middle cut fillet, middle cut gigot, top end, top of fillet leg, top leg

Chump
Broad chops, chump chops, chump end, chump end chops, chump end leg, chump loin chops, end fillet, fillet, fillet leg, gigot, gigot chops, lamp chops, lamb steaks, leg chops, leg steaks

Loin
Best end, best end rib, best loin, best loin chops, cutlets, double loin chops, grilling cutlets, lamb chops, lamb cutlets, loin chops, middle loin, middle loin chops, sirloin chops

Best End of Neck
Best end, best end chops, best end cutlets, best end neck cutlets, cutlets, fine end chops, fine end loin, lamb chops, lamb cutlets, loin chops, neck chops, neck cutlets, rib chops, rib loin, single loin, wing chops, wing end chops

Breast
Breast lap, bosum, flap, flank, lap, lap breast

Shoulder
Can be divided into shoulder, blade side and knuckle end
Shoulder
Forequarter
Blade side
Back chops, back rib, back rib chops, blade, blade end, blade half, blade half shoulder, half shoulder, half shoulder blade, half shoulder

bosum, middle piece, middle runner, neck side shoulder, oyster butt, rack chops, rack side, shoulder blade, shoulder chops, spade end, stewing chops, top shoulder
Knuckle end
Breast knuckle, half shoulder, half shoulder knuckle, half shoulder shank, knuckle, knuckle half, knuckle side, lamb knuckle, lockside shoulder, middle cut runner, runner chops, runner cut, shank, shank end, shank side, shoulder chops, shoulder end, shoulder knuckle, stewing chops, thick end

Middle Neck
Best end, best end neck, best end neck chops, braising lamb, casserole lamb, middle neck chops, neck, neck chops, scrag, scrag and middle, scrag chops, stewing, stewing lamb,

Scrag
Casserole lamb, double scrag, middle neck, neck, neck chops, neck end, neck of lamb, neck rings, round neck, ring neck, scrag and middle, scrag chops, scrag end, scrag end neck, scrag middle neck, scrag rings, stewing, stewing lamb, Scotch chops, Scotch neck, Scotch rounds, thick neck

PORK
Trotter
Foot, hock, hough, knuckle, pestel, shank, trotter
Knuckle
Gigot, foot end, half leg, half leg knuckle, hock fillet, knuckle end, knuckle leg, leg end, shank, shank end, shank end gigot, shank end leg,

short knuckle
Fillet of Leg
Best end leg, centre cut, cutlet, fillet, fillet cutlet, fillet end, fillet end leg, gigot, half leg, half leg fillet, leg fillet, middle cut, middle fillet, middle fillet leg, pork fillet

Chump
Broad chops, broad end chops, chump chops, chump end, chump end gigot, chump fillet, fillet of pork, fillet pork, fillet pork steak, gigot, gigot chops, pork chops, pork cuttings, pork fillets, pork slices, pork steaks

Loin
Best end, best end chops, best end neck, best loin, centre loin, chine, crop loin, cutlets, double loin, fore loin, griskin, hind loin, middle loin, neck chops, neck end chops, pork chops, pork cutlets, rib chops, single loin, spare rib chops

Belly
Belly bacon, belly draft, belly slices, belly strips, breast of bacon, breast of pork, flank end, flank pork, flitch, interlean, pork bacon, pork rib, pork slices, pork strips, streaky, streaky pork

Spare Rib
Best neck, blade, blade chine, bladeside, butt, chainside, chine, collar, collar end, collar pork, crop, cropside, foreleg pork, forequarter rack, frying pork, neck, neck chops, neck end, pork steaks, rack of pork, shoulder, shoulder ribs, spare rib chops, thick neck

Blade
Blade bone

Hand and Spring
Can be divided into

hand and thick end of belly:
Hand
Bottom side of shoulder, breast and hand, breast of pork, cropside, fore leg roast, forequarter pork, goose of pork, half shoulder, hampkin, hand of shoulder, handside, hankin, knuckle end shoulder, knuckleside, pork steaks, shankside, shoulder, shoulder and fillet, shoulder knuckle, shoulderside, shoulder steaks, spring, spur
Thick end of belly
Belly bacon, belly draft, belly slices, belly strips, breast of bacon, breast of pork, flank end, flank pork, flitch, interlean, pork bacon, pork slices, pork strips, streaky, streaky pork

VEAL
Shank
Leg, hough, knuckle, osso buco, shin
Thick Flank
Bed, escalope, leg, steak, top rump
Topside
Leg, round
Silverside
Leg, round
Rump
Escalope, heuk bone, hip bone, leg, steak ·
Breast
Flank, brisket
Loin
Chine, cutlet, escalope, sirloin, steak
Chuck
Blade bone, rib, shoulder, top rib
Shin
Knuckle, hough, osso buco, shin
Neck
Shoulder
Clod
Shoulder

A FEW USEFUL ADDRESSES

I make absolutely no attempt to give a comprehensive manual of useful meaty addresses. There are many excellent butchers throughout the country and an increasing number of producers of free-range, or semi-free range, meat of high quality. Here I give just a peppering of names known to me. Some are people I have encountered while filming the television series that accompanies this book. For much more detailed information, can I suggest that you buy a copy of *Henrietta Green's Food Lovers' Guide to Britain* (BBC Books).

BUTCHERS

PORTWINES
24 Earlham Street
London WC2H 9LN
Tel: 0171 836 2353

Graham Portwine, whose family have been butchers in Covent Garden for over 300 years, was my co-presenter on the television series.

FRANK GODFREY LTD
7 Highbury Park
London N5 1QJ
Tel: 0171 226 2425

The Godfreys, father and sons, used to be my butchers when I lived in London, and taught me much of what I know about cuts of meat. Their shop is exemplary, their advice excellent, as is their meat.

C. LIDGATE
110 Holland Park Avenue
Holland Park
London W11 4UA
Tel: 0171 727 8243

MACKEN BROS LTD
44 Turnham Green Terrace
London W4 1QP
Tel: 0181 994 2646

WHOLEFOOD BUTCHERS
24 Paddington Street
London W1M 3RG
Tel: 0171 935 3924

ALLEN'S LTD
117 Mount Street
London W1Y 6HX
Tel: 0171 499 5831

GARY WALLACE,
Chesterton Farm Shop
Chesterton Lane
Cirencester
Gloucestershire GL7 9JP
Tel: 01285 642160

A shop specializing in meat from rare breeds. Delicious Gloucestershire Old Spot sausages and bacon, home-made steak and kidney pies packed to overflowing with Hereford beef.

MAIL-ORDER MEAT

There is an increasing number of suppliers of mail-order meat, most of whom specialize in organic or free-range meats. You do, naturally, pay a premium for the service, but it means that everyone has access, in theory, to the best.

GRAIG FARM
Dolau
Llandrindod Wells
Powys
Wales LD1 5TL
Tel: 01597 851655
Contact: Bob Kennard

Organic meat, including mutton, and other organic products, ranging from cheese to smoked tuna from St Helena.

HEAL FARM
Kings Nympton
Umberleigh
Devon EX37 9TB
Tel: 01769 572077
Contact: Anne Petch

Traditionally raised meat from traditional breeds.

EASTBROOK FARM
Bishopstone
Swindon
Wiltshire SN6 8PW
Tel: 01793 790460

Organic meat.
PURE MEAT DIRECT
Rectory Farm
Upper Stondon
Bedfordshire SG16 6LG
Tel: 01462 851561

Organic and Conservation Grade Meat.

THE REAL MEAT COMPANY
East Hill Farm
Heytesbury
Warminster
Wiltshire BA12 0HR
Tel: 01985 840436

As well as offering an efficient mail-order service for humanely raised, high-welfare, additive-free meat, they also supply many butchers around the country.

MAYNARDS FARM BACON
See Bacon

FLETCHER'S OF AUCHTERMUCHTY
See Venison

MACSWEEN
See Haggis

TRADE AND MEAT PRODUCERS ASSOCIATIONS ETC.

Q-GUILD LTD
PO Box 44
Winterhill House
Snowdon Drive
Milton Keynes
Buckinghamshire MK6 1AX
Tel: 01908 677577

An umbrella organization for butchers who maintain the highest standards in hygiene, butchery skills, presentation and anything else that matters. Q stands for quality and membership is not accorded to any old Tom, Dick or Harry.

BRITISH MEAT INFORMATION
26 Fitzroy Square
London W1P 6BT
Tel: 0171 388 7421

RARE BREEDS SURVIVAL TRUST
National Agriculture Centre
Kenilworth
Warwickshire CV8 2LG
Tel: 01203 696551
Contact: Peter King

The RBST runs an increasingly successful scheme to encourage selected butchers to supply the meat of rare breeds of farm animal. For details of suppliers in your area ring the RBST. Being able to sell surplus animals for meat supports the conservation programmes operated by the Trust. Since the Rare Breeds Survival Trust was established in 1973, no further breeds of farm animal have disappeared.

BRITISH WILD BOAR ASSOCIATION
30 Fen Road
Milton
Cambridgeshire CB4 6AD
Tel: 01223 860116

BACON

MAYNARDS FARM BACON
The Hough
Weston-under-Redcastle
Shrewsbury
Shropshire SY4 5LR
Tel: 01948 840252

Maynard Davies' life is dedicated to making traditional bacon, and it shows in the finished product – he produces some 29 different types, from mild to strong, as well as his own sausages and some hams. This is some of the best bacon I've ever eaten, and luckily it can be bought by mail order.

VENISON

LAYER MARNEY TOWER FARM SHOP
Near Colchester
Essex CO5 9US
Tel: 01206 330784

Housed in a magnificent Tudor gate house, this farm shop is definitely worth the detour. Sheila Charrington and her husband raise their own deer on the farm, as well as keeping a variety of rare breeds of sheep, goats and chickens.

FLETCHER'S OF AUCHTERMUCHTY
Reediehill Deer Farm
Auchtermuchty
Fife KY14 7HS
Tel: 01337 828369

The Fletchers pioneered deer farming in this country, and remain enthusiastic promoters of venison. They will send vacuum-packed venison out by mail.

HAGGIS

W. MATHESON'S MOBILE
BUTCHER'S VAN
based in Aberfeldy
Perthshire
Tel: 01887 820565

Willy Matheson drives his butcher's van around a stunning route in the Perthshire hills, stopping at cottages here and there along the way. Faithful customers make a beeline for his haggis.

MACSWEEN
130 Bruntsfield Place
Edinburgh
Lothian EH10 4ES
Tel: 0131 229 1216

The most famous haggis maker of them all, and with some justification. The haggis is superb, and can be bought by mail order if you can't get to the shop in person.

BLACK PUDDING

MORRIS'S PORK BUTCHERS
120 Market Street
Farnworth
Bolton
Lancashire BL4 9AE
Tel: 01204 571763

Jack Morris's black puddings are reckoned by some to be even better than those sold at the Bury market a few miles away, and that, I am told, is high praise indeed. He has been known to mail them out.

BIBLIOGRAPHY

MEAT

Charcuterie and French Pork Cookery, Jane Grigson, Penguin, 1987
Great Meat Cookery, ed. Tony de Angeli, Hamlyn, 1989
The Real Meat Cook Book, Frances Bissell, Chatto, 1992

GAME

Classic Game Cookery, Julia Drysdale, Papermac, 1983
Good Game, Victoria Jardine-Peterson and Colin McKelvie, Swanhill Press, 1993
Nicola Cox on Game Cookery, Nicola Cox, Gollancz, 1993
Wild Game Cooking, Jonquil and Edward Barr, Rosendale Press, 1988

GENERAL

Observer Guide to British Cookery, Jane Grigson, Michael Joseph, 1984 (o. p.)
Complete Cookery Course, Delia Smith, BBC Books, 1992
Constance Spry Cookery Book, Constance Spry and Rosemary Hume, Weidenfeld & Nicolson, 1994
English Food, Jane Grigson, Penguin, 1993
Henrietta Green's Food Lovers' Guide to Britain 1996-1997, Henrietta Green, BBC Books, 1995
French Provincial Cooking, Elizabeth David, Penguin, 1993
Italian Food, Elizabeth David, Penguin, 1993
Leith's Cookery Bible, Prue Leith and Caroline Waldegrave, Bloomsbury, 1991
Leith's Cookery Course, Prue Leith and Caroline Waldegrave, Fontana, 1985
Mastering the Art of French Cooking, Simone Beck, Louisette Bertholie and Julia Child, Penguin (in two volumes), 1987
New Larousse Gastronomique, Hamlyn, 1988
On Food and Cooking, Harold McGee, HarperCollins, 1991
Reader's Digest Complete Guide to Cookery, Anne Willan, Dorling Kindersley, 1989
Sainsbury's Book of Food, Frances Bissell, Sainsbury, 1989

INDEX